Everything You Need to Know to Get to Heaven

Decoding the Bible
The Secret Behind 2012

Gary J. McDonald

I dedicate this book to the One Universal God,
and to my mother, Joan, as she was most
instrumental in my spiritual development.

With unending love to my daughter, Amber, of whom
I am so proud, and my Companion Soul Mate, Minerva.

Thanks to all my friends, family, loved ones, and associates who
supported my efforts to write and edit my book, including
Ken Lambert, Christine Messier and Stella Togo.

Table of Contents

❧

List of Illustrations:

Illustrations by Jennifer Coughran, Print2WebDesign.com

Author photograph by Paul Savage Photography, ShotByASavage.com

**What we do for ourselves
dies with us.**

**What we do for others
and the world
remains and is immortal.**

Albert Pike

Section I

RAISING OUR CONSCIOUSNESS

Author's Note

Everything You Need to Know to Get to Heaven represents a belief system based on intuitive reasoning, thought-filled deduction, personal experiences and spiritual insights. These beliefs stem from an intense meditation practice, supernatural experiences, visions, dreams, group discussions, lectures, and the works of numerous spiritual authors. This book represents an integration of various religions and philosophies with science and metaphysics. I merge Intelligent Design with Evolutionary Theory. I provide a thought provoking explanation for Darwin's Missing Link and for the Big Bang. Many of my hypotheses are supported by holy scripture, albeit a broader interpretation of scripture.

Everything You Need to Know to Get to Heaven is an overview of spirituality with fresh understanding and new insights. As such, it redefines the Holy Trinity, merges science with God along with tenets of various religions and ancient belief systems into one spiritual system eliminating narrow-minded thinking and senseless religious dogma. Through intense study and seemingly unending analyses, I believe I have decoded critical verses contained within the Christian Bible and present the revised interpretations here in this book. Maybe most importantly, it presents what I believe will occur in the year 2012 as we attempt to transition into the next dimension and beyond.

I have read a hundred or more spiritually-based books over the past 20 years. Consequently, to cite specific references to books I read years ago would be impractical. I would be merely guessing as to where the acquired knowledge actually came from. It may also appear that *Everything You Need to Know to Get to Heaven* is in part based on information found on the internet. However, my use of the internet was to substantiate what I already knew in my head and heart to be true. Beyond that, some of the internet research was necessary to simply remind me of what I already knew but had forgotten over time.

In all cases, the Divine played a critical role in directing me to the information that needed to be in this book, sometimes in very mysterious ways. As challenging as it was, I believe that I have uncovered *Everything You Need To Know To Get To Heaven*. When reading this you might regard the contents of this book to be a religion unto itself. It surely is for me personally. However God is limitless, without boundaries, and in truth beyond anyone's understanding. Knowing this, what I present in the following chapters, I present as possibilities with hope that this book will help expand your mind to a bigger truth. As always, it is up to you, the reader, to determine your own spiritual truth.

Introduction

What *Everything You Need to Know to Get to Heaven* offers to the reader is a complete one-stop-shopping overview of spirituality. In one way, this book decodes the Bible because I present new mind-expanding possibilities on how to interpret the Bible. I often quote scripture to support what I propose to be true. *Everything You Need to Know to Get to Heaven* may also accurately describe the evolutionary progression of mankind's consciousness. It may further explain what we each must individually and collectively do to avoid any unnecessary devastation as we enter the next dimension, the next level of our evolution in consciousness set to occur in the year 2012. For me, this book is an incredibly huge gift from God because it answers my questions about who I am, what I am, and my purpose for being here. It addresses all the major spiritual questions I have about life, death, and the afterlife, and hopefully will do the same for you.

For the majority of my earlier years, I felt a huge void in my life. I tried to fill this void with alcohol, relationships, and material possessions without much success. One day while returning home from work I again felt this void, but this time it manifested as an actual physical pain surrounding my heart. Recognizing the cause of my pain I looked up, as if turning toward God, and said "Let's do it your way." Little did I have any inclination that by uttering those five simple words my life would be turned completely upside down. Since that life-altering day I have had many incredible spiritual experiences some people might think a little strange or even crazy, but I know in my heart that with God anything is possible. I know without a doubt that there is so much more to life than what we typically witness every day in this material world. There is so much more to life beyond this everyday illusion of physicality. I know this because I experienced it in the most astonishing of ways!

Writing *Everything You Need to Know to Get to Heaven* was like peeling an onion. The more I peeled, the more I began to understand the interconnectedness of the universe. At times it made my hair stand on end. Other times I wept with joy better appreciating the hidden beauty within God's master plan for us, His children. This book aided me in processing and organizing data and consequently moved me forward in my own spiritual development. It was like piecing together a great spiritual puzzle. During periods of writing this book I decided to remarkably increase my *Chi energy* (pronounced Chee) by not having any sexual orgasms in hopes of increasing my inner levels of creativity and better connecting me to Spirit (God), much like an athlete abstains from sexual relations before an event in order to improve his or her athletic performance.

Chi energy, also known as *Kundalini energy* (pronounced Kuhn-dah-lee-nee), is the spiritual life force energy of the body. By abstaining from any and all types of orgasms, there was a substantial buildup of the life force energy within my body and a significant rise in my consciousness and psychic ability. At times this additional energy became extremely uncomfortable and overwhelming. As a direct result of this energy extraordinary spiritual phenomena began to occur within me and around me, some of it quite frightening.

The night before I began writing this book, I had a very vivid prophetic dream. I noticed three pricks on my left hand in the soft fleshy area between my thumb and my first finger. The three pricks were blood red in color but were not bleeding. Together they formed a perfect triangle. Upon awakening, I knew intuitively what it meant. I was being directed by Spirit to begin my book with an explanation of the Trinity: the Father, the Son, and the Holy Ghost. I soon realized that I had no idea how or where to begin defining the Trinity. Furthermore, *who was I* to define God? I suddenly felt insignificant and small in comparison to my task. This dream launched me on a journey in which I torturously struggled to understand God and the nature of God, which ultimately proved most enlightening for me.

Several nights later as I contemplated the Divine, I felt as if my mind began to physically expand. It felt as if the crown portion of my head had exploded open and a flower was unfolding petal by petal. Initially I thought I was having a stroke, and fear began to sweep over me. As soon as I figured out what was happening, the spiritual experience ended. I realized this was the *thousand-petaled lotus flower* the Buddhists and Hindus speak of beginning to unfold in my mind. According to Eastern Mysticism, the unfolding of the flower is a sign of advancing levels of spiritual development. Fully open, the lotus flower is indicative of an enlightened being. I lay in bed desiring more, surprised to discover that when the Eastern religions speak of the thousand-petaled lotus flower opening in the head area, it's a metaphor for something you actually feel when your spiritual consciousness expands. It was amazing!

As I struggled to manage the increased Chi energy (Kundalini energy) within my physical body, incredible things continued to happen to me. Early one morning as I lay in bed, I felt the sensation of a small earthquake. It was a slight vibration, so I really didn't think it so strange at the time that nothing other than my bed seemed to vibrate. A few days later, I awoke in the middle of the night and decided to focus my attention on my inner *third-eye chakra*, which is also referred to as the *Christ Consciousness Center* or, more simply, the *Christ Center*. Within the next few moments my Christ Center (third-eye) began to light up as if it were radiated, gradually becoming living, breathing consciousness. The back of my head became expansive as well. I could feel the rear portion of my third-eye chakra enlarge as if two hands had pierced the back of my head and began to pull it apart. Suddenly the back of my head began to vibrate much like the earthquake I felt the previous day. It lasted for what seemed like fifteen seconds. When it was all over, I lay in bed feeling as if I had just experienced a moment of major spiritual expansiveness. Interestingly enough, it felt very feminine in origin.

Nearly a week had passed since I felt the first vibration when another similar vibration hit me. I had gone to bed later than usual and had fallen asleep almost immediately. A short time later I awoke to the vibration, this time centered in my heart area. *My heart began quaking inside my chest!* It lasted for fifteen to twenty seconds. This verified for me that neither this vibration nor the previous ones were related to earthquakes. Up to this point I had fantasized that the first vibration was something spiritual, more than just an earthquake, and now I was certain it was true.

The next morning I decided that I would start my meditation at sunrise, which is a powerful time to meditate. After a few minutes passed, I fell back asleep. Sometime later I awoke to yet another vibration in my chest. It lasted maybe a few seconds at best. As soon as the quaking subsided, a warm sensation filled my heart, increasing in magnitude to the point that my heart felt on fire. Some sort of purification was occurring. I felt as if I was being filled with the Holy Spirit. The fire within my heart lasted about twenty seconds before it finally subsided. It was truly amazing. All these events occurred within the first two weeks of beginning to write this book.

My advice as you read *Everything You Need to Know to Get to Heaven* is to spend some time contemplating the content found within each chapter. Consider the possibility that what I am suggesting might be true. There may be sections that you feel are difficult to understand or accept as truth based on your current belief system but please reserve judgment to the end. As I stated earlier, *Everything You Need to Know to Get to Heaven* is like a huge spiritual puzzle because it merges numerous seemingly contradictory concepts in a new thought provoking meaningful way. I also highly recommend not skipping any portions you think you already know. You may be suddenly surprised to discover a new insight or perspective.

Finally, this is not meant to be a feel-good type of book as many self-help or metaphysical-based books are intended to be. Rather, I wrote it to provide answers to life's major questions about God and spirituality. Why are we here? What is my purpose? Where are we in terms of our conscious development? What do we need to do individually and collectively to move forward toward spiritual fulfillment? Where and what is heaven? What will happen in 2012? Who goes to heaven? How do I make sure I get there?

As I was writing I certainly began to question whether or not I was ready to live the lifestyle I suggest here in this book. I questioned the necessity of living such an austere lifestyle just as a child doesn't want to hear that it is time to stop playing and do homework. But that is what *Everything You Need to Know to Get to Heaven* is about; getting serious about shifting our consciousness to one of experiencing greater levels of love. In doing so, we must surrender certain aspects of our ego-based selves and materialistic ways. It's not always an easy path.

Everything You Need to Know to Get to Heaven is about making difficult choices regarding our humanness and spiritual advancement individually and collectively as the human race. I believe if you read this book and remain open to its content, you cannot help but feel positively affected and possibly one step closer to realizing heaven. That is my hope and intent. You may be surprised, maybe even shocked or appalled, by what you read, and therefore I present these chapters as possibilities. I do not presume to be an authoritarian. I am simply presenting the information as it flowed through me; and now I feel compelled to share it with you. So let's get started.

CHAPTER 1

Universal Laws

✧

Before I attempt to explain God, or the concept of the Trinity, I will begin by building a foundation for this book by briefly explaining God's universal laws. A *universal law* is a *property or principle that is always true* whether you are talking about the nature of God or the material world. These divine laws provide order in the universe as well as guidelines for human behavior because they set parameters for our spiritual development. Universal laws, moreover, help us by providing a framework in which to conduct our lives. In one way they restrict us, but alternatively they are guideposts for our return back to heaven. The science of quantum physics and thermodynamics are at last beginning to prove some of the universal laws spiritually conscious people have known for ages. There are a number of universal laws outlined below and some of them are quite complicated, yet none are contradictory or mutually exclusive. These laws will hopefully help to provide additional clarity and insight as you venture through this book.

Law of Free Will: God does not dictate what we say or do. We are not spiritual puppets. The choices we make are not predestined. We have complete and total free will in our decisions, even though we may not always believe it. We do indeed have one hundred percent free will. The problem lies in the fact that we don't always act according to what is best for us spiritually speaking, and consequently life becomes increasingly difficult and complicated.

"Everything is permissible, but not everything is beneficial."
1 Corinthians 10:23[1]

Law of Relativity: Everything is relative. Relativity is the duality found in nature. If there is an up, then there is a down. If there is an east, then there is a west. If there is cold, then there is hot. Only within duality can we experience relativity. How can we experience joy if there is never sorrow? Relativity is necessary to have choice. By the same token, we could not experience being human without other humans. The fact is we need each other to experience ourselves.

Law of Nature: The Law of Nature states that for every positive aspect of something there is a corresponding negative aspect. Some people believe mankind is generally good. Some believe mankind is generally evil. There are some that say mankind is mixed between good and evil. The Law of Nature suggests the latter. People have the propensity for good and evil. Goodness is associated with the higher nature of God. Evil is associated with the lower nature of humanity. We all have a light side and a dark side associated with our human nature. Under certain conditions we may act in accordance with either side. The key to choosing correctly lies in understanding the complex relationship of good and evil within us.

Law of Gender: Everything has either a masculine and feminine quality to it, sometimes referred to as *yin* and *yang*. The feminine (yin) is characterized as water, cold, dark, and the gentle, receptive side of human nature. The masculine (yang) is characterized as fire, hot, light (versus dark), active (versus receptive), and the more aggressive and forceful side of human nature. In reality, all of us possess both feminine and masculine qualities in varying degrees. It is up to each of us to strike an appropriate balance between the two.

Law of Correspondence: There is a direct relationship between heaven and earth. What is true above is true below. What is true in the spiritual world is reflected in the physical world. Whether or not we recognize it, the words we choose and the actions we take are often based on a greater truth. Things of a physical nature reflect the nature of the *Godhead* (an alternate word for Trinity).

> "For the invisible things of him from the creation of the world are clearly seen, being understood by the things that are made, even his eternal power and Godhead." Romans 1:20

Law of Karma: This is also known as the *Universal Law Cause and Effect*. Karma is commonly defined by the phrases, *What comes around goes around*; *An eye for an eye*; and *As you sow, so shall you reap*. Karma can also be defined as *spiritual lessons yet to learn*. Later in the book, I discuss karma in much greater detail.

Law of Grace: As humans, we must abide by the laws of man, not just the laws of God. Upon reaching a point of enlightenment, the soul, whether still in a physical body or not, lives under the Law of Grace. These souls are not subject to the Law of Karma because their karma has been eliminated. They have risen above the Law of Karma. At this point, evil no longer has any power or control over an enlightened soul; the soul has been purified. At the point of spiritual enlightenment, a soul has immediate access to heaven whether in a physical body or not. The Law of Grace could also be interpreted as *absolute forgiveness*.

shabd sound current *Universal Laws*

Law of Vibration: Everything created by God has form whether visible or invisible to the naked eye. Science states that nothing is truly solid; there is a certain amount of emptiness in everything. Everything created by God also has a certain degree of energy associated with it and consequently everything in this universe vibrates. As a result of the vibrational component within creation, everything emits a sound whether audible or inaudible to the human ear.

Law of Attraction: Like attracts like. Negative energies attract negative energies. Positive energies attract positive energies. In relationships, we choose people, places, and things that are more like us than not. In those situations where this is not the case, the relationship will tend to be volatile and typically short-lived. Likewise, souls will attract souls that have a similar vibration. Sometimes we say *opposites attract* but in reality they have a similar soul vibration.

Law of Creation: Consciousness precedes thought. Thought precedes emotion. Emotion precedes action. Action precedes results. In order to create, we must first think a thought, and then we must act upon that thought. Emotion is what creates the desire or drive to take action. By exerting enough energy into the *action,* creation occurs, assuming the universal laws are not violated in any way. As an individual soul, we create our own personal reality, whether we wish to take responsibility for it or not. Jointly, all souls create our collective reality.

Law of Unity: The Law of Unity may be better known as the *Universal Law All is One.* All matter is made of the same basic elements in nature. These elemental materials are consistent throughout matter. What varies is the amount of each material in each object. The same holds true for God because everything is God. In the beginning before creation, there was only God and God was everything. There was nothing that was not God. This still holds true. As a result, everything is connected in one way or another because we all come from the same source. How could God create something outside of Himself since He is everywhere?

Law of Abundance: Everything you need you already have or will be provided to you when you need it. As souls in human form, we will be given everything we need to carry out what we are intended to experience within this lifetime. God wishes nothing but goodness and happiness and abundance for us. However, being rich in life does not necessarily equate to possessing great wealth. Possessing wealth may not be in our own highest good. It may be in our own best interest to experience this life without wealth. To further complicate things, sometimes we can be our own worst enemy by acting outside of our own best interests.

Jesus said there will always be poor among us.

"The poor you will always have with you…" Mark 14:7

<u>Law of Consciousness</u>: Everything on this earth has consciousness. Even nonliving objects such as rocks have a certain degree of consciousness. It is all relative. A man has a greater degree of consciousness within him than an animal has within it. An animal has a greater degree of consciousness within it than a plant. A plant has a greater degree of consciousness within it than a rock, and so on down the line. Everything is simply consciousness or matter with consciousness. Collectively, we form group consciousness.

<u>Law of Change</u>: The Universal Law of Change is sometimes referred to as the *Universal Law of Progress*. Progress implies change but change doesn't always imply progress. Everything in this physical world changes eventually. It either progresses to a state of higher form or regresses to a lower state of form. Nothing is static. Some consider death the ultimate or final change, although in reality, it is merely a shift in consciousness and form to another dimension.

> "For death begins with life's first breath, and life begins at the touch of death." John Oxenham

<u>All Is Chosen</u>: Everything, without exception, is chosen on some level. Chaos and randomness are a *non-reality*. This may seem very harsh when we look at the perceived injustices that occur daily in our world. But as you read on, you may come to the same conclusion as me, that there is a greater consciousness that exists within the fabric of the universe we can never fully comprehend or appreciate given our current state of spiritual development. But upon reaching a state of enlightenment, we will discover that there is a reason for everything, even the difficult challenges we face in our lives.

God's Universal Laws together form the basis in which we are constrained or liberated. Our mere presence in this universe by default means that at some point we agreed to these rules. Collectively, we may have even created them. Either way, understanding these rules in advance can only serve to augment our journey back to heaven.

CHAPTER 2

Challenges Are Blessings

❦

Challenges are *change agents* we consciously or unconsciously manifest in our lives for our own betterment. Our personal challenges are intended to move us forward in our spiritual progression. However, the challenges we face should not define who we are as individuals. We should not be defined by our challenges because *we* define our challenges. Since one of God's universal laws is All Is Chosen, we are necessarily the creators of every moment we experience. I have a personal philosophy, a mantra so to speak. Right or wrong, it's how I approach life's disappointments and personal challenges. Here it is: *The universe is constantly rearranging itself for a better outcome.* By the universe rearranging itself, I obviously imply change, sometimes difficult hard-to-accept change, not always what we might perceive as positive change, but positive change nonetheless.

I would like to expand on my philosophy here for a moment. If it is true that certain events generally perceived as negative actually steer us away from greater tragedies, or move us forward to better material outcomes, or toward greater spiritual progress, we might begin to look at our challenges in a different light. A mother might understand that by getting stuck in traffic two blocks from her home, she avoided an accident that might have lead to her child's death. A couple on their honeymoon might understand that by missing their connecting flight to Hawaii, they were saved from being attacked by sharks while snorkeling. These are extreme examples that may occur less frequently than some others. And, of course, we would have no idea as to what tragedy we might have been spared in any given moment, but I believe these types of situations happen a lot more than we realize.

Here's another example that might seem a little more realistic. Let's say that a businessman misses the 7:10 bus and is now going to be late for work. On the very next bus he sits next to someone who gives him a vital piece of information he needs for an important project. This could only have occurred if the businessman remained open to striking up a conversation with someone on the second bus. Even though challenged, the businessman kept himself open by maintaining a positive mind-set and received a material gift from the universe. It is also possible that our challenges are more spiritual in nature and are meant to teach us about some aspect of love such as patience, compassion, forgiveness, and so on. Actually, in every instance, challenges provide an opportunity for us to grow spiritually.

The key to all of this is *how we react* to difficult situations. By staying in the moment and turning to *discernment*, that is, judging every challenging situation we face wisely and objectively, we remain open to the loving flow of the universe. By staying in the moment of discernment, we accept life as it is presented to us. Through conscious discernment we save ourselves from the negative thoughts and emotions that normally accompany challenges. We also save ourselves from any negative karma resulting from our negative reactions. When we live our lives believing that *the universe is constantly rearranging itself for a better outcome*, we can better let go of the negativity associated with our challenges. If this works for you, memorize my mantra or create your own. The universe can only help us if we continue to make positive choices in our lives through conscious discernment. Choosing to focus solely on the negative aspect of a challenge only makes the universe's job more difficult.

As souls in human form, we are tested every day by the challenges we face. The quality of the outcome is directly proportional to the quality of our decision. Being tempted to react negatively is a part of being human. It is a part of the rules we created for ourselves since All Is Chosen. The choice between good and evil allows us not only the opportunity for choosing, but for choosing love. When we choose love, we know deep down in our soul that we have chosen correctly. We instinctively know that we are acting in accordance with our higher self and take one step closer to the all-loving God. Eventually, we develop a deeper understanding of one of the greatest secrets of life, that being *wisdom* or *God-mind*, another aspect of the all-loving God. And why is God-mind one of life's greatest secrets? The reason is as follows: in instances where we have chosen an act of love, we are for all intents and purposes the receiver. In assisting others, we are given an opportunity to move closer to God and reduce our negative karma. In giving, we receive. This is necessarily true because of the Universal Law of Unity or All Is One. If we help another person, we are inevitably helping ourselves.

Every person in his or her lifetime will face a specific set of predetermined challenges as specified in his or her own *spiritual contract*. These challenges are not predetermined by God, but rather predetermined by the soul itself. Spiritual contracts are discussed in further detail in a later chapter, so I will not delve into it here.

Overall, life's challenges serve one primary purpose. Challenges make us grow. Challenges, more often than not, involve a certain degree of pain. Pain reminds us to seek God and the god within us. Please note that I intentionally did not capitalize god in this last sentence to represent that we as individual souls are only an aspect of the whole God being. As both man and god, we are all sons (or children) of God. Continuing on, it is sad to say that often it is only within our pain that we choose to seek God or the god within us. Inherent within all pain is a compulsion, a compulsion to eliminate pain. One way or another, God or the god within us will expose our spiritual weaknesses through pain and will continue to do so until we acknowledge it and correct it. Boxer Joe Louis summed it up quite succinctly when he spoke of his upcoming boxing match with Max Schmeling: "You can run but you cannot hide." We cannot hide from our spiritual challenges. It is not possible because we will continually be presented the same challenging opportunities until we get it right.

It bears credence to ask the question *If life was easy, would we turn to God?* I doubt highly that I would have had I not been challenged to the degree I was challenged. We therefore cannot blame others or God for the challenges we face. They are the lessons we draw to us because we have yet to learn them. It is our karma; other people only play a role in the fulfillment of our karma. We should be grateful, not angry or resentful, for our challenges; and it is within the extremeness of the challenge that we have the potential for the greatest growth. Challenges are a blessing in disguise in that they force us to grow by looking deep within ourselves. You've heard of the term *soul searching*, haven't you? It is literal. In times of pain we often look inside ourselves and ask the question *Why?* Looking within is a healthy response to our challenges. Blaming God or others is not.

Challenges generally come to us in one of three categories: relationships, finances, and health. If you consider what your major concerns have been this lifetime, I am sure that you would agree that all of them fall into one of these three categories. Before coming to earth each soul will typically decide to fully experience a minimum of two of the three categories of challenges during its upcoming lifetime. Understand that when I suggest that we take on two of three of the three categories of challenges, that is not to say that we won't have minor issues in the third category as well, because we will. Hopefully, it is clear that I am suggesting that we will face major challenges in two of the three categories with minor challenges in the remaining category.

Very evolved spiritual beings may decide to take on all three categories of challenges at once in a major way, but that indeed can be a heavy load to bear as a human. Rather, most spiritual entities (souls) limit their life-altering challenges to two primary categories at a time. However, as one of the challenges tends to dissipate over time, another will most likely arise. For me, my two primary categories of challenges for the majority of my life have been personal relationships and financial problems. As my financial problems over the years seem to dissipate, my health seems to be transitioning in a negative direction. In this way I continue to deal with a minimum of two of three categories of challenges at the same time. Again, to take on all three categories in a full-blown fashion would be a heavy burden to bear, but there are those souls who decide to do this. God bless them for their efforts. Their success or failure affects us all.

Relationships are our teachers. We learn by being in relationships. Typically the more difficult the relationship, the bigger the lesson we face. Often the aspect we find most difficult to accept within someone else is usually the aspect in us that we need to most heal. Our relationships reflect back to us who we are and the healing that needs to take place in our lives. If we discover something in another person that bothers us, we need to look deep within ourselves and ask the difficult questions. *How do I act in the same way? In what manner do I possess the same trait as the other person?* The people who often rub us the wrong way hold a special lesson for us; they are our spiritual teachers. Life is similar to a classroom where each person who touches us in a significant way, positively or negatively, reflects back to us who we are and what we need yet to learn. The fact is we need other people.

In general, when we run away from a troubling relationship, we may be running away from a potential lesson we need to learn. That is not to say that we should stay in any emotionally or physically abusive relationship. That is not the case at all. If anyone is in an abusive relationship, most likely the lesson for them is to reject the abuse realizing that we are all creatures of God that should never be abused in any way whatsoever. There is never an excuse for abusive behavior. If you are involved in an abusive relationship on either end, please seek professional help immediately before it worsens. Healthy relationships are meant to teach us about ourselves; the more we know about our own personal dynamics, the easier it will be for us to shift into what we wish to evolve into spiritually.

In all relationships, whether with people, places, or things, we draw to us what we need to learn. It is the Universal Law of Attraction. God will provide to us whatever we need to learn this lifetime. We will draw to us the people we need to teach us. We do not need to look for them. They will come to us when we are not looking for them in the unlikeliest of ways. Rest assured that if we are intended to meet someone special this lifetime, they will find us. If we are intended to meet our special significant other, we will. Waiting for the right person to come along can be tough but everything happens in divine timing. Meeting the right person before we are spiritually ready can be disastrous. Remember that we are all provided everything we require to accomplish everything we set out to accomplish this lifetime in divine order, including our relationships. But beware, everything in this world is transitory; therefore, seeking anything beyond a deeper, more permanent relationship to God will eventually lead to disappointment.

The result our challenges ultimately are intended to produce is this: *We need to surrender our lives to God.* In surrender, we offer everything up to God. There is nothing that can come between us and God when we put Him first above everything else. Placing God second in our life to any person, place, or thing will not get us to where we need to go. The Bible states that when we seek God above all others, we will be rewarded.

"...he rewards those who earnestly seek him." Hebrews 11:6

God is asking us to invest our energies in seeking Him and not in things of this earth.

"Do not love the world or anything in the world." 1 John 2:15

That is what was meant when Jesus said we are to die to sin. Then we can wake up to the joy inherent in life because the stress that weighed us down, as if it were the weight of the world, is now lifted off of our shoulders.

God promised that He would take care of us.

"Look at the birds of the air, they do not sow or reap or store away in barns, and yet your heavenly Father feeds them. Are you not much more valuable than they?" Matthew 6:26-27

Our individual struggles in relation to money, people, and health are meant to draw us closer to God. You won't find everlasting happiness in any relationship outside of God. We can only discover our bliss within our relationship to God. God is there waiting for us to offer ourselves up to Him in surrender. He will never leave us or disappoint us. So the next time you are faced with a major life struggle, you may consider thanking God for the opportunity for growth. As difficult as it may be to understand, our challenges are really our blessings in disguise. They show us where we need to grow and where to make changes in our lives. Life doesn't always seem to make sense, but there is a higher intelligence at work here that knows what is best for us, better than we know it ourselves. So remember, our greatest pain can be our greatest gift and our greatest blessing.

CHAPTER 3

Effecting Change in Our Lives

To effect positive change in our lives we must take some sort of action. Every day we take action in one way or another because we feel we ought, should, or must, to fulfill our needs, wants, or desires. In some instances we must act to survive. In most instances we act to fulfill a need, want, or desire much less life-sustaining or life-threatening. Our actions often incorporate our values and beliefs as long as they remain consistent to our needs. We might make a choice that is inconsistent with our values and beliefs when the need is greater than the desire to remain congruent with our values and beliefs. An example here is a mother who steals to feed her children because they are hungry. The act of stealing is neither consistent with her value to be honest or her belief that stealing is wrong.

Because of our needs, values, and beliefs, we establish certain patterns in which we act.

Let me backtrack a little and provide some definitions for the terms I use here:

- Need: a necessity or lack; requisite
- Value: that for which something is regarded as useful or desirable
- Belief: an accepted opinion
- Pattern: a model of behavior that is copied or repeated

Our most basic need is survival; we need food, water, and shelter. When faced with the possibility of death, an individual might do most anything to survive, including committing an act of murder.

Beyond survival, we have other basic needs, some of which are listed here:

- A need for individuality (exclusion)
- A need for love (inclusion)
- A need for growth (change)
- A need for stability (order or consistency)

As you can see, our needs are not always consistent with each other.

Values add another dimension to decision-making. What is it that you value? Do you value love, security, money, appreciation, or honesty? Values help us make certain judgments or discernments. Is this valuable to me? How much will I pay for this? In many cases it benefits us to determine worth or worthiness. A value system helps to prioritize as one value may be more strongly held than another. Values that are held more deeply within a person's value system are not easily transmuted into an opposing viewpoint or value.

A belief, on the other hand, is an assertion, claim, or expectation about reality that is assumed to be true or false even if evidence exists that may counter the belief. Sometimes a belief may be based on no evidence whatsoever. An example in which a belief has little or no basis for measurement is a belief in a higher power such as God. There is little or no proof that God exists. There is no proof heaven exists either. Yet for many there is a very strong need to believe in a higher power and heaven, or at least some type of afterlife. In some instances, a belief may be easily altered if enough evidence is presented to counter the initial belief, assuming the belief is not a strongly held belief. A strongly held belief may remain unaltered even when presented evidence to the contrary.

The interaction of needs, values, and beliefs are integral to the decision-making process. When an individual makes decisions based on needs, values, and beliefs and the decision is replicated time after time, a pattern has developed. An individual's need for consistency is met by constructing patterns. This becomes even more important in an increasingly complicated, changing world.

The decisions we make are generally intended to bring us greater levels of happiness. It pretty much goes without saying that we all want to be happy. So then, what does it take to be happy? The answer lies within our *state of mind*. If we possess a positive state of mind, then we are naturally happy. To begin with, it is important to define what happiness means to each of us. Is happiness defined as being in a relationship? Is happiness defined as wealth? Is happiness being in love? Is happiness simply being healthy? Is happiness getting the right job? Is happiness based on how much we own or what in particular we own?

Obviously some of you can already recognize the flawed thinking associated with a few of the questions above. For example, being in any type of physical relationship with another human being will only bring transitory pleasures. We have all been temporarily upset or discontented with loved ones at one time or another. We all have fallen in and out of love with someone at some point in our lives. Likewise, there are plenty of people with lots of money who are not happy, and there are many poor people struggling every day to put food on the table who are happy; so money does not guarantee happiness. Being healthy helps, but there are plenty of people suffering from an illness that have come to a place of resolution and are quite happy with their lives. So health is not an absolute factor in happiness; in fact, it can be quite the reverse. Ironically, sometimes an illness or disease is what brings us around to discovering true happiness. Similarly, we have all lost or changed jobs. When it comes down to it, *peace of mind* is probably the best determinant of happiness, isn't it?

What are some of the factors that lead to peace of mind? Forgiveness could be one. If we are harboring anger against someone else, then peace of mind is not possible. Moving past negative emotions that close down the heart is important. How can anyone be happy if their heart is closed? The heart must be open to love. Faith in a higher power that we are loved and being taken care of is vital for peace of mind, at least for me. Trusting in God's intelligence is consistent with understanding and believing that we each play a divine role within God's plan on this earth no one else can fill. This should bring greater levels of peace to us. Taking responsibility for our own actions, while not accepting responsibility for the inappropriate actions of others, creates a sense of empowerment. Empowerment can lead to greater levels of peace. Peace of mind naturally includes even-mindedness.

Living in the moment is crucial for establishing peace of mind. If we are living in the past, we may be trapped in an emotional state of regret. If we are living in the future, we may be trapped in an emotional state of constant worry. Only by staying in the moment is joy and peace of mind possible. We also need to love ourselves. We need to love ourselves no matter what we do for a living or what we look like. We need to recognize that we chose our temporal bodies and the specific details surrounding our lives, but it is not who we truly are. We are children of God, and the soul within us is the immortal aspect no one or no thing can harm. We should recognize that there is a tremendous source of love and beauty within us, and that outer beauty fades with time for everyone. If you can think of other aspects of life that positively impact your peace of mind, you may wish to write them down so that you may more quickly recall them at a later time.

So how do we begin to create positive change within our lives? First, we need to establish or determine our *intentions*. By setting an intention, we inform the universe of what we wish to create into being. Our intentions stem from our thoughts and desires. Without desire, typically nothing will happen. Without a desire, we would not be motivated to act. Desire plus action creates an outcome. That is where most people fail. They never act on their desire most often due to some type of fear. But here is a little secret, whatever it is that you desire, believe it is already yours. In this way the universe seeks to fulfill it. Spirit working on our behalf does the heavy lifting, so to speak. We are in effect simply the channel for the intention. Through the act of intention, we use our consciousness to affect the totality of consciousness found within this universe.

The next step of creation is to expend the amount of energy necessary to accomplish the outcome. Finally, let go of the outcome. In this way we let go of the fears associated with failure which then allows the universe to provide us what is best for us without polluting the eventual outcome with our expectations. Expectations are all about our desire for control, but control is really in the hands of God, not us. If we are not meant to achieve any particular outcome, it will not come into being because it will not benefit our highest good.

Remember, in all cases, to let go of the need for a specific outcome. This is vitally important. If you do not let go of the outcome, you may reside in the state of neediness, and that is what the universe recognizes and attempts to provide you. The state of neediness is not congruent with the state of satisfaction we feel when we experience fulfillment. Of course there are at least two types of fulfillment: temporary and everlasting fulfillment. Temporary fulfillment may lead to temporary peace of mind. Everlasting fulfillment leads to everlasting peace of mind. Therefore we must seek that which provides us everlasting fulfillment. Things of this earth cannot provide everlasting fulfillment. Thus far I have only described some aspects of peace of mind, but I have not as yet given you the tools to achieve it. So how do we create peace of mind? Here are two hugely important tools outlined for you.

Here is tool number one: *Change what you are thinking; change your thoughts.* It is important to understand that peace of mind is exactly that, peace of *mind.* It is not peace of money. It is not peace of health. It is not peace of job. It is not peace of relationship. It is peace of mind; therefore, the key to happiness lies within the mind. Peace of mind can only occur by working with the mind. It comes down to what we think that matters. It is not tied to our emotions. Our emotions are tied to what we think or rather how we think. It is not what we have or what we don't have in our lives. It is not about whom we have or whom we don't have in our lives. It is about the mind. It is about *changing the mind.* So the next step then would be to write down your thoughts. It is surprising how many thoughts we have during the day we really don't acknowledge. By periodically writing them down through journaling, we bring what we are thinking to our attention. Are they primarily negative or positive? What is it that we are thinking? Are we worrying about something in particular? Do the thoughts we have during the day support our intention to achieve peace of mind or hinder it?

During the course of the day a variety of events can occur that would normally cause us to feel positive or negative. How we react to these occurrences is the key to creating peace of mind. What we create within our mind as a result of the events of the day is what makes all the difference. Let me give you an example. If you were just fired from your job yesterday how might that make you feel? Would you feel anxious, nervous, sad, or distressed? Most likely you would experience any combination of these feelings. What if I told you that tomorrow you would be offered your dream job and you would be making more money than you ever had before? Would that make you feel differently? Of course it would. That is how it typically works. Let me explain.

Our minds most often simply *react* to outside stimuli. We perceive and judge each event as good or bad, positive or negative. What would happen if we brought our attention to a point of consciousness within ourselves, and let's say that within that point of consciousness we hold the understanding that *everything is going to be fine no matter what happens?* Would your attitude now change on how you felt about your old job or new job? Let's say that the new job didn't work out the way you expected and you were suffering miserably at your new job. Things have changed again, haven't they? But did your attitude change with it? Remember that I said *everything is going to be fine no matter what happens.* That is the way life is. Life is a series of ups and downs. Life is like a rollercoaster ride. With every upswing life is exciting and fun, and with every downswing life is scary or distressing. But after the ride is finished, where do we arrive? In every case with every ride, we arrive at the very same place in which we started the ride, at the beginning.

What if then I explained that there are a few variables in the rollercoaster of life that we could manipulate to make the ride easier for us or harder for us? Would you be interested in learning more? I will share a few more insights with you. The beginning and the end of the ride is heaven, whatever heaven at present means to you. Assume first that you are going to be one of the many who make it to heaven. What we subsequently need to do next is to level out the ride, right? By definition, if we take out the downswings in life then as a result we have to take out the upswings in life. We can't have only ups with no downs. Life doesn't work that way. But if you again center your mind back to the perception that *the universe is constantly rearranging itself for a better outcome,* then what would be a normally distressing occurrence in life is not going to affect you the same way it once would have.

Remember, our challenges are blessings that afford us an opportunity for greater material or spiritual growth. Keeping that in mind, life's ups and downs are not going to bring on the anxieties they once would have. We have in effect taken out the downswings, which will take out the upswings. Why? Because we now appreciate the fact that the end result does not change either way. The end result is heaven. It is our place of origin. It is where we began our ride, our spiritual journey. It is also where we finish our journey. Now we have created peace of mind because we come from a place of greater understanding and even-mindedness. Since we have appropriately changed our attitude toward life, the only thing left to consider then is our choices. Do we make decisions that help or hinder our new attitude toward life?

To know in our heart of hearts that *everything is going to be fine no matter what happens,* we recognize that there is a higher power out there that loves us and has our best interests at heart. By keeping this thought pattern in the forefront of our minds, we are better situated to achieve and maintain peace of mind. Didn't I put forward the idea that peace of mind is really about focusing on *a piece of our mind?* What are you focusing on during your day? If we are having thoughts that bring about anxiety and worry then we need to quickly switch our thoughts back to a positive mantra such as *There is a loving God out there that has my best interests at heart.* You can come up with any mantra you would like that suits you. Create your own, something positive you can repeat over and over in your head as time allows or as necessary given your current condition or stress level.

It also helps to develop a spiritual practice that includes meditation. Meditation calms the mind and brings a deeper sense of peace. I promise this is true. So meditate daily for at least fifteen minutes. Establish a daily practice. Please make it a priority. The longer you meditate each day, the greater the peace of mind you will discover within yourself. Use creative visualization to direct your thoughts to those that bring a deeper sense of peace. For instance, think of a place you consider to be very beautiful where you might have sensed a higher power present. Will that change how you are feeling at any particular moment? Most likely it will.

So, if you wish to change your life, try using the tool *change what you are thinking.* Another way of saying this is to *change your mind.* By changing your mind, you can instantaneously change your life if you decide to do so. If you have negative thoughts, reverse them and turn them into positive thoughts and act in accordance with the positive thought. As an example, state aloud, "I am happy," versus dwelling on the feeling of sadness. By doing this we use *cognitive dissonance* to our advantage. Cognitive dissonance is *the perception of incompatibility between two cognitions.* For simplicity sake, we will define the term *cognition* as *a belief, idea, or perception.* Cognitive dissonance occurs when two beliefs do not resonate with each other; they conflict and only one can be true. Cognitive dissonance can be made to work in our favor. By choosing to accept or adopt the more favorable belief, we cause a disturbance in our mind until we eventually come to a point of resolution by eliminating the other belief less desirable to us. In other words, we cannot hold both contradictory beliefs to be true. By holding onto the more positive thought, such as *everything is fine,* we eventually dispel the more negative thought of *everything is not fine.* In the long term, we cannot hold both of these statements to be true at the same time. It is impossible. This is cognitive dissonance.

Here is a specific example of how cognitive dissonance works. Let's say you are depressed about breaking up with a significant other. It would be very easy to fill your head with ideas and notions that could and would distress you. "I will never be happy again" or "I am so alone" or "This really hurts" are all statements that we could make up in our mind that might describe the situation we feel we are in, correct? Let's say you decide to think much more positive thoughts. For example, you could change your mind to something like "This will give me time to really explore myself spiritually" or "Now I finally have the opportunity to take that trip I have always wanted to take" or "This opens the door to find a more suitable mate." I am sure you can see the difference. After my last significant breakup, I actually took my own advice and went to Egypt. My trip assisted me in transitioning past the loss of the relationship.

It is important to focus your mind only on the positive aspects of something, even if you have to initially make it up. Eventually your mind will adopt the new belief system. The key is to keep repeating positive statements in your mind until they become your new reality. They will become your new reality as long as you put forth the effort to make them come true. For me personally, because I stayed in a positive frame of mind open to the universe rearranging itself for a better outcome, I discovered my *true companion soul mate* for this lifetime. The spiritual benefits of meeting your true companion soul mate is discussed in a later chapter.

Here is the second tool to enact positive change in your life: *Change what you are doing; change your behavior.* The first tool is to *change what you are thinking* with the anticipation that this will eventually lead to a more permanent positive change in your thought patterns. The principle for *changing what you are doing* is once again based on cognitive dissonance. It works this way. If you change what you are doing to a more positive behavior, there will follow a change in the way you are thinking, as long as you continue the new behavior long enough to solidify a new thought pattern. Let me give you a personal example. When I feel depressed, or rather when I have decided to think in a depressing way, I sometimes find it difficult to hold onto the new positive thought long enough to make the transition to a more permanent positive thought pattern. When this occurs I do something that consistently clears my mind and cheers me up. For me, that is hiking. However, I normally do not have any physical energy given that in the moment I am depressing positive thought patterns. I nevertheless make myself to go for a hike. This is where willpower, a function of the mind, is vitally important. In places where there are no nature trails, I go to a park or walk around the neighborhood.

So then for me (and maybe for you) the key to overcoming depressive thoughts is to hike or minimally go for a walk. It may or may not surprise you to hear that there is a scientific rationale behind walking. The process of walking marries or balances the left side of brain with the right side of the brain. The right side of the brain is considered to be the feminine and more creative side. The right side is more apt to intuit an answer to a problem. The left side is considered to be the masculine side of the brain and is the more concrete thinking (versus abstract thinking) part of the brain; everything here is more black and white type thinking. The left brain is better at solving mathematical questions or problems where a specific step by step process is needed to determine an answer. In other words, the left brain tends to work in a more linear fashion.

The very first stage of linking the left side of the brain with the right side of the brain occurs at a very young age. Crawling is the earliest basic activity that trains the mind to link or marry the right brain creative function to the left brain concrete analytical function. When a child learns to crawl, normally between the ages of six and twelve months, the child learns to move his or her right hand forward with the left leg, and alternatively the left hand with the right leg.[1] Crawling is therefore a crucial part of a child's development and is carried forward into our adult life through the process of walking. As adults, we perform the same function when we swing our arms alternately with our legs as we walk. So if simple contemplation doesn't work, and feeling your way through a problem doesn't bring you the satisfaction you are looking for, then go for a walk and swing your arms. The process of walking may help you clear your mind, and in doing so, balance your emotions. Walking definitely helps me overcome any depressive thought patterns and has at times allowed me to tap into my creative genius to solve perplexing problems.

There are at least two types of depression. The first type is *situational depression*. This occurs when something we consider to be negative happens to us and we are upset about it. This most commonly occurs when we feel we have suffered a loss of something or someone, but it is usually temporary and we eventually overcome it. The second type of depression is much more severe. It is *long-term depression*. It generally comes into being when people are not living an authentic life consistent with their soul's true purpose. What they are doing, in a literal sense, is depressing their truest nature. They are completely unaware of their higher purpose or are avoiding it out of laziness or fear. They are choosing to not awaken to the spirit (soul) that lives within them. They are spiritually asleep. They have not as yet made the connection to their soul. They reside almost fully within their egocentric state of illusion and material nature. Most people, unaware of why they are suffering long-term depression, turn to medicating themselves or worse, drugs and alcohol. What they should be doing is turning their attention inward and listening to their inner voice. The best way to do this is by meditating, not medicating.

Of course, this much abbreviated note on depression is a generality, but as most generalities are, they are based on some spiritual truth. However, people that have a chemical imbalance or a mental illness may very well require some type of prescription medication to facilitate healing. As a Licensed Professional Counselor (in Colorado only), I am not qualified to give medical advice. A person seeking medical advice for depression or otherwise should always be treated by a qualified licensed practitioner. That being said, let's get back to effecting positive change in our lives.

Tapping is another exercise where you marry or balance the right side of the brain with the left side of the brain. It is a great exercise when you are faced with a problem in which you are finding it difficult to reach a satisfactory solution. First, sit in a comfortable chair with your feet placed flat on the floor with your back upright so that your upper body is neither leaning forward or backward. Then concentrate on your problem as intensely as you can. Try not to let anything interfere with your concentration. Holding the problem within your mind, begin to tap your left hand on your left knee and alternately your right hand on your right knee. It is easier to maintain this exercise if you rest your palms on each leg as you tap with your fingers.

Once you begin, try to maintain the tapping process for several minutes. At times you may become so relaxed by this exercise that you may find it difficult to continue the tapping process. If this occurs, take a brief rest and start again when you feel you are ready. If possible, tap for three to five minutes for a total of three intervals resting for a couple of minutes in between each interval. Remember that it is crucial to concentrate on your problem while you are engaged in the tapping process. The intent of this exercise is to marry the left brain function with the right brain function while you are focusing on the problem. The concrete side of your left brain marries with the abstract side of your right brain and then all of a sudden, out of nowhere, a resolution surfaces. I have done this with various clients I have counseled over the years and have had many successes; rather, the success was theirs. This tapping process also appears to have a calming effect on students before taking exams, and consequently students may test higher than their previous overall averages. Tapping of course cannot be used as a replacement for studying.

For you, the concept of *changing what you are doing* may mean something else. Maybe knitting is what you love to do. Maybe reading a good book snaps you out of a negative state. No matter what, the key is to make yourself do something positive. Taking positive action forces cognitive dissonance to kick into gear. How can you be thinking negatively when you are doing something you love? By changing what you are doing, eventually through cognitive dissonance, the mind adopts a more positive thought pattern. In this same way, if you change a negative behavioral pattern, you can make significant long-lasting positive changes in your life.

So I have now given you two great tools: *change what you are thinking* and *change what you are doing*. The beneficial change will naturally follow. To create lasting change, you may have to continually interrupt a negative thought pattern that has become well established. You have heard of "fake it until you make it," right? Well, it works. It has been scientifically proven. The key is to stick with the more positive thought pattern or positive action until the positive transition occurs.

During my days of counseling clients in Colorado, I was working with one particularly difficult client. For confidentiality sake, let's refer to him as John. John had been seeing various counselors for years with little result. His chronic depression led him to believe that he was worthless, and consequently he had few, if any, friends. John hated his line of work. John literally felt that no one else on earth had as many problems as he faced on a daily basis. With a job he hated, no friends to speak of, and feeling forsaken by life, John spoke to me about committing suicide. In the beginning I primarily treated John using Cognitive Therapy. Cognitive Therapy is a technique that attempts to alter the client's established thought patterns. By changing the way the client thinks the client is better able to make positive choices in their lives usually increasing peace of mind. In John's case this was critical. Without altering his continuing thought patterns, I feared he might carry out his ideation of suicide. In short, John did not respond favorably to Cognitive Therapy. He had been thinking depressively for too many years and was not able to hold onto the new thought pattern long enough to create positive change in his life. My concern for his personal safety grew.

Next I tried using Behavioral Therapy techniques with John. John's belief that he had no friends may have been accurate. John's belief that he was the forsaken by life in that he was worse off than any other human being on this planet was obviously an inaccurate self perception. In attempting to change John's behavior, I suggested that he discover new hobbies. In doing so, John put himself in a position to meet new people that had similar interests. As far as feeling forsaken by life, I took John to the homeless shelter to see what challenges other less fortunate people were dealing with in their lives. I also took him to the Salvation Army mobile food truck to see the men, women and children in line in the dead of winter for a hot meal. I explained to John that many of these people were homeless with some facing major additions of various types. I went on to say that many of the homeless women were sexually abused or battered. Needless to say this had a dramatic impact upon John. I would like to say that John had a complete turnaround after our brief visit to the homeless shelter and the mobile food truck, but I would be less than honest if I did. John did not change his behaviors to the point necessary to live a significantly more positive productive life. John did however change his perception on just how bad life was for him as compared to other people and in doing so he may have saved his own life.

Every day we are faced with choices. Our choices either serve to promote the lower nature of our own humanity or the higher nature of the Spirit that resides in us. Our choices serve to build up our outer personality as ego or inner personality as our soul. Our choices serve to promote peace of mind or continual dysfunction. What you think and do in this life says volumes about you. A personal spiritual practice that includes meditation will only serve to solidify the positive changes you wish to make in your life. Faith in a divine being along with the understanding that we all face our own set of challenges will help you to develop a deeper spiritual acceptance of life's mysteries. The key to establishing lasting peace of mind is to know that we in the truest sense are eternal immortal souls loved by God; and as aspects of God, we are on a rollercoaster ride back home to heaven. We can make the journey home a little easier for ourselves by utilizing these two important tools: change a thought or change a behavior.

CHAPTER 4

What Are Thoughts?

❦

What are thoughts? What is the difference between our brain and our mind? Does our mind exist after our brain has stopped functioning? Where do thoughts come from? Do thoughts come from the brain? Do they come from our mind? Have you ever considered that we are not the creator of our thoughts? These are all very good questions and I will attempt to answer them all.

What are thoughts? A thought is a form of energy just as is everything else created. Do you remember the Universal Law of Vibration about everything having an energetic property to it? The same is true for thoughts. Thoughts are energetic forms. Thoughts are energy transmitted in a way similar to that of electricity. Once a thought is created it exists within the planes of consciousness and is available to anyone that can tap into it. That is called *telepathy,* which is *the direct thought transference between one person and another.* Let me provide you with a word of warning. All of our thoughts are recorded by God in the *Book of Life,* not just our actions. The Book of Life is nothing more than an omnipresent God experiencing our thoughts, emotions and actions recorded into His eternal memory.

What is the difference between our brain and our mind? The mind is obviously not the same as the brain. The brain represents the physical container of the mind. The brain is the physical manifestation of the non-physical mind. The brain is simply the physical receptor of thoughts, just as our physical body is the physical vehicle for our soul. The Law of Correspondence is at work here; what is true above is true below. What exists in the spiritual plane will eventually manifest itself somehow somewhere on the physical plane.

Does our mind exist after our brain has stopped functioning? Our mind consists of our thoughts, imagination, perceptions, intelligence, reason, willpower, and memory. In a broader sense, an individual's higher nature mind is God Consciousness or God's wisdom within each of us. The lower nature mind is obviously not pure God Consciousness. Lower nature mind is God Consciousness we polluted. We create this lower energy. Without our higher conscious mind, no learning can occur for the soul because our higher conscious mind in effect is the same energy as the soul. When the soul leaves the body, there are no more thoughts in the brain because the mind is gone; it has left the body.

This would be consistent with the descriptions of near-death experiences where a person recalls hovering above his or her own lifeless body before returning to that body. The mind or soul as consciousness for a brief period in time was outside of the body. Without our higher nature mind we would be nothing more than animals. We would once again be like an ape. Without the Holy Spirit life force energy, the body along with the brain would be dead.

"As the body without the Spirit is dead...." James 2:26

Where do thoughts come from? Do thoughts come from the brain? Do they come from our mind? Have you ever considered that we are not the creator of our thoughts? It might come as a surprise to you to hear that the human brain is not the true generator of thought. In at least one sense of the word, neither is our mind. For the most part, as an unenlightened being, our mind is a receiver of thoughts. So, if the brain is no more than the physical manifestation of the mind and our mind is primarily a receiver of thoughts, then thoughts can come from a whole variety of sources. Thoughts entering our minds may stem from a variety of sources including but not limited to our individual soul as our higher nature self or sliver of God Consciousness. Besides our individual soul, we may receive thoughts from outside sources such as our spiritual teachers, angels, spiritual guides, and yes, even evil influences. Have you ever had a thought that was so ridiculous or so very evil that you shook your head in wonderment and asked yourself something to the effect "Where did that evil thought come from?!?" Because we exist within a state of lower consciousness (less than that of being enlightened) our mind is polluted, polluted with lower nature desires related to material nature or materialism, in effect *evil*.

Our thoughts can also come from another person sharing his or her ideas with us. A thought may come from a conversation with a teacher, friend, or a relative. Television as well as radio can affect our thoughts. As human beings, we are sensitive to all of these thought energies. Intuition can help us to tune into other people's thoughts. We all have intuition, whether developed in us or not. Have you ever felt like someone was looking at you and you turned around and you were right? You felt their thought energy directed at you. In reality, thoughts can come from almost anywhere.

So, if we are not always the creator of our own thoughts, how do thoughts reach our mind? The answer lies within the mind itself. Our mind acts like a radio receiver. Our mind picks up these energies as thoughts. It receives them just as a radio receiver would pick up radio waves. Thought forms exist on the planes of consciousness as previously mentioned. These planes are filled with a multitude of thought energies. I can only describe what thoughts on the planes of consciousness are like in this way: It would be like turning on ten thousand radios all at the same time and with all of them tuned into a different radio station. Luckily our mind has a filtering device or we would be flooded with random thoughts of all sorts. If a person is mentally ill or has had significant brain damage, his or her thought filter may be corrupted and consequently cannot process or filter out thoughts properly. This person may therefore be a great deal more receptive to negative thought patterns and/or evil energies. He or she might even be considered insane or schizophrenic.

Within each thought wave, there can be either a positive force/vibration, a negative force/vibration, or a neutral force/vibration. Just as the Holy Spirit can build up, tear down, or be neutral energy, our thoughts can build up, tear down, or be neutral energy. The Holy Spirit is defined in greater detail in a later chapter. Thoughts are corrupted when humans attempt to control situations normally associated with a lower desire or fear. These lower desires or fears corrupt the originally pure energy contained within the thought. Pure and holy thoughts are energies of the Holy Spirit and assist the world in raising its consciousness. Negative thought energies in turn affect the physical world negatively. Neutral thoughts possess neither positive nor negative energy. What thoughts we act on depends upon our level of spiritual development.

Now that you understand thoughts do not always necessarily come from our true higher self (soul), it may be easier to understand why we at times think evil thoughts, or worse, verbalize them or act on them. The greater sin of course is to act on the evil thought. Remember that each of us in effect has two minds, a lower nature ego-based mind and a higher nature God-mind. This split in mind function occurred because of the fall in man's consciousness (discussed later in greater detail). Suffice it to say that previously our individual minds were consistent with God-mind. Through the process of continually choosing correctly, we will eventually return to the higher nature God-mind and of course heaven.

We create our own reality with the thoughts we think, individually and collectively. Our thoughts are the first step in creation as co-creators with God. Thoughts may then lead to an emotion and then an action. Action leads to results, good or bad. Where we focus our attention and energies determines our quality of life and our peace of mind. If we focus our attention on the negative things in life, we see only the negative. We can easily manifest hell on earth if we are not careful. Conversely, we can create heaven on earth. If we place our focus on the positive things in life, we draw the positive things in life to us. What we think, visualize, and act on is created into form or being; it becomes our reality, good or bad. Fear may be our greatest adversary.

Fear, as does any emotion, plays a vital role in life. Fear's job is to make us aware that we may be in some sort of danger. We should be fearful of getting into a cage with a lion. We should also be fearful of jumping off a bridge. These are intelligent wholesome fears that keep us safe and alive. F.E.A.R. is sometimes defined as False Evidence Appearing Real. This type of fear generally stems from either believing that we are not enough, which is *fear of failure*, or the fear of not having enough, which is *fear of scarcity*. Fear of scarcity can sometimes manifest itself as greed. Neither of these two fears represent our truest reality. Fear always manifests itself as anxiety, and any anxiety tends to shut down or corrupt the life force energies of the Holy Spirit within us. Fear of a specific type of failure may actually bring the feared failure to fruition. We draw these unhealthy failure-based energies to us by simply focusing on them for too long of a period of time.

Everyone at one time or another has heard the phrase "You are what you eat." But have you ever heard "You are what you think"? Scientists have concluded that every cell in the body is replaced approximately once every seven years. In theory we have the potential to recreate ourselves every seven years. The thoughts we think, not only the foods we eat, are crucial to our physical, emotional, and spiritual wellbeing. So logically then, we should ask the following question: *Does our mind control our thoughts and desires, or do our thoughts and desires control our mind?* A spiritually elevated person has control of his/her mind and avoids delving into the lower nature for material gratification. It is our lower nature as ego that attempts to fulfill our desires for material nature. It is our higher nature that wishes to fulfill our desire to *re-member with God*, as in *reuniting with God*. However, reuniting with God may take many lifetimes. Heaven may not be the next step in our spiritual transition after our death. Remember, I asked you to stay open to all possibilities.

Since the thoughts we have are not necessarily our own, we must make a decision in regard to each thought, and in fact we do. With each thought, we make a decision whether or not to believe it. The problem is our thoughts happen way too fast, and since we have established certain patterns, we often accept a negative thought as valid. Too often we accept the negative thought as our own without really giving it due consideration. What we really need to do is to slow down our thought process and look at each thought and ask if that thought serves our higher good. We need to decide whether or not it adds more love to our consciousness, or whether or not it adds greater levels of anxiety, hate, or other negative emotions to our consciousness.

By slowing down our thought process and by discriminating between each thought, we create an opportunity for choice. We segment time. We use time in a more positive manner. In a way, we stop time. When we take the time to do so, we can choose the positive thoughts that serve us and ignore the negative thoughts that tend to injure us or injure others. Since our thoughts do not necessarily come from our higher selves, it becomes necessary for us to discriminate between each thought and not simply accept all of them as being true or having validity. When we accept all thoughts as our own and having validity, we create the opportunity for dogmatic thinking. In choosing lower nature thought forms, we create a lower nature consciousness steeped in dogma and fear. These negative thought-form energies are very real and very damaging to us individually and collectively. Negative thought-form energies can harm us physically, emotionally, mentally, and/or spiritually as it relates to our soul's karma.

Dogma, defined as *a religious doctrine proclaimed as true without proof*, is simply compilations of thoughts and ideas mankind professes to be true. But not all of mankind proclaims the same things to be true. Each religion has created its own dogma by arbitrarily setting limitations upon God. By saying God is a certain way is to suggest that He is not the other way. But in effect isn't everything God and/or minimally from God? Religious dogma has led to incredible hardships and even death for many people by means of countless wars and crusades. But isn't everything we believe in simply what we declare as truth and what we declare as lies or untruths based on our current level of information and consciousness? If this is correct, then in all probability none of us have it right a hundred percent of the time, which means we are all wrong in one belief or another. Maybe we should open our minds to greater possibilities and not limit how God manifests Himself in the world. What makes one religion more accurate or more truthful than another? The answer sadly lies in our own dogmatic belief systems. One dogmatic belief system I was brought up to believe was that only Christians go to heaven. I was surprised to discover that many other religious leaders have the same belief system. If they are correct in their assumptions, then no one will go to heaven because religion is exclusionary, versus what I believe God to be, which is inclusionary.

CHAPTER 5

Subconscious Mind and Memory

⚜

Subconscious thought is unconscious thought. The *subconscious mind* refers to thoughts and desires that occur below the conscious mind's awareness. The term *subconscious* is sometimes used interchangeably with *unconscious* although they vary slightly in meaning depending upon how the word is used in a sentence. The subconscious in psychotherapy refers to that which is below the surface of awareness that affects conscious behavior. Alternatively, within the level of our awareness in which thoughts and ideas are generated and/or expressed is conscious thought. Rational thinking and cognitive awareness of our own existence that guide our daily decisions and activities occur on the conscious level. A person aware of his or her thoughts and feelings is said to be *conscious of self*. However, the expression *self-conscious* has developed a slightly negative variation of the original meaning.

The subconscious mind is always recording, even in sleep. The subconscious mind also keeps track of time. Often I awake from a deep sleep knowing the correct time within a few minutes before looking at the alarm clock. Even space is recorded by the subconscious mind. Time and space are important tools for us to achieve Christ Consciousness (enlightenment). However, they can also be hindrances when used for lower nature purposes. The unconscious mind helps us process what the five senses perceive during the day. Not everything we see, hear, taste, smell, or touch during the day can be processed by our unenlightened mind. Because we can't immediately assimilate all of what we perceive in our daily lives, it is recorded in the subconscious mind. The conscious mind can process approximately fifty bits of information per second, while the subconscious mind can process approximately fifty trillion bits of information per second.[1] The conscious mind may attempt to organize or categorize bits of information it receives into memory to be used now or retrieved later if it determines the information is necessary or important. The subconscious mind stores additional information for later recall or may attempt to make it known to the conscious mind more expeditiously. Some memories too traumatic to be recalled are buried in our subconscious. Dreams help us process what we experience during the day and are one of the ways unconscious thoughts become conscious. That is one of the reasons why analyzing dreams is so important.

The world of conscious thought and unconscious thought comprise our total memory. It includes our *soul memory* from all of our previous lifetimes, which is normally stored in the subconscious. During a past life regression, past life memories are brought forth into the conscious mind. Other exceptions to past life memories being stored in the subconscious mind include past life memories that are made conscious through dreams or *spontaneous past-life memory recall*.

The unconscious mind has unlimited capacity for memory. It can store an infinite number of thoughts. An unenlightened mind can only hold a limited number of thoughts within its conscious memory. When the Holy Spirit enters you fully and completely, there is no longer an unconscious individual mind because the Holy Spirit energies contain within it the memory of God. Everything is made conscious by the Holy Spirit. In effect the unconscious mind has been upgraded to the *all-conscious all-knowing God-mind*. That is why the apostles, when filled by the Holy Spirit after the ascension of Christ, could speak many foreign languages.

> "All of them were filled with the Holy Spirit and began to speak in other tongues [or languages] as the Spirit enabled them." Acts 2:4

I believe that *speaking in tongues* is nothing more than the power to speak in many languages. The apostles could do so because they tapped into the memory of the manifested God, the Holy Spirit Consciousness, where nothing is unconscious. They were enlightened beings.

Therefore it is important that we cultivate our spirituality each lifetime. Our soul memory aids us in our spiritual development. It helps us remember our mistakes. It helps us remember spiritual lessons. It is vitally important to remember how to discriminate between what is good and what is evil. In one way it is through our memory that we re-member with God. Memory is one of the Holy Spirit energies carried within our soul. Our soul memory is therefore inherent within each of us as we travel from one incarnation to another incarnation. Memory is in effect a key to immortality. By storing each past life memory in the soul, we can begin each lifetime where we left off from the previous life, rather than having to relearn the same spiritual lessons over and over each lifetime. Our soul memory is what keeps us from dropping back into lower levels of consciousness each reincarnation. How can we learn from our mistakes if we don't remember them? The spiritual lessons we learn as a result of our experiences are stored in our soul memory. If that were not the case we would be starting over every lifetime from the beginning.

By cultivating a new life experience into our conscious memory, we are increasing our knowledge and concurrently decreasing the amount of our memory stored in the subconscious mind. We are in effect preparing our minds for enlightenment. Soul memory is a gift we were given to remember our spiritual lessons until such time we reunite with God. The Holy Spirit as God Consciousness is our higher memory. It is the holder of all memories of which we are just an aspect. When we are filled with the Holy Spirit, we are filled with divine memory and nothing is unconscious. We then remember that we are in reality one with God. When an individual becomes fully conscious the subconscious mind is eliminated and all is known. We return to a state of being where we recognize the presence of God in all things including the god within us, which by at least one definition is heaven.

Section II

MERGING RELIGIONS WITH GOD

CHAPTER 6

Faith

꧁꧂

Contrary to popular Christian doctrine, I do not agree that faith automatically gets us into heaven. However, I also recognize that we will not gain access to heaven without it, because without faith, there is often no hope for salvation. Overall, I believe the word *faith* has been incorrectly defined. We have defined **faith** as *a belief in the truth* when faith is more accurately defined in the Bible as *a state of knowing the truth*. Believing something to be true is not the same as knowing something to be true. Faith, as we think of it, is merely an interim step. Faith then is a necessary precondition for believing. Let me explain.

Jesus talked about faith in the Gospel of Matthew.

> "He replied, 'Because you have so little faith. I tell you the truth, if you have faith as small as a mustard seed, you can say to this mountain, "Move from here to there," and it will move. Nothing will be impossible for you.'" Matthew 17:20-21

And when Jesus said this He was addressing His own apostles! Why is it that Jesus suggests that we have so little faith? Jesus says that if we had as much as a small mustard seed of faith we could move a mountain. Was Jesus once again speaking metaphorically? Or was Jesus speaking literally? I do not believe faith in God as we understand it is going to get us into heaven. I believe *knowing* there is a God will get us into heaven. Knowing is not what we normally think of when we talk about faith. It is by and large the opposite. It is often because we don't know whether or not God exists that faith becomes a necessary precondition. We all struggle with our faith at times. Supposedly even Mother Theresa struggled with hers. I know I have often struggled with mine.

Did Moses part the Red Sea because he had faith or did the sea part because *he believed* God would part it? I believe Moses knew that if he went into the water, the sea would part for him. In that moment Moses' faith in God transcended all doubt.

"As Jesus was on his way, the crowds almost crushed him. And a woman was there who had been subject to bleeding for twelve years, but no one could heal her. She came up behind him and touched the edge of his cloak, and immediately her bleeding stopped." Luke 8:42-44

Was it faith that healed the woman or was it an inner knowing that she would be healed? I believe she knew in advance of touching Jesus' cloak that she would be healed. Her faith was not faith in the sense that we think of it today. Her faith was an absolute knowing, without doubt.

Did Jesus turn two fish and five loaves into enough food to feed five thousand people because of His faith? Or did Jesus know He had the power to do so?

> "Another of his disciples, Andrew, Simon Peter's brother, spoke up: 'Here is a boy with five small barley loaves and two small fish, but how far will they go among so many?' Jesus said, 'Have the people sit down.' There was plenty of grass in that place, and the men sat down, about five thousand of them. Jesus then took the loaves, gave thanks, and distributed to those who were seated as much as they wanted. He did the same with the fish." John 6:8-11

Do you really think that Jesus had any doubt whatsoever that He could do what He intended to do? The answer is absolutely not. As a fully enlightened, fully conscious being, Jesus knows the Father (God), and in knowing the Father, Jesus knew that He could perform any miracle in His name.

After the apostles received the Holy Spirit they went out into the world to heal the sick. Was it faith or did they know with absolute certainty they could heal the sick?

> "Then Peter said, 'Silver or gold I do not have, but what I have I give you. In the name of Jesus Christ of Nazareth, walk.' Taking him by the right hand, he helped him up, and instantly the man's feet and ankles became strong." Acts 3:6-7

Was there any doubt in the crippled man's mind that he would walk? If there were any doubt, I find it difficult to believe that he would have walked. His faith resided in the knowing that he would walk, not in thinking there was a possibility he might be healed. Likewise, Peter knew he could heal beyond any doubt.

In the Gospel of John, Jesus speaks about the glory of God.

"My prayer is not for them alone [the apostles]. I pray also for those who will believe in me through their message, that all of them may be one, Father, just as you are in me and I am in you. May they also be in us so that the world may believe that you have sent me. I have given them [the apostles] the glory that you gave me, that they may be one as we are one." John 17:20-23

When Jesus refers to the glory, He is speaking of the Holy Spirit that He himself received from God. Jesus likewise gave the gift of the Holy Spirit to the apostles. Jesus requests in prayer *that they may be one as we are one.* Jesus clearly states that He is one with the Father. Jesus here is referring to the Universal Law of Unity (All is One) since we are all children of God. When the apostles became enlightened, they too could perform miracles and knew themselves to be one with God. Nowhere in the verses above does Jesus use the term *faith.* He consistently uses the word *believe* throughout the verses. Only when one believes can a person reunite (re-member) with God by receiving the glory of the Holy Spirit. Only then can one enter heaven. Only by *believing* do we enter heaven, not through *faith* as we currently understand it.

"This righteousness from God comes through faith in Jesus Christ to all who believe. There is no difference…" Romans 3:22

It is clear that faith as described in the Bible is not defined as a state of trusting so much as believing and knowing. Faith is believing and knowing there is a God.

"Now faith is being sure of what we hope for and certain of what we do not see." Hebrews 11:1

Maybe the reason we lack faith is because we don't understand the true nature of God.

Faith is not as much about hope as it is about being sure that we will enter into the kingdom of heaven. It is about knowing we will one day return to our God in heaven. And where is faith without deeds?

"You foolish man, do you want evidence that faith without deeds is useless? Was not our ancestor Abraham considered righteous for what he did when he offered his son Isaac on the altar? You see that his faith and his actions were working together, and his faith was made complete by what he did…You see that a person is justified by what he does and not by faith alone." James 2:20-24

"…so faith without deeds is dead." James 2:26

"And without faith it is impossible to please God, because anyone who comes to him must believe that he exists…" Hebrews 11:6

The last verse makes it clear that to get to heaven, we must believe in God. Faith, as we currently define it, will not get us there. Faith without action is not faith at all, for if a person truly believes in God, that person would feel mandated by his or her own conscience to help others. Faith is embracing the belief that the universe is acting on our best behalf, and that this intelligence knows what is best for us—better than we do ourselves. Faith is accepting the darkness and the light as equal within the context of our spiritual development when we consider a negative occurrence in our life to be simply an adjustment to our path. In other words, we require both light and dark in order to choose the light. Without darkness there is no choice. This is addressed by the Law of Relativity.

Knowing and believing in God is the same and comes to us as we increase our levels of consciousness to a point of enlightenment and a soul vibration consistent with being enlightened, a vibration consistent with heaven. This is addressed by the Law of Vibration and the Law of Attraction. Don't worry if you are not yet at the point of believing without doubt; that will come with the ongoing conscious development of the soul over time. As we increase our soul's vibratory rate or soul development, we will develop a newer, more complete understanding of God and will come to a place of absolute knowing (enlightenment) and a place called heaven.

CHAPTER 7

Prayer, Intent, Affirmations, and Mantras

༺✤༻

Just as faith is not *thinking* or simply *hoping* that something is true or will come true, the same holds true for our prayers. Its foundation rests in *knowing* and *believing*.

> "Therefore I tell you, whatever you ask for in prayer, believe that you have received it, and it will be yours." Mark 11:24

According to the verse above, by acting as if we have already received what we requested, it will be given to us. The key then may be to pray, and to then let go of the outcome, knowing and believing we have already received it. And then if it is meant to be, it will be. If it wasn't meant to be, it will not come into being, hopefully. In the case of prayer, maybe it is then better to begin in a state of gratitude for receiving even before we receive that which we are praying for. However, prayer necessarily comes with a warning. Often we do not know what is best for us, and consequently we pray for the wrong things.

> "We do not know what to pray for, but the Spirit himself intercedes for us with groans that words cannot express. And he who searches our hearts knows the mind of the Spirit, because the Spirit intercedes for the saints in accordance with God's will." Romans 8:26-27

Referenced as *saints* in the verse above, it is clear that we may not always ask God for what is best for us. It is the old adage, "Be careful what you pray for, you just might get it!" Sometimes we get what we ask for even though it is not in our best interest, spiritually speaking. The reason we receive things not consistent with our higher nature is because we have free will and/or it might be tied to a spiritual lesson we have yet to learn. Sometimes the lesson is learning about *what* we should ask for. But as the promise goes, when we look within our hearts we find Spirit; and Spirit intercedes for us on our behalf providing us what we need, not necessarily what we desire, because the Spirit within us knows what is best for us consistent with God's will. That is reason enough to let go of the outcome, isn't it?

So, then, what are prayers? Prayers are energetic thought waves (vibrations) sent out into the universe in order to create a specific outcome or condition. Prayers are thoughts expressed directly to God, typically with some emotion and/or a specific request behind them. Sadly, too often these requests are meant to gratify one of our five senses versus asking for something that brings us closer to God. However, the universe's job is to fulfill our desires, as holy or unholy they may be because we are *mini-gods*. For that reason, we need to be careful where we put our intentions and prayers; we could be creating additional karma for ourselves. If through our intention and actions we are able to bring wealth to us, it would come with added responsibility. It is vital that the energy of money be used to better mankind's situation on earth. This can be accomplished in many ways.

Tithing, of course, should be one of the ways in which we use the energy of money.

> "The Bible is a book about giving, with more promises related to giving than to any other subject. For example, the subject of 'believing' appears 272 times in the Bible, 'prayer' 371 times, and 'love' 714 times, while 'giving' is mentioned 2,162 times! Jesus talked more about giving than anything else; more than half of the parables have to do with money and worldly goods."[1]

Donating to worthy causes is beneficial for all mankind. Besides tithing to a church and charities, making the world a better place can come about through the creation of jobs that pay a fair wage. Money can be used to create more environmentally friendly products. Money can be used positively in many ways. However, if we use wealth to satiate our lower nature desires related to our own material pleasure, we may be increasing our karma and the likelihood of having to return to this earth for another lifetime. If we place money before God, which is easy to do, we are in effect worshiping a false idol.

> "No one can serve two masters. Either he will hate the one and love the other, or he will be devoted to one and despise the other. You cannot serve both God and money." Matthew 6:24

The fact of the matter is that God knows everything and therefore knows what we desire even before we ask Him.

> "Do not be like them, for your Father knows what you need before you ask him. This, then, is how you should pray: 'Our Father who art in

heaven, hallowed be thy name, your kingdom come, your will be done on earth as it is in heaven. Give us today our daily bread. Forgive us our debts, as we have forgiven our debtors. And lead us not into temptation, but deliver us from the evil one.'" Matthew 6:8-13

Jesus instructed us on how to pray, yet often we continue to pray for certain materialistic-based pleasures. If you notice in The Lord's Prayer, we ask God to give us what we need by saying, "give us our daily bread," not necessarily giving us what we desire. We are all God's children, and He will give us everything we need for our spiritual development. Why do we continue to ask for so much more and then worry about whether or not we are going to receive it?

"Do not be anxious about anything, but in everything, by prayer and repetition, with thanksgiving, present your requests to God." Philippians 4:6

Notice that we should couple our request with thankfulness (in thanksgiving) as if we have already received it.

Someone once told me that Jesus had another prayer, and sometimes when I want to understand something spiritual on a deeper level I use it. It goes like this: "Dear Father, open me up to know." On a daily basis, I find myself praying for clarity, strength, and wisdom. *Clarity* to see the truth and the highest path. *Strength* to make the difficult choices. *Wisdom* to choose wisely and always for the highest good, no matter what the outcome. Sometimes the greatest good emerges from the darkest outcomes. Asking God to show us the deeper meaning behind tragedy often brings forth illumination and understanding. Lastly, and maybe most importantly, *pray for others*. I use the same prayer for others as I use for myself. Strangely enough, when I find myself praying for others, I quickly forget about *my* issues, worries, and desires. In praying for others, sometimes I find my greatest peace.

Since prayer is a vibratory thought pattern, it is important that this vibration be congruent with the vibration of God Consciousness. A prayer can raise our consciousness or lower our consciousness. Correct prayer raises our consciousness. Prayer can shift our consciousness to a new belief system. When this occurs, the mini-god *within us* then vibrates more consistently with the God *without us*, meaning that part of God that exists outside of us. The new higher vibration then replaces the older one, creating new higher vibrational thought patterns within us and a new spiritual reality. Remember, everything has consciousness, whether in physical form or not.

What we think in each and every moment becomes our daily prayers. In other words, every thought we have is a prayer. What we repeat in our minds over and over become our mantras. With each thought, we are saying, this is what I believe in. This is what *I AM*. If we focus on the negative things in life, we will attract the negative things in life. Our prayers will have been answered. If we focus on the positive things in life, we will draw the positive to us. Again, our prayers have been answered. When we pray, we tend to think that we are praying to a God outside of ourselves. The fact is everything is God. We are a part of the infinite consciousness. Knowing this, we should refocus our minds so that we make them once again consistent with God-mind. So when we pray, whether it occurs in the form of formal prayer or our daily thoughts and actions, it is important that our minds be congruent with God-mind.

What should be the *intent* of prayer? We should pray in our thoughts, desires, and actions to become the consciousness that vibrates consistent with God Consciousness. That is what praying should be. We should pray to the consciousness of which we are all an integral part. We are not separate from God. We are an aspect of God. We are a wave in the ocean of God Consciousness. The intent of prayer should be to once again align ourselves with the vibration of God Consciousness. In accomplishing this, we become more like God. We become more like Buddha. We become more like Krishna. We become more like Jesus. We become our true selves as we are so intended. We become enlightened. We return to our original state of consciousness consistent with God-mind. We awaken the Christ inside us by raising our vibrational consciousness.

Affirmations have various meanings depending upon which context they are used. The term ranges in meaning from *a court judgment* to *a declaration* to *a statement asserting truth*. The definition I will use in this particular context of spirituality and increasing consciousness deals with *making a statement or declaration of truth without possessing any particular proof*. Under this definition of the word *affirmation*, we make statements about ourselves that are generally very positive and uplifting. The intent of creating an affirmation is to change a thought process from a more negative one to a more positive one with the idea that we will eventually accept the affirmation as being our personal truth as it relates to ourselves. Affirmations are intrinsically used to change negative thought patterns to more positive thought patterns. We in effect *change our minds*.

Mantras are similar to prayers and affirmations. The word *mantra* is derived from a Sanskrit word that essentially means *to free from the mind*.[2] Mantras are sacred words or phrases that are considered to be very healing. Through repetition, mantras re-channel the flow of thought energy through the brain in order to create new brain wave patterns of positive thought. *Chants* are repeated mantras that often have a melody or music tied to them. Mantras can also help open up the chakras (the spiritual energy centers of the body). Mantras can also serve to block evil thoughts from entering our minds. Mantras can calm you down prior to meditation because of the repetitive nature that completely engages and relaxes the mind. Mantras can be used for worship, healing, or advancement of the consciousness.

Mantras provide a vehicle for spiritual attunement in that they are vibrationally recuperative for the soul and can decrease karmic debt. Mantras are intended to deliver the soul from all states of worldly illusion. Mantras can be used to attract certain things or people to you. They can be used to attract wealth or your soul mate. With mantras, as with thoughts, faith, and prayers, you must act as if the outcome has already occurred. That is why mantras are best said in the present tense. They also need to be positive statements versus *reverse negatives* such as "I am not unhappy." Here are some sample mantras: "I am joyful" or "I am healthy" or "God provides me everything I need" or "I am goodness" or just "I AM." "I AM" is a very powerful mantra when used correctly. You are in effect claiming yourself to be one with God. If you say your mantras in the future tense such as "I want to be enlightened" or "I need more money," you reinforce the neediness and wanting. Again, always approach God in gratefulness and thanksgiving as if it has already occurred. If it is something you need for your spiritual advancement then you will receive it, because God gives us our daily bread. God gives us everything we need to get to heaven.

CHAPTER 8

Meditation

During meditation, we travel inward. The practice of meditation is really about *contacting the soul*, which is the God aspect inside each of us. The soul is the deepest and truest individuated essence of us. In meditation, we attempt to tap into that sense of being-ness, and sense of one-ness. When we meditate, we seek that aspect of God Consciousness within ourselves. We are attempting to make contact with God, the part of God hidden within us at our deepest level. Meditation is creating a space in our lives for an inward focus on God. Enlightenment cannot be found outside ourselves. When we seek enlightenment outside of ourselves, we repeatedly get lost in material form, in *materialism*. The path to enlightenment can only be found within us. By focusing our energies inward, we attempt to contact the Totality of Being-ness and Ultimate Consciousness via our soul. Meditation is one of the most important means to reaching enlightenment.

An ongoing meditation practice will change your life for the better, guaranteed. Even meditating as little as fifteen minutes per day with the proper spiritual intent of creating a deeper connection to God will change your life significantly. Meditation has a major calming effect on the mind-body-soul continuum. Besides prayer, meditation is the only method I know of contacting God. However, they are fundamentally different. Prayer is *speaking* to God. Meditation is the reverse. Meditation is *listening* to God. Meditation is an act of receiving. In meditation we attempt to quiet our minds so that we can receive. Occasionally, while in meditation I receive visions or messages from *my higher self*. These types of messages are intended to provide us spiritual direction in our lives. Other times these messages help us with problems we may be facing in our everyday human lives.

Sometimes the messages we receive are very simple.

"Be still, and know that I am God…." Psalm 46:10

To practice meditation, it is helpful to go to a secluded, quiet place. This is how I suggest meditating. First, sit in a comfortable chair or on a cushion set on the floor. It is important to be comfortable, but not too comfortable; you don't want to fall asleep. The spine should be straight up and down with the chest slightly out. Hold your head level with your back and neck straight up and down as if in a line and not curved in any way. If seated in a chair, the soles of your feet should be planted firmly upon the floor. Do not cross your legs or hands at all. If seated on the floor, crossing you legs is fine. Either way, in a chair or on the floor, your hands should be resting upon your lap comfortably with your palms up. Begin to breathe deeply and slowly from your abdomen.

If you find yourself in an uncomfortable position, it may hinder you from achieving a greater sense of peace and stillness while in meditation. Once situated, feel for any tension in your body that you may be holding onto and immediately try to stretch out that area. Sometimes by increasing the tension in the affected area, it will relieve the original tension you felt in that area. If the tension is not released, continue to stretch your body until you find some relief.

Your eyes can be slightly open if you wish, but do not focus on anything in particular. Rather, look forward with a soft gaze. This is sometimes referred to as *soft eyes*. Some teachers of meditation say that it is best to light a candle and focus on the candle. However, I find a candle very distracting because it will often flicker. You can focus on anything you wish, again preferably with soft eyes. Avoid straining your eyes in any manner. I personally prefer to close my eyes. I then focus on the third-eye chakra which is one of the seven spiritual energy centers of the body. In order to see the third-eye chakra (with eyes closed) you must focus your eyes slightly upward toward the center without crossing them. It is also referred to as the Christ Consciousness Center or Christ Center. The Christ Center may appear as a four-pointed or five-pointed star. Sometimes it may appear as a tunnel or as swirling energy. Again, your eyes should not be straining or crossed. The slightly upward glance into the Christ Center should remain as a soft gaze even though your eyes are closed. Focusing on the Christ Center during meditation can on occasion activate our sixth sense, our psychic ability. Don't worry if you don't see the Christ Center. The process and intent is what is most important.

Once I am situated in my meditation pose, I will begin to repeat a mantra. Often I will use a Hindu or Tibetan mantra. Constant repetition will typically relax my body. As I chant my mantra I purposely slow the rate in which I am repeating it. Eventually I will no longer say the mantra aloud, but will continue to repeat it for a time within my mind. If I am in a group meditation, I will begin by repeating it in my mind only. When I feel much more relaxed I discontinue saying the mantra altogether and switch my focus to my breath. I will focus on my breath as I breathe in and as I breathe out. Each breath in and out should be relaxed and not forced. Each breath in and out should be roughly equal in length, maybe four or five seconds each. If that length of breath is too long or too short, adjust your breath accordingly until you feel comfortable. On occasion I will purposely hold my breath for a moment between each exhale and inhale and between each inhale and each exhale. Stopping the breath before and after each breath is a technique I started using to obtain deeper levels of meditation. It came to me intuitively much like my meditation style came to me intuitively. I have never heard of anyone else doing this while in meditation. However, I understand some yogis have actually attained an evolved state in which they can stop breathing entirely for incredibly long periods of time while in meditation. Concentrating on the third-eye chakra alone is not nearly as effective as concentrating on the third-eye chakra coupled with conscious breathing.

Around this time in my meditation, I set the intention to connect to the Impersonal God energy (masculine energy) above by sending an energetic cord from my head up into the sky. I sometimes playfully imagine that this cord wraps around God's foot. Alternatively, I at times imagine that the cord goes up into a cloud and I imagine God in that cloud. Once connected to the God above, I pull the masculine energy down to me, encompassing me. In this way, I connect to the masculine energy above me. I then send an energetic cord from the base of my spine down into the center of the earth. I imagine the cord anchoring to the center of the earth. After that, I pull the energy up from the center of the earth up my spine to the top of my head. In this way I anchor to the feminine energies associated with Mother Earth. By connecting with and blending these energies in and around me, I create a perfect balance between the feminine and masculine (see illustrations). I lock these energies into place using intent and imagination. Once these energies are secured, I again focus on my third-eye.

As you continue to meditate, thoughts will come into your consciousness, but simply dismiss them as they enter your mind. Do not judge yourself negatively for having random thoughts. This is all a part of the process of settling down and quieting the mind. The Buddhists call these random thoughts *monkey mind*. Your mind is racing around like a monkey in a cage. In the beginning stages of learning how to meditate, it may be best to keep a pen and paper next to you. It is preferable to dismiss any and all thoughts you might have altogether; however, sometimes a thought may pop into your mind you feel is vitally important to write down. At least if you have a pen and a piece of paper next to you, you will not have to abandon your meditation pose completely in order to write it down.

Occasionally you may begin to drift into a state of *nothingness* or *no thought*. This is very good. This means your mind has temporarily given up thinking and has reached a complete state of receptivity. Every now and then when I reach this point, I will have a vision or receive an incredible insight. If you are a beginner, reaching and maintaining a state of nothingness during your meditation may be difficult. When you reach a very deep state of meditation, you may notice for a time that you have stopped breathing altogether. For me, I become aware this has transpired when I find myself suddenly gasping for air. This of course completely takes me out of my deep state. Frustrated by this, I subsequently restart my meditation process beginning with a mantra.

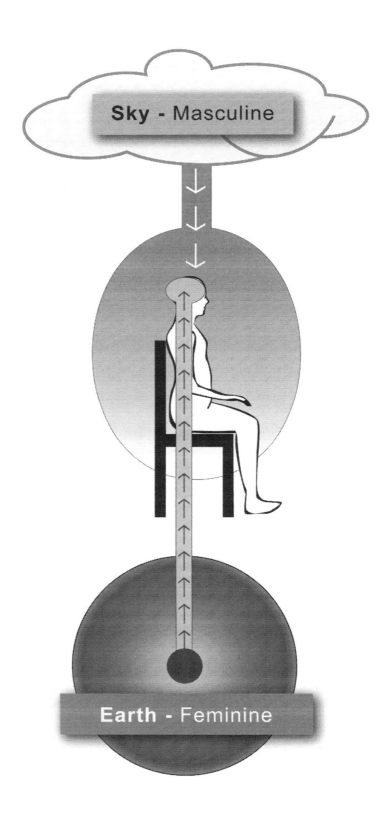

Meditation

Meditation, just like prayer, must be done with devotion. It is work. It is not an easy practice, but it is most definitely a rewarding practice. One of the goals of meditation should be to reach an inner peace free of all material desire or sense gratification. Only through constant practice will you achieve any level of God realization. If you find that you are experiencing pain in your body while in your meditative pose due to a previous accident or injury, then a lying-down meditation might prove useful. It is important not to fall asleep, and of course, falling asleep is much easier to do in a lying-down meditation. If you must lie down to meditate, you should do so when you are not tired. Everything else in terms of the process remains the same. Again, first release the tension in your body, and then begin your chant or mantra. Later, focus your mind on your breath with your eyes focused on the Christ Center (third-eye chakra).

I was once told by a spiritual teacher that the most powerful times to meditate are at dawn and sunset. These are the moments of the day where there is neither darkness nor light. At these two times, I am reminded of the Great Nothingness, the Great Void, and the Impersonal God, which are all differing names of the same God that reflects the space between the relative dichotomies of nature. Maybe that is why we are so fascinated with sunsets and sunrises. Maybe the beauty we see in these moments remind us of the beauty we see in heaven.

CHAPTER 9

Sin and Penance

It used to be troublesome and at times quite annoying for me when I would hear someone make the statement "I am perfect as I am." I was not certain if it was my inappropriate judgment of them or if it was simply my Virgo-nature coming through; Virgos are typically perfectionists and consequently can be very critical of others and themselves. Either way, it would bother me. I would ponder their comment and my corresponding negative judgment and ask myself, *Why do I get so upset by this statement?* In the end I came to the conclusion that we are *not perfect* as we are, and accordingly there is always room for improvement. In that case, I beg the question *How could anyone ever believe that we are perfect as we are?* I could only assume that they were trying to get across the idea that, given their current state of consciousness, they were doing the best they could in any given situation. If so, I find these types of statements a little more acceptable, as long as that is their intended meaning.

In terms of our daily challenges, I have come to the realization that we all have our own little toolbox with which to deal with life. When I refer to tools, I am referring to our ability to act correctly in any given situation, just as a laborer would use the correct tool in any given work situation. It would be incorrect for a worker to use a saw to drive a nail into a piece of wood, just as it would be incorrect for a person to become intoxicated after having had an argument with his or her spouse. The correct tool to use to pound a nail would of course be a hammer. The correct tool to use after an argument would be to sit down and discuss the situation with one's spouse in a healthy manner without raising one's voice or getting inebriated. Some of us have a broader array of tools than others either because of our education, the manner in which we were raised by our parents, our karma, or our level of spiritual development.

My lack of certain tools at an earlier age would explain why I did some things in my life I am not very proud of. It would explain why I hurt people in my life. My lack of the appropriate tools could explain why I chose to lie in situations rather than tell the truth. It might explain why I reacted poorly in any challenging situation. Let me be clear about something: I am not attempting to make excuses here. What I am saying is that hopefully I acted as best I could given my toolbox at the time. As we grow older, we hopefully become wiser and add more tools to our arsenal to deal with problematic situations. That is why counseling or professional coaches generally help us move forward in our conscious development. I have come to the conclusion that when people utter the words "I am perfect as I am," they do in fact recognize their imperfection and understand that they are doing the best they can given the toolbox they have at the moment.

This new way of looking at it feels right to me. It is something I can live with. It also expresses an advanced level of self-acceptance, which is excellent. It is clear to me that we all need to love and accept ourselves a little more and to not judge ourselves as harshly as we often do. That is not to say, however, that this is a valid excuse for not trying to grow spiritually. We all must do what we can to grow and consciously make better choices to avoid sin. But where and at what point in time does a sin begin or, for that matter, end? For example, we all have heard the terms *little white lies* or *grey area* to express the idea that it's not really a lie but that it came close to being a lie, or that it was an acceptable lie based on some abstract or obtuse excuse. I guess whatever we said didn't cross the line as it relates to the truth. But is it really feasible to rank sins? Is one sin worse that another? Or is a sin a sin and that's all there is to it? For that matter, what is sin?

Sin, by some people's definition, means *to err*. Sin can also be defined as *to ignore the truth* or *to act in ignorance*. The word sin in Aramaic means *to miss the mark*; it's the same in archery. Sin may be considered *any act of ungodliness* or *a transgression against God's laws*. But which laws are to be obeyed, the Ten Commandments, the universal laws, or both? Over time, I have created my own definition of sin. My definition of sin is *anything that takes you away from God or serves as a diversion to your direct return home to God in heaven.* This definition is very similar to *missing the mark*. In Spanish, the word *sin* (pronounced *seen*) means *without*. I like this definition too (even though it is a transliteration) because I also think of sin as *without God* or as *the absence of God.* This is consistent with all of the various definitions of sin listed above. For the balance of the book, I will use the term *missing the mark* or similar variations of it.

It is very important in my opinion to understand that sin is not what we think it is, at least in one respect. Sin is not something horrible we at any cost must avoid. Rather, at our current level of consciousness it is next to impossible to avoid sin at all times. The concept of sin need not be steeped in judgment or guilt. It should not be intrinsically tied to self-deprecation or condemnation either. In my definition, sin is an obstacle to our journey back home to God. If we are taking a path that will not take us directly back home to God, then we have missed the mark. We have taken a wrong turn or a wrong path. We have sinned.

Here is a more concrete illustration. If I am in New York and I want to get back home to San Diego driving straight south, I will not arrive in San Diego via the most direct route. That is not to say that once I reach Florida I couldn't head due west and eventually reach San Diego. It is clear in this example that I would not be taking the most direct route home to San Diego if I traveled south toward Florida. However, my path will eventually get me there, won't it? The journey to San Diego is analogous to our return to God and heaven.

But there is an important question to ask here. At whose demise did I take the long route home? Was it God's demise? The answer is absolutely not. Taking the long route home made it more difficult for me, not for God. The route I took could in one way be considered a sin or merely my karma, understanding then that sin comes at my own expense. If I choose some thing that is not consistent with the direct path back to God it only delays my return to God. It is *my* consequence. So sin, as it is in archery, is just missing the mark, isn't it? Sinning is like taking the long road home back to heaven, with consequences. In missing the mark we take a step away from God.

Let's now turn our attention to what the Bible says:

> "Those who live according to the sinful nature have their minds set on
> what that nature desires; but those who live in accordance with the Spirit
> have their mind set on what the Spirit desires." Romans 8:5

Sin, as the absence of God, is our *sinful nature* as referenced in the Bible. Sin is then something we should attempt to avoid if we wish to avoid the potentially negative consequences (karma) associated with it.

Jesus said that we must repent or perish:

> "…unless you repent, you too will all perish." Luke 13:1-5

This sound pretty ominous; however, *perish* in this verse could simply mean that our bodies will experience death and does not necessarily constitute an eternity in hell. Further, let's focus on the word *repent* for a moment. One definition of repent is *to reform*. The meaning of reform in this instance could mean *to give up evil ways*. John the Baptist talks about repentance in the Gospel of Luke:

> "Produce fruit in keeping with your repentance." Luke 3:8

By stating this, John the Baptist is suggesting that we not sin any longer, that we give up our sinful ways and act in goodness, and in this way we *produce fruit* by our actions.

John the Baptist goes on to say that there can be severe consequences for living a life filled with sin.

> "The ax is already at the root of the trees, and every tree that does not produce good fruit will be cut down and thrown into the fire." Luke 3:9

This last verse suggests that if we continue to sin there may be a huge price to pay. The reference to fire, at first blush, could be understood as a reference to hell.

But is it really possible to stop sinning altogether? We are just fallible human beings, aren't we? We all sin, don't we?

> "No temptation has seized you except what is common to man. And God is faithful; he will not let you be tempted beyond what you can bear. But when you are tempted, he will also provide a way out so that you can stand up under it." 1 Corinthians 10:13

These verses are suggesting that *with God anything is possible* because God will not allow us to be tempted beyond what we can endure. But who isn't sinning in some fashion or another in today's world?

The truth is that the Holy Spirit fills us up incrementally with God's light as we move closer to God. In other words, we as souls will gradually increase in our consciousness to the point of our perfection. Without knowing this, I imagine one might perceive it to be impossible to stop sinning altogether. Knowing this, we can consciously make incremental steps toward God. As we increase our consciousness we will miss the mark less often. An alternative explanation to being *thrown into the fire* could be some type of accelerated purification potentially perceived as punishment or a highly unpleasant consequence for our sins, and not necessarily hell as we typically think of it.

When we stop sinning completely, via some sort of purification process, and confess our sins, all will be forgiven:

> "If we confess our sins, he is faithful and just and will forgive us our sins and purify us from all unrighteousness." 1 John 1:9

I am assuming *purify us from all unrighteousness* means that as we grow spiritually to the point of enlightenment, we will not sin again. It is in our own ignorance that we believe we can continue to sin over and over again without any consequence. When we give up sinning altogether, we will be awarded eternal life. Maybe this is more correctly stated this way: When we grow spiritually to a point of enlightenment, we will no longer sin, and as a consequence of being enlightened, we reach a state of eternal existence whether in our human body or in our immortal body.

Let us now delve into the various types of sin. Generally speaking, there are three types of sin. The first type of sin is *sin against the self*. The second type of sin is *sin against another person, place, or thing*. The third sin is *sin against God*. Any of these three types of sin distance us from re-membering who we really are, spiritually hampering our journey back to enlightenment and hampering our journey back to heaven. In sinning, we *dismember* (distance) ourselves from God. Energetically speaking, sins come in three forms: negative thought, negative speech, and negative action.

The first type of sin is a *sin against yourself*. You sin against yourself when you create negative thoughts about yourself, say negative things about yourself, or take a negative action against yourself, none of which serve your higher good. A sin against the self injures the self and eventually affects the body in a negative way. Long-term obsession of the same negative thought, feeling, or emotion can manifest in the form of *dis-ease* or disease. Unhealthy habits are sins against the self. There are many more negative actions that a person can take against himself/herself. If we engage in these activities, we are missing the mark.

The second type of sin is *sin against another person, place, or thing*. This type of sin could occur in countless ways, most of which would fall under the Ten Commandments in one way or another. Again, sins come in three forms: negative thought, negative speech, and negative action. We sin against another person, place, or thing when we create negative thoughts about some entity or person outside our self. We sin against another person, place, or thing when we express negative statements. In effect we send out negative energy into the universe which in turn affects everything, according to the Universal Law All is One. And next, we sin when we take a negative action against another person, place, or thing. This is what we commonly think of when we consider the topic of sin.

The last type of sin would be *sin against God*. Any negative thought, statement, or action made against God is considered a form of blaspheme. A sin against God would include systematically and consistently turning away from one of God's doctrines or ignoring His authority and universal laws. Normally one might consider the greatest sin to be against God. But if you think about it, and you might already be ahead of me on this, you would realize that since All is One, there is only one type of sin. Sins against yourself, any person, place or thing, and sins against God are *all* sins against God. As such, all sins could be considered sins against the whole of which we are all an integral part. In this regard, all sins are then sins against our self. The only thing left to consider with sin is the impact it has on each of us, which is directly related to karma. The greater the impact of the sin, the greater the karma one has incurred and likewise the greater the consequence or penance required.

As a child I grew up believing that penance is what the Catholic Church was trying to acknowledge by karmically ranking sins. The less severe sins were called *menial sins* and required less penance. The more severe sins were called *mortal sins*, and as I understood it, if a person committed a mortal sin he would certainly go to hell and no level of penance could save him. Consequently, as a young child I had the fear that if I had to go to war, I would have been doomed to an eternity of hell. I missed being potentially drafted into the Vietnam War by less than one year. I was a senior in high school when it ended. Thank goodness I know better now that it isn't the act of killing that determines whether or not we go to heaven. Rather, it is in the motive and what lies in our hearts and minds. God knows our intentions. He knows our thoughts.

So then, what is the saving grace that saves us from our sins and the consequence of hell? What course of action can we take to actively and consciously make strides toward attaining heaven? One way is *penance*. Penance is simply creating a situation that reverses the negative karma associated with the sin previously committed. Generally speaking, there are three types of penance. The first penance is directed primarily toward the self. The second type of penance is directed toward another person, place, or thing. The third type of penance deals with God. Are you beginning to recognize a pattern here? Any of these three types of penance assist us with re-membering with God back to a state of enlightenment as they serve to eradicate our sin and bring us positive karma.

Penance comes in three forms: positive thought, positive speech, and positive action. This is the same as sin, except in a positive light. Penance directed toward the self includes positive thought, positive speech, and positive action aimed at the self. Thinking positive thoughts about the self reverses negative thoughts made previously about the self. You are basically undoing what you have previously done to yourself. What we think about ourselves is organically important because we become our thoughts. Thinking thoughts such as "I am a beautiful creature of God because God made me" or "I am happy" or "I am successful" are all positive thoughts that counter previous sinful thoughts made against the self. You may be surprised by the beneficial effect repeating positive statements over and over will have on your life. It basically becomes a mantra. You begin to draw positive things and positive people into your life. It is the Universal Law of Attraction. It becomes your new reality.

Positive speech is simply verbalizing the positive thoughts you hold about yourself, but don't confuse it with bragging. A positive action for your self could be choosing anything of a higher nature. This would include anything that might generate peaceful or loving thoughts within yourself. Meditation and practicing yoga are two examples. Meditation is similar to a form of penance because it has the same effect of reducing karma. Studying scripture or reading spiritual books is positive action as well. There are many more positive actions that a person can take to nurture his or her true self.

What might be considered a more *negative aspect* of penance toward the self would be abstinence. Abstinence could take the form of fasting or withdrawal of any pleasure such as food or drink or some other thing that might gratify the five senses. Please understand that when I make a reference to the *negative aspect of a positive action* that is not to say it is bad. Rather, I am trying to say that fasting could be perceived as something we may *not* wish to do or a type of punishment, something negative. Fasting, however, can be a very positive and powerful spiritual practice.

The various types of penance directed toward others include positive thought, positive speech, and positive action toward another person; this also applies to other forms with consciousness such as animals and nature. Positive thoughts for others would include holding them in your mind and thinking pleasant thoughts about them. Another form of positive thought would be praying for others even if you consider them to be your enemy, especially if you consider them to be your enemy. This would generate even more positive karma. Positive speech could take the form of saying anything nice about someone else. What might be considered the negative aspect of positive speech is humbling yourself by making an apology to another person. Apologizing is actually a positive form of humiliation. Positive action could be an act of generosity toward someone or a financial gift made to a church or nonprofit. Positive action could also take the form of service. Volunteering is definitely a positive action and is often fun and rewarding. It is vitally important to teach these things to our children since they are our future.

Penance directed toward God includes positive thought, positive speech, and positive action toward God. Positive thoughts include praying and all positive thoughts in general. The act of confession is penance as a negative aspect of a positive action. Positive action toward God would include worship through song and praise, and tithing of your time and money. Another negative aspect of a positive action would be to prostrate before God. I hope you understand that being prostrate before God is not negative in any sense even though some may consider it an act of being punished. Rather, it is a highly respectful form of praise and worship. Maybe surprisingly so, God does not require our praise and worship. We worship and praise God as a part of our spiritual development. It is an integral part of our developing consciousness. For us to grow and vibrate at higher levels of conscious spiritual development, praising and worshiping God assists us in accomplishing this.

What is important to understand is that penance means we don't have to be perfect; penance can be an effective way in which to balance out the negative effect of our sins, meaning the negative karma associated with sin and missing the mark. Doing more penance than what is required to balance out our sins in this lifetime reduces our karmic responsibility from previous lives and brings us one step closer to enlightenment and heaven. That is not to say that we can go out and commit a sin since we now know the *secret formula* for reducing karma. It doesn't work that way. A person has to be sorry for their sins and do everything within their power to not repeat them; otherwise the intent of penance has been corrupted. There needs to be remorse for the sin itself, for missing the mark. There needs to be repentance. Otherwise the lesson associated with the negative karma has not yet been learned by the soul.

Penance in the form of self-deprecation or self-injury is a sin against the self and is not really penance. Penance made by inflicting pain or damage to the body is a sin against the self. Damaging your body in any way or mistreating it is a sin because your body is the temple of the Holy Spirit. Instead of inflicting pain upon yourself why not use this same energy to create more good in the community through service? Doing penance for reward is selfish and means that you have attachment to an outcome. Any attachment to performing penance corrupts the intent of penance. Penance needs to be selfless. Penance should be made without expecting something in return. Otherwise, it would be like expecting to be paid for volunteering your time. Any sacrifice made for material benefit is not penance. Sacrifice should be made out of duty and love of God. Sacrifice, penance, and charity performed as a matter of spiritual duty or moral obligation to God purifies the soul by raising its vibration.

To summarize the critical points within this chapter would be to acknowledge anything that takes you away from God as a sin. Sin is simply missing the mark or veering off the direct path back to God. It is a diversion to truth and goodness, with consequences. It is taking a step away from God, and since we are human, most of us sin everyday in some small way or another, without even realizing it. It is where our collective and individual consciousness currently lies. It is a part of life, for all of us. Therefore we all sin in some regard. None of us are free from sin. Therefore we must *atone* or make amends for our sins through acts of penance as we progress back to a state of enlightenment. At the moment of *atonement* or *at-one-ment*, we are no longer capable of sin and merge back into the Oneness of God truly experiencing a heaven beyond our wildest imagination.

CHAPTER 10

Forgiveness

"An eye for an eye makes the whole world blind." Mahatma Gandhi

Forgiveness comes in many forms. Naturally, we must forgive others as written in Romans. We must not retaliate by seeking revenge.

"Do not repay anyone evil for evil." Romans 12:17

There is also the forgiveness God grants us. Interestingly enough, it appears that God's forgiveness is tied to whether or not we forgive others.

"For if you forgive men when they sin against you, your heavenly Father will also forgive you. But if you do not forgive men their sins, your Father will not forgive your sins." Matthew 6:14-15

It is clear here that we are not forgiven unless we forgive others. Is it possible that if we do not forgive others, we cannot possibly be forgiven because of the Universal Law All is One? In other words, how can the body be forgiven if the right hand does not forgive the left hand, or if the right foot does not forgive the left foot?

Another type of forgiveness comes into play when we forgive ourselves. We cannot purify our consciousness until we forgive ourselves. In reality we cannot truly love others if we do not love ourselves. It is not possible. Forgiveness is about compassion and empathy, which are both different facets of love. It is only through an open heart that we come to a point of forgiveness, either for ourselves or others. We must have compassion and empathy for others as well as ourselves.

The fact is *everyone is fallible*. Only when we fully understand this within our hearts, and that *we are fallible too*, will we be able to forgive others and their fallible nature. If we possess feelings of hate, envy, or jealousy, there can be no room for forgiveness. Forgiveness is about *letting go*. Letting go is vitally important and will, if implemented, assist us in the process of forgiveness. We can also approach forgiveness from our minds versus our hearts. By approaching forgiveness from a *mind perspective*, we may begin to realize that the action taken against us is most likely due to our own past negative karma, since all of us unenlightened souls have a greater amount of negative karma than positive karma. Let me explain. Let's say that you offended someone in some way in a previous lifetime which in turn created a karmic debt to this person. This accrued negative karma is holding you back from becoming an enlightened being. In this lifetime the other person offended you much in the same manner in which you offended them in a previous lifetime. The action taken *against you* by another *benefits you* by reducing your karmic debt. The reason it reduces your karmic debt to the other person is because the universal scales of justice are now balanced. Is this, then, something you should be angry about or pleased that there is a reduction in your karmic debt to the person offending you?

Now let's look at it another way. Let's say in this instance that the act taken against you was not to balance out your karma, but to help you understand a specific spiritual lesson concerning *revenge*. Let's say that the lesson of *not* enacting revenge is something that your soul has been attempting to learn over many lifetimes, but learning this lesson has seemingly escaped you each lifetime. By this person taking an action against you, he or she in effect may be carrying out a promise made to you before either one of you were born. The act was planned in advance appearing in your spiritual contract (and his/her contract) so that you would learn the lesson of *not* enacting revenge. And in learning this valuable lesson, your soul is that much closer to obtaining a state of enlightenment and heaven. Is this something you should be thankful for or something you should be angry about? Do you see how releasing the judgment associated with the actions of others frees you from negative emotions, and possibly negative reactions (revenge), which would only serve to increase your karma? Forgiveness in these last two scenarios gives forgiveness new meaning. In both of these scenarios we should be thankful to this person *for-giving* us an opportunity to reduce our negative karma or *for-giving* us an opportunity to learn a valuable soul lesson about love. For-giving should then be closely followed by gratitude *for-getting* the lesson. Be thankful in both. Forgive then forget.

So if the reduction of karma scenario was most likely preplanned, or minimally chosen by you on a soul level, the next time you are injured in any way, don't immediately get angry. It may be something that was meant to occur to you this lifetime. The worst thing that could happen is that the other person increased his or her karmic debt to you. As long as you do not react in a negative fashion, you are freed from that karmic experience, at least on your end. Remember, we attract to us people who are like us, and the lessons we still need to learn. These people then reflect back to us our weaknesses as if a mirror. That is why our friends and loved ones sometimes frustrate us to no end. We draw people into our lives that reflect back to us where we need to grow spiritually. They may be from our soul group or even the same soul as us living a parallel existence, a parallel life. Remember that in this universe of infinite possibilities, one soul may be living several lives at once. In this case, one soul has decided to live several lives at once in order to maximize its growth and experiences.

As far as my personal experiences with parallel lives go, I would like to share just one story. It was a pretty average day as I was driving back to work. I was working at the food bank that serves southern Colorado at the time. While I was driving, I had a vision of a man and a woman. The vision flashed in front of me as if I were there watching from a location somewhere above the couple. Thank goodness the vision was short-lived, as I was traveling approximately sixty miles per hour on the expressway. The vision I had was of a beautiful place near an ocean. Somehow I knew that this location was somewhere in Greece. The couple was walking together through a grassy field toward a spot overlooking the ocean high above a somewhat sheer cliff. I sensed immediately that they were a couple very much in love. They were older, maybe in their late fifties or early sixties.

Sadly, I sensed that the man had cancer and was dying and that this was one of their final moments together. I also knew that this man was somehow me. That didn't make sense to me at first, but then I realized that it must be a parallel life I was living. This man shared my soul; I was that man, and he was also me. Before this experience I had never given the possibility of parallel lives much thought. All of this information I received in a flash of time. Several months later, I awoke very sad and this sadness dragged on throughout the day, at times overwhelming me. At some point in the day I asked myself why I was so sad, and as it nearly always happens, my higher self answered me in that quiet little voice. The little voice told me that the old man with cancer had died that day. Somehow my soul was mourning his departure. I felt a strange unconditional love for him.

Above all, we should remind ourselves that we all make mistakes. We are all flawed in our own way. No one is perfect. Therefore we all have to forgive. By refusing to forgive, we increase our karma individually and collectively. We negatively affect the whole. Understanding that we all are an aspect of God trying to make our way back home to heaven will hopefully open our hearts to a greater understanding, compassion, and forgiveness—reducing karma. Again, the first step in forgiveness is forgiving ourselves. Start by saying, "I forgive myself no matter what I've done." This is a very powerful statement. However, this is not to be used as an excuse to continue to do harm to others or ourselves. The next step is for us to forgive others by saying, "I forgive all others no matter what they have done." In forgiveness, we give ourselves permission to move on; to move beyond the hurt, anger, or possibly even hate. In forgiveness, we open our hearts to greater levels of compassion. Conversely, without complete forgiveness we cannot enter heaven. We anchor ourselves into the necessity of reincarnation. We must reincarnate again to finish the lesson of forgiveness and must again suffer physical death.

"Before you seek revenge, be sure to dig two graves." Chinese Proverb

Without forgiveness, we suffer. Forgiveness is really a gift to ourselves. Absolute forgiveness opens the gates of heaven.

CHAPTER 11

Karma and Universal Justice

❧

Think of karma as nothing more than some mathematical formula. In mathematics we plug in a few numbers and we achieve a mathematical result. It is the same for karma. We plug in an action and we create a consequence. It is nothing more than cause and effect. The problem in understanding the direct relationship between the cause and effect of karma lies in the fact that there is generally a substantial space in time between the initial cause and resulting effect. In other words, the effect of an action does not immediately follow the cause, also referred to as the causal factor. Because of this time and space lag between the causal factor and the corresponding effect, we don't immediately understand the result as being directly tied to the original action. We see them as being separate even though they are not.

What we send out into the world in terms of energy is like a boomerang. It comes right back to us. It always does. This is ultimate *universal justice*. We just don't always see this relationship or understand it as such. In our present level of consciousness, we often do not know the cause of certain occurrences because of the time-space gap. Consequently we then see daily mishaps as injustices against us or others. Alternatively, we may have agreed to an injustice occurring in our lives in order for us to experience and learn or to inspire others to do something about it. It is up to us to decide what we do with our injustices. Do we ignore them or act upon them in a positive way? Often the greatest deeds performed by mankind stem from a previous injustice.

To make things a little more confusing, universal justice does not necessarily occur over just one lifetime. It is actually the reverse; it occurs over many lifetimes. One consequence may occur this lifetime because of an action taken many lifetimes ago. If I told you that a baby was born with a disability due to the sins of a past lifetime, would you still feel that the disability inflicted upon the baby in this lifetime was unfair? Or would you suddenly appreciate the connection between cause and effect and possess a deeper understanding of karma and universal justice? Inequalities at birth are accordingly just and fair when one understands the Universal Law of Karma (cause and effect) in this manner. These inequalities could be physical abilities or disabilities, or they could manifest as economic advantages or disadvantages. The effects of past karma can obviously present themselves in a myriad of ways. Correspondingly, inequalities at birth may provide us opportunities to act more compassionately.

Karma is not eternal. It has a beginning and an end. It is my contention that karma began individually for each of us with *original sin* in the Garden of Eden, which I will explain in more detail later. I believe it ends for an individual when the individual reaches enlightenment and no longer creates it. Until such time, wherever we leave off in terms of our karma as we exit one lifetime is the point in which we pick up our karma the next lifetime. In other words, the balance of the negative karma associated with past lives stays with the soul as he or she reincarnates. Additionally, the soul's karma often determines the specifics of the next reincarnation, that is, the soul's next life is to a great extent dependent upon how well it executes its spiritual contract this life and the lessons the soul has yet to learn.

Karma can also be measured by *the degree of impact* of an action. The degree of injury is most often returned to us as in *an eye for an eye*. If we rape, we will be raped in some lifetime. If we steal, someone will steal from us. If we murder, we will be murdered in some lifetime.

> "'Put your sword back in its place,' Jesus said to him, 'for all who draw the sword, will die by the sword.'" Matthew 26:52

Even something as insignificant as a thought has karma because thoughts have energy behind them. A positive thought sent out to someone else produces positive karma for the one sending the thought. A negative thought sent out to someone else produces negative karma for the one sending the thought. How much negative karma is there in a thought? Not much, but isn't the reason we keep coming back to earth because of our cumulative negative karma? Wouldn't it be better to subtract from our negative karma than to add to it, since freedom from the Law of Karma is generally associated with enlightenment? A thought that enters our mind will not necessarily increase or decrease our karma if it is but a fleeting thought; however, we are one hundred percent responsible for the thoughts we decide to ponder, fantasize about, or place into action. The level of karma is determined by how much energy we put into the thought because the thoughts we hold onto reflect what is in our hearts and minds. Vibrationally speaking, they reflect where our soul has yet to heal.

Sometimes karma is returned to us in alternative ways and varying degrees. Just because we took a very specific negative action against another person, that doesn't necessarily mean that the same action will be returned to us in the exact same manner or in the same degree of impact. For example, if you gossiped about someone else and it caused that person to lose his or her job, this does not necessarily mean that someone will gossip about you and then as a consequence you lose your job. The negative karma you have created by gossiping could be returned to you in a completely different way, such as a loss of money, or it could be that another relationship of yours suffers, however not as a result of gossip. Either way, you will eventually need to learn to *not* gossip.

Negative karma may also be returned to you in a bundled manner. Using the previous example, the one karmic action of gossiping could be bundled with other previous acts of gossiping and may come back to you later with a much higher degree of impact. In other words, the karma returned to you may be substantially more severe, especially if this has been an ongoing problem lifetime after lifetime. This occurs because your soul is attempting to get the lesson of not gossiping across to you once and for all. Remember, it's all about mathematics. If we keep increasing our karma, we create a backlog of negative karma that eventually needs to come back to us. At some point in time this backlog of negative karma may be returned to us in a lump sum manner in a potentially devastating way.

Likewise, if we refuse to learn a spiritual lesson by repeatedly choosing the same negative thought pattern or action, the consequences may increase for the same misgiving. Let's say, for example, that one of the lessons I am meant to learn is to slow down my life by living more in the moment. I would initially be provided opportunities to learn this lesson before any major upset occurs. If I continue to operate my life in a frenzied manner, an upset will occur in my life that will provide me a hint that I need to slow down. If I don't heed the message, then I may be stricken with a number of other upsets to get me heading in the right direction. It is kind of like a courtesy parking ticket or a warning ticket for speeding. The first time is just a warning. However, if I don't slow down my life, the consequences may worsen. The important thing to remember here is that if I don't learn the specific spiritual lesson, the consequences may eventually increase each time I make the same mistake. A scary thought, huh? It's almost like God initially taps me on the shoulder to get my attention. If that doesn't work, then God will give me a little slap. If that doesn't work, then God may knock me to my knees with a tragedy related to the lesson I still need to learn.

In this vein, Jesus forewarned an invalid He had previously healed, as detailed in the Gospel of John:

> "Later Jesus found him at the temple and said to him, 'See, you are well again. Stop sinning or something worse may happen to you.'" John 5:14

Any way we look at it, God, or possibly the god in us, is going to get our attention so that we finally learn the lessons we came here to learn via our life experiences.

An important question to ask is this: *When something bad happens, how will we know whether it is a result of our negative karma or purely an error made by another person, a sin he or she committed?* The answer is, we won't know. That is another reason why forgiveness is so important. And if something bad happens to us as result of our sin, how will we know if it is a result of negative karma accumulated from this lifetime or a previous lifetime? Again, the answer is, we won't know. We will not know at the time when something negative happens to us if it is due to this lifetime's karma or a previous lifetime's karma. Actually, how important is it for us to know? Would it make a difference if we did know? Either way, we must forgive. And if we don't forgive, who suffers most? The bitterness we feel inside tends to eat us up. Are the negative feelings we feel inside an immediate and direct return of the energies associated with our own reluctance to forgive as an instantaneous return of our own karma? Do our own negative thought energies tear down our own body via an illness or dis-ease?

It is important to remember this important rule for reducing our karma: if we think a thought or perform an act with positive intention, there cannot be any negative karma associated with it. Knowing this, if we act with only good intent, there can be no negative karma associated with the results, even if the results are disastrous. This is true because God can see within our hearts and judges us accordingly. Consequently, we should act with only positive intent and our negative karma will eventually be reduced to a point of balance with our good karma. Of course, reaching enlightenment is easier said than done; otherwise, we would have reached enlightenment a long time ago. When karma is finally balanced, there is neither positive karma nor negative karma attached to the soul. The soul has balanced the scales of universal justice and is released from the cycle of rebirth. Karma is just another way of saying that we are one hundred percent responsible for our actions, and all that we send out into the world as positive or negative energy is returned to us one way or another. Any way you look at it, we cannot return to the kingdom of heaven until we balance out our negative karma with our positive karma. I refer to this as the Universal Scales of Justice. Until the scales are balanced, our souls feel an urge to return to another lifetime.

CHAPTER 12

Reincarnation

❦

Belief in reincarnation dates back to ancient times. Actually, many early Christians believed in reincarnation. Some early Jewish sects such as the Essenes believed in reincarnation. As Christianity grew, the concept of reincarnation was hotly contested within the early church. As a result of this ongoing debate, it is believed by a number of religious scholars today that early church elders elected to delete most of the original references of reincarnation in the Christian Bible. Furthermore, these scholars believe that the Bible over time has been periodically altered, implying new contextual meanings as well as having been edited to erase inconsistencies between the various writings. This in effect implies that scripture is really the work of men, admittedly God-inspired, but still the work of men.

"All Scripture is God-breathed..." 2 Timothy 3:16

If you think about this rationally, is it really that plausible that the Gospels of Matthew, Mark, Luke, and John were originally that similar? What is the likelihood of four different men who spent three years with Jesus writing virtually the same four gospels verbatim? There certainly must have been major collaboration or editing by the early church somewhere along the way, or substantial plagiarism between the four apostles, which, by the way, I am not suggesting. I am suggesting the former.

"Jesus did many other wondrous things as well. If every one of them were written down, I suppose even the whole world would not have room for the books that would be written." John 21:25

So if this is true, and I believe it is, then how could four different books written by four different apostles be so similar and limited in content?

But why have these changes in the Bible occurred over time? What was the rationale of the church? And who wrote the Bible? The Bible is really a collection of sixty-six books written by many various authors, not just the four apostles. These books were compiled into one book while countless other books, likewise divine in nature, some with competing ideals and beliefs, were purposefully left out by the early church. To complicate matters even further, the books contained in the Bible were written in several different languages and had to be translated, eventually to the English language.

In the book *Misquoting Jesus: The Story Behind Who Changed the Bible and Why* by Bart E. Ehrman, he states the following:

> "The more I studied the manuscript tradition of the New Testament, the more I realized just how radically the text had been altered over the years at the hands of the Scribes, who were not only conserving scripture, but changing it."[1]

Scribes were used to write down and/or copy the original manuscripts.

Ehrman also suggests many more disturbing changes were made:

> "In some instances, the very meaning of the text is at stake…"[2]

> "…the New Testament is a very human book."[3]

None of the original manuscripts exist today. They are copies or copies of copies. Therefore there is no original Bible that still exists today. Dating as far back as the fourth century, the *Codex Vaticanus* is thought to be the oldest complete copy of the Bible still in existence. It is housed in the Vatican Library, along with other controversial scriptures that potentially contradict traditional Christian beliefs.

The Bible may be God-inspired, but most definitely was subject to man's influence by interpretation. The following is a substantially abbreviated history of scriptural changes that occurred within the early church that may have significantly altered the original messages contained in the Bible.

The Orthodox Church was founded upon the original teachings of Jesus Christ and His apostles.

> "He said to them, 'Go into all the world and preach the good news to all creation.'" Mark 16:15

Five churches were eventually established after Jesus' death. They were located in Jerusalem, Antioch, Alexandria, Rome, and Constantinople. They did not all immediately call themselves Christians.

> "The disciples were called Christians first at Antioch." Acts 11:26

Early on, yet many years after Christ's death and resurrection, the churches became divided each holding contrasting beliefs and ideologies. The Roman emperor Constantine I was a Christian convert who recognized that the various religious sects were in conflict over scripture. As a result, he called the first ecumenical council directing them to resolve their conflicts and determine one doctrine for the Christian church. An *ecumenical council is an assembly of theologians and church dignitaries called together to discuss and establish the teachings of the church.* The first ecumenical council, called the *Council of Nicaea,* met in 325 AD and was believed to have lasted over two months.[4]

At this ecumenical council, the church declared as heresy or a heretic anyone that believes that *Jesus did not exist before He was begotte*n, or that *He was made out of nothing,* or that *Jesus was created versus begotten.* The church also declared as heresy or a heretic anyone that believes *Jesus was subject to change,* or that *Jesus was capable of good and evil,* all of which I suggest in this book to be true.

Out of this council came the *Nicene Creed*—the symbol of faith for the church:

> We believe in one God,
> the Father, the Almighty,
> maker of heaven and earth,
> of all that is seen and unseen.
>
> We believe in one Lord, Jesus Christ,
> the only Son of God,
> eternally begotten of the Father,
> God from God, light from light,
> true God from true God,
> begotten, not made, of one being with the Father.
>
> Through him all things were made.
> For us and for our salvation
> he came down from heaven,
> and by the power of the Holy Spirit
> he was born of the Virgin Mary and became man.
>
> For our sake, he was crucified under Pontius Pilate,
> suffered, died, and was buried.
>
> On the third day he rose from the dead
> in accordance with the Scriptures;
> he ascended into heaven,
> and is seated at the right hand of the Father.

He will come again in glory to judge the living and the dead,
and his kingdom will have no end.

We believe in the Holy Spirit, the Lord, the giver of life,
who proceeds from the Father and the Son,
who, with the Father and the Son, is worshiped and glorified,
who has spoken through the prophets.

We believe in one holy Catholic and Apostolic Church.
We acknowledge one baptism for the forgiveness of sins.

We look for the resurrection of the dead and the life of the world to
come. Amen.

The Nicene Creed institutionalized *Jesus Christ as the Son of God* disallowing any
and all of the supposedly heretical notions mentioned earlier about Jesus.

The second ecumenical council, referred to as *The First Council of Constantinople*,
convened in the year 381 AD "affirmed the divinity of the Holy Spirit."[5]

In the third ecumenical council, called the *Council of Ephesus*, which met in 431 AD,
the bishops of the various churches crafted twelve new *anathemas*.[6] An anathema
is *a belief that has been condemned by the Christian church*; holding such a belief is
usually followed by excommunication from the Christian church. One of the twelve
anathemas states that anyone who believes that *Jesus was able to perform his miracles of
healing the sick by virtue of the power of the Holy Spirit versus His own power* is subject to
excommunication. The Council of Ephesus also declared Mary, the mother of Jesus, the
Mother of God.[7]

Prior to this point in time, Nestorius (Bishop of Constantinople, an influential figure
in the early church) emphasized the human nature of Jesus and taught that Mary had
given birth to the man named Jesus, not God. He did concede that as an enlightened
Christ, Jesus' body served as a temple for God. Nestorius then argued that this by definition
would make Mary the Mother of Jesus, not the Mother of God. This is steeped in logic;
however, the church did not see it that way and decreed such beliefs an anathema. The
church also unified Jesus and the Christ as one person indivisible; whereas I believe that
the word *Christ* is a title and a level of spiritual development we all can achieve, making
Jesus a man separate from the title of Christ. I believe that there is a Christ in all of us.

As far as Mother Mary is concerned, the virgin birth of Jesus is straightforward
and requires no explanation. However, it wasn't until church leaders met at the fifth
ecumenical council that Mother Mary was declared *perpetually a virgin*, making Jesus
her only biological son. This, however, directly contradicts the Bible if taken literally.

"While Jesus was still talking to the crowd, his mother and brothers stood outside, wanting to speak to him." Matthew 12:46

To further clarify, the *Immaculate Conception* is not the same as the virgin birth of Jesus, but is sometimes confused with the concept of the virgin birth. The Immaculate Conception is a belief of the Catholic Church that Mary was born without the stain of original sin. Mary the Mother of God wasn't declared an immaculate conception until the year 1854 AD by Pope Pius the IX.[8]

As previously mentioned, I believe the concept of reincarnation was certainly a fundamental component of the early Christian church. It surely was for the Gnostics, a spiritual sect that revered wisdom and the attainment of spiritual knowledge necessary to attain enlightenment. A number of other significant people in the early days of the Christian church were fervent believers in reincarnation, such as Saint Gregory of Nyssa, Saint Augustine, and Saint Jerome. Another very important proponent of reincarnation was Origen. In his work *On First Principles*, Origen established his main tenets, including the pre-existence of souls, the Fall of Man, the rebirth of souls into temporal bodies, and the eventual return to enlightenment as our original state of consciousness. He was considered one of the greatest of all the early Christian theologians and most likely one of the primary people responsible for the onset of the ecumenical councils.

The *Second Council of Constantinople*, which was actually the fifth ecumenical council, met in 553 AD under Pope Vigilius and Emperor Justinian I. Nearly three hundred years after Origen's death, Emperor Justinian at the fifth ecumenical council declared fifteen anathemas (condemnations) against Origen.

"The very first of the 'Anathemas Against Origen' states: 'If anyone asserts the fabulous pre-existence of souls, and shall assert the monstrous restoration which follows from it: let him be anathema.' The fifteenth anathema stated in part: 'If anyone does not anathematize Arius, Eunomius, Macedonius, Apollinaris, Nestorius, Eutyches, and Origen as well as their impious writings...let them be anathema.' The condemnation of Origen's teachings was taken to imply rejection of pre-existence and reincarnation by the entire church."[9]

They also declared that *Jesus Christ's resurrection was not ethereal (etheric body) and anyone who believes that our bodies will not be raised as mortal, no longer matter, will be excommunicated.* It also states that *anyone who believes that the life of the spirits (souls) should be like the spirits in the beginning before the fall, so that the end will be the true measure of the beginning, they too shall be excommunicated.* In other words, we were originally perfect; there was a fall in consciousness; and now we are on the road back to our original immortality. I suggest that these additional points, considered anathemas, are all true as well.

The council also resolved that if anyone should say *Christ is in no way different than other reasonable beings (souls), that is, we are all equal as sons of God, they shall be excommunicated from the church.*[10] Further, *if anyone believes that hell is a temporary place of punishment, he too shall be excommunicated.* It is amazing to consider that all of these decisions regarding what constituted Jesus Christ's original teachings were made centuries after his death. Do you think that maybe the church got some of them wrong? Is it possible that the religious leaders in power at the time mistakenly misinterpreted or intentionally manipulated portions of the Bible for their own benefit?

It is becoming increasingly accepted among some religious scholars that Jesus had a very close personal relationship with Mary Magdalene, who, by the way, was most likely never a prostitute. Sometime in the late sixth century, around the year 591, Pope Gregory the Great in a sermon mistakenly stated that the prostitute mentioned in the Gospel of Luke (Chapter 7) was the same woman mentioned later in the Gospel of Luke as Mary Magdalene (Chapter 8). It wasn't until much later that the Vatican recanted their error. Was Pope Gregory's assumption purposefully made in order to degrade women and subsequently lessen the power of women in the church? This is the most likely scenario since the men in power wished to retain control over the church and over the general populace. Even today women lack significant power in the Catholic Church in that they are still not allowed to be priests or hear confession.

Eventually, after a long period of continual conflicts over interpreting scripture, the Roman Church separated from the other Orthodox churches and formed the Roman Catholic Church in 1054 AD.[11]

The *Council of Trent*, the nineteenth ecumenical council, occurred between 1545 AD and 1563 AD in three separate periods with each assembly challenging the Protestant Reformation started in large part by Martin Luther. The church at this council reaffirmed many of the doctrines firmly held by the Catholic Church. They also held firm to the Seven Sacraments, the necessity of celibacy for priests, the virginity of Mother Mary, along with other important signs of their faith such as relics and indulgences. Historically, indulgences included purchasing items from the church such as relics or making gifts to the church as a means for pardoning their sins. Without indulgences, there would be no forgiveness of sins by the church.

To date, there have been more than twenty such councils where interpretation of the scriptures have been redefined, altered, or declared as heresy. What is important to realize in all of this is that the leaders of the Christian church over time changed doctrine. What may have been considered accepted church doctrine immediately following the days Jesus walked the earth is clearly no longer accepted today. Reincarnation was in all probability a readily acknowledged component of Jesus' original teachings. The fact that Jesus rose from the dead in His etheric body may also have been a widely held belief during the early days of Christianity. For that matter, many of the doctrines unacceptable to the current Christian church may have been an integral component of the early church's doctrines. Remember, the first ecumenical council occurred nearly three hundred years after Jesus' death and resurrection. I would strongly suggest within one hundred percent probability that the church misinterpreted Jesus' teachings in numerous instances.

In an important Gnostic text named *Pistis Sophia,* one of the few texts devoted wholly to the cryptic teachings of Jesus to his disciples, circa 200 AD, Jesus Christ is quoted as having said the following:

> "Souls are poured from one into another of different kinds of bodies of the world."[12]

This certainly suggests that Jesus taught the concept of reincarnation to His followers.

What does this say about today's religious beliefs and the Bible? It most certainly brings into question the validity of church doctrine. The fact that many of the church's doctrines were addressed in the first place signifies that many components of the existing religious doctrine were at the time in contention, and that anyone who didn't go along with the changes made by the church would have been subject to anathema, excommunication, punishment, torture, or possibly even being burned to death. It just goes to show you that you can't without question simply accept everything as the truth, not even if it appears in the Bible. I highly recommend to the reader to further delve into the ecumenical councils, as it makes for scholarly religious study.

Throughout history, there have been many famous, very educated people who are said to have believed in reincarnation: Leo Tolstoy, Ralph Waldo Emerson, Mark Twain, Henry Ford, Norman Mailer, Carl Jung, General George S. Patton, Albert Schweitzer, Walt Whitman, Benjamin Franklin, Charles Dickens, Friedrich Nietzsche, William Shakespeare, Leonardo da Vinci, Thomas Edison, Gandhi, George Harrison, Dalai Lama, Charles Lindbergh, and Edgar Cayce.[13]

> "The only survival I can conceive is to start a new earth cycle again."
> Thomas Edison

> "I adopted the theory of reincarnation when I was twenty-six. Genius is experience. Some seem to think that it is a gift or talent, but it is the fruit of long experience in many lives." Henry Ford

There are many others who also believed in reincarnation, some very influential in science as well as in literature: Pythagoras—Greek philosopher and creator of the

Pythagorean Theorem; Cicero—possibly the greatest Roman orator; Edgar Alan Poe, Henry D. Thoreau—America authors; Napoleon Bonaparte, and William Randolph Hearst.[14]

> "I am confident that there truly is such a thing as living again, that the living spring from the dead, and that the souls of the dead are in existence." Socrates

Today various religions have reincarnation as a major tenet. Reincarnation is an integral component of Hinduism, Buddhism, Sikhism, Jainism, Taoism, Theosophy, Kabbalah, Sufism, and the New Age movement.

> "To millions of Christians, reincarnation is a familiar word. This is not at all surprising since reincarnation is the belief of literally billions (thousands of millions) of human beings on earth today."[15]

If the Christian church had not changed the Bible to remove reincarnation from its doctrine, more people than not would believe in reincarnation, as Christianity is the world's largest religion. Surely the majority of people living today are not aware of the changes made to early religious doctrine by the church over time.

Millions of people make the assumption (or no assumption at all) that the religious beliefs today are the same religious beliefs from when Jesus walked this earth. This is simply not true. Which chapters were to be included in the Bible was dictated by the church over time, dictated by men, not by God or Jesus or even the apostles. And how they were to be interpreted was determined by the church as well; this occurs even today. If the world knew the truth about the early church and its manipulation of religious doctrine throughout history many would begin to question the church's authority even more than what is occurring at the present time. For instance, I believe the manipulation was an attempt to control the masses, place absolute power within the church, and minimize the power of women.

Evidence of reincarnation ranges from reports of verifiable past life memories to the remaining references of reincarnation in the Bible not deleted by the Second Ecumenical Council of Constantinople. These lingering quotes in the Bible once again imply that reincarnation was a common belief back in the days of Jesus. Even the words Jesus spoke Himself, not deleted from the Bible by the early church, indicate the possibility or likelihood of reincarnation as a common belief at the time.

> "I tell you the truth: among those born of women there has not risen anyone greater than John the Baptist; yet he who is least in the kingdom is greater than he. From the days of John the Baptist until now, the

kingdom of heaven has been forcefully advancing, and forceful men lay hold of it. For all the Prophets and the Law prophesied until John. And if you are willing to accept it, he is the Elijah who was to come." Matthew 11:11-14

It is clear here, at least to me, that Jesus is saying that John the Baptist is the same soul as the prophet Elijah. The only reasonable explanation can be reincarnation.

There are additional references in the Bible that suggest that reincarnation is true. When Jesus heals a man born blind, the apostles as reported in scripture ask Him an interesting question.

"As he went along, he saw a man blind from birth. His disciples asked him, 'Rabbi, who sinned, this man or his parents that he be born blind?' 'Neither this man nor his parents sinned,' said Jesus, 'but this happened so that the work of God might be displayed in his life.'" John 9:1-3

The apostles' reference to the man's sin suggests that if the man's sin caused him to be born blind, that sin must have occurred before the man's birth. Minimally, it would suggest the apostles believed in reincarnation. And since the apostles spent their days and nights together with Jesus who better would understand Jesus' teachings? Overall, these verses not only reference potential karma in relation to sins from previous lives, but interestingly enough, it also references potential karma for the parents for some sin they might have committed.

Here is another biblical verse that could imply reincarnation:

"Him who overcomes [sin] I will make a pillar in the temple of my God. Never again will he leave it." Revelation 3:12

The obvious implication here is that the one who overcomes sin will not have to be reborn.

Possibly the most revealing of all the potential references to reincarnation is found in Ephesians.

"What does 'he ascended' mean except that he also descended to the lower, earthly regions? He who descended is the very one who ascended higher than all the heavens, in order to fill the whole universe." Ephesians 4:9-10

Is this verse suggesting that Jesus is the reincarnation of Adam? Jesus clearly is the soul *who ascended higher than all the heavens. He who descended* may be a reference to Adam descending into the lower earthly regions to become sinful man. *He who descended is the very one who ascended* clearly states that they are the same soul.

There are other verses in the Bible that further suggest the possibility that Jesus is the same soul as Adam.

"So it is written, 'The first man Adam became a living being; the last Adam, a life-giving spirit.'" 1 Corinthians 15:45

"Nevertheless, death reigned from the time of Adam to the time of Moses, even over those who did not sin by breaking a command, as did Adam, who was a pattern for the one to come." Romans 5:14

Could the phrase *"Adam, who was a pattern for the one to come"* be referencing Jesus Christ? It is increasingly apparent that even Jesus may have reincarnated. Notice also that *"death reigned…even for those who did not break a command"* could mean that the original sin taints all of mankind from the point of original sin on.

There are at least two other references I could locate in the Bible that suggest Jesus had previous lives beyond Adam.

"Altogether Enoch lived 365 years. Enoch walked with God; then he was no more; because God took him away." Genesis 5:23-24

Another well-known person referenced in the Bible *"walked with God."*

"This is the account of Noah. Noah was a righteous man, and he walked with God." Genesis 6:9

Is *walking with God* a code for additional reincarnations of Jesus? Why are these prophets referenced in this manner? The answer may be that they are additional reincarnations of Jesus, or would it be more appropriate to say *additional resurrections of Adam*?

Another interesting verse in scripture that warrants further exploration is the following:

"After he (God) drove the man out (Adam), he placed on the east side of the garden of Eden a cherubim and a flaming sword flashing back and forth to guard the way to the tree of life." Genesis 3:24

Adam with Eve, because of their original sin, reportedly closed the gates of heaven, and these gates subsequently remained closed until Jesus died and rose again. If Jesus was the same soul as Adam (and vice versa), then Jesus opened the gates of heaven by His sacrifice that He was responsible for closing as sinful Adam. In this way, perfect universal justice as karma comes full circle. It is important here to make a further clarification. Adam (which in Hebrew means "man") may serve both as a metaphor for the first man or men on earth, as well as the soul that later reincarnates as Jesus. Jesus may then be the reincarnation of Adam in the sense that He may have been the very first man to sin, or minimally may represent the men that sinned originally in the more general sense of the word. He also may be symbolic of the Christ in all of us.

"For as in Adam all die, so in Christ all will be made alive."
1 Corinthians 15:22

Jesus completed his purpose on earth, and in doing so, scripture tells us that He will not enter a physical body again. He will not be reincarnated according to scripture.

"The death he died, he died to sin once and for all; but the life he lives, he lives to God." Romans 6:10

One more bit of evidence suggesting that Jesus is the reincarnation of Enoch, I would like to point out, appears in scripture, specifically in Hebrews:

"By faith Enoch was taken from his life so that he did not experience death; He could not be found, because God had taken him away." Hebrews 11:5

Since we are all sinners due to the tainting of our soul by original sin, and consequently we must all suffer death, how is it that Enoch was able to avoid physical death before Jesus was even born? I was taught in Catholic grade school that the gates of heaven had been closed since the point of original sin. It says so in Genesis 3:24, and in 1 Corinthians 15:22. The Bible also states that because of Adam, all men must die. However, Enoch did not die even though his life came after Adam's original sin and before Jesus' life, death, and subsequent resurrection which reopened the gates of heaven. How is it that Enoch was spared death? The only explanation is that Enoch and Jesus are the same soul and that Enoch was allowed to return home to heaven without tasting death. Did the soul of Jesus as Enoch already achieve enlightenment? If this is the case, that would explain why Enoch did not have to suffer physical death. Subsequently, Enoch as Jesus may have reincarnated as an unenlightened human to show us the way back to enlightenment.

This and more is declared in the book *Lives of the Master, the Rest of the Jesus Story* by Glenn Sanderfur, a book based on the psychic readings of Edgar Cayce, who is considered to be the greatest of all modern-day prophets. Edgar Cayce while under hypnosis made the subsequent claims about Jesus' reincarnations as reported in Sandefur's book:

"The readings of Edgar Cayce indicate that the Jesus soul lived as many as thirty lives and from among them clearly identified the following:

Amilius—an incarnation in Spirit-form only.

Adam—the first man, described in the opening of the Bible.

Enoch—a man who "walked with God," according to Genesis.

Melchizedek—a priest at the time of Abraham.

Joseph—son of Jacob who was sold into slavery by his brothers.

Joshua—the successor to Moses who led the Israelites into the Promised Land.

Asaph—a musician in King David's court.

Jeshua—a priest who helped re-establish the worship of God after the Israelites' return from captivity in Babylon.

Zend—the father of the religious leader Zoroaster.

Jesus—the Christ."[16]

Could one of the greatest prophets proclaimed to have ever lived, Edgar Cayce, be correct? If so, it is clear-cut evidence that our soul as consciousness never dies, and that it may take many lifetimes for us to reach enlightenment and, of course, return to heaven.

Section III

REDEFINING THE TRINITY

CHAPTER 13

The Trinity or Godhead

❧

In Christianity, the Trinity, sometimes referred to as the *Godhead*, represents the Father, Son, and Holy Ghost. The Holy Ghost is also known as the Holy Spirit. They refer to the same entity. However, I will be using the term *Holy Spirit* for the remainder of this book because I believe that the term *Spirit* is a better descriptor of this entity than *Ghost*. Also, please note in advance that for lack of a more accurate manner in which to address God, I will at times use the words *He* or *Him*, and related pronouns. However, please understand that I recognize that God is not a man. I recognize that God is neither a woman. God is not a person. God is a divine infinite being with both feminine and masculine characteristics. God is arguably an androgynous being.

Throughout history mankind has attempted to identify and understand God. Many forms of nature have been made deities: sun, moon, earth, fire, Mother Nature herself, even thunder and lightning. In the past, God has been made into idols of gold, silver, or other precious metals often accompanied with precious gems. In today's society we have many false idols we occasionally place before God, such as cars, jewelry, and addictions such as alcohol, sex, drugs, and even our physical bodies.

God and the countless facets of the Godhead have been called many names by various religions and philosophies: Father, Allah, Lord God, Elohim, Eloi, Abba, Yahweh, King of Kings, Logos, Odin, Ra, Zeus, Rama, Shiva, Vishnu, Void, and Nothingness. God has many more names in which man has attempted to explain or personify Him. Sadly, the many names we have assigned God only serve to divide Him into a separate God for each set of different peoples and religions. The religions of the world have therefore become exclusive rather than inclusive, with many falsely believing that only the people of their individual faith can enter heaven.

Most often the religious personification of God portrays God as having a masculine overtone possessing traits we might expect of an earthly father, sometimes stern and authoritarian, possibly even lacking in some of the more feminine characteristics. In my attempt to discover the truth about God, I compared the Bible to other holy books and philosophies to see if they were at all consistent. Often they didn't conveniently fit together as I would discover an inconsistency I could not overlook. As a result, I would have to begin the process of redefining the Trinity all over again. I quickly came to the conclusion that the Godhead is not so easy to comprehend!

Within the Christian Bible, the Old Testament on occasion portrays God as an unforgiving God, and at times, when angered, a punitive God. The New Testament seems to portray God as a more forgiving, less vengeful God, supposedly due to the new covenant God made with mankind through His Son, Jesus Christ. In Christianity, Jesus is considered to be *The Only Begotten Son* of God. Some religions and philosophies have associated the concept of a Holy Spirit with the feminine side of God. As I continued my general research, I discovered that various religions and philosophies at times define God and the Trinity in somewhat similar ways or aspects.

However, in numerous other instances there appear to be monumental discrepancies between religions; even within Christianity itself, there are huge inconsistencies. For example, how can one marry the concept of an unconditionally loving God with one that would judge and condemn His children to an eternity of hell? This has never made any sense to me. Within this book, I will be proposing alternative meanings to longstanding belief systems in an attempt to discover what I believe to be a truer, more accurate description or understanding of the Godhead.

Only by comparing religions and philosophies was I able to generate a greater understanding of the three beings of the Godhead residing within the Trinity. In each religion I studied, I saw a different facet of the Godhead. My quest reminds me of the story of the three blind men attempting to describe an elephant. One is touching the tail and describes the elephant in terms of a tail. The second blind man is touching the trunk and describes the elephant in terms of the trunk, while the third blind man is touching the body of the elephant and describes it as such. Each part described by each man is an equally important facet of the whole elephant, yet not enough to describe the entire animal when taken individually. By the way, none of them were incorrect. So it is in studying various religions and philosophies that I was able to piece the "God puzzle" together. But to begin to understand the Godhead, it is important to break it down into smaller, bite-size chunks.

The Trinity in a sense can also be likened to a diamond. A diamond represents love, is very beautiful, and has many facets. When describing or discussing a diamond, it is important to realize that when we are doing so, we are typically referring to just one aspect of the diamond. We may be referring to its cut, color, clarity, carat weight, cost, or another one of its many facets. However, in all cases, we are referring to the one diamond. The same holds true for the Trinity; whether we're referring to the Father, the Son, the Holy Spirit, or one of their infinite facets or aspects, we are referring to the one God. One cannot divide up the Godhead. Only in theory can we attempt to do so. The Trinity really is one being. There is only one God, no matter how we slice or dice Him.

For the purposes of this book, the Godhead—as represented in the Trinity—is defined as *a Being consisting of all the consciousness in the universe (or universes)*. It really is the *totality of being-ness*—that is, the *Being of all consciousness*. The Godhead is all things of form and non-form. The Godhead holds within it both energetic and non-energetic properties. The Godhead is both the light and the darkness. The Godhead holds within it all creation and that which has yet to be created. God is everything you can see and all that remains unseen to human eyes. The Godhead is all you could ever imagine and much more. God is in everything. That is what is meant by God being omnipresent.

To understand the individual facets of the Godhead is not particularly easy or straightforward. Therefore, before we continue, I ask that you set aside for the time being what you were taught about the Trinity and their relationship to each other. Forget everything you have been taught in religion and open your mind to fresh new ideas. Try not to immediately judge what I say here. Think about it for a while and see if it makes sense, then decide. Be open to the possibilities. Let us begin with the Impersonal God.

CHAPTER 14

The Impersonal God

I refer to this part of the Trinity as the *Impersonal God*. I've read about an *impersonal* God in a couple of spiritual books, but whenever I did, I refused to believe it and set the book down usually feeling somewhat discouraged. Initially, it didn't make any sense to me. How could there be an impersonal God that doesn't care about me? I could not embrace the concept of an impersonal God until I realized that there is a *Personal God* aspect to the Godhead as well.

God at the uppermost level is an impersonal being, a being beyond emotion, at least in the way we humans normally think of emotion. What I further discovered is that the Impersonal God is the truest part of the Godhead. It is the original state of God Consciousness or *state of being* before creation. It is the *Alpha and the Omega—the Beginning and the End*. The Impersonal God is the *unmanifested, unformed, non-energetic, supreme consciousness, all-knowing God*. Inherent within the unmanifested Impersonal God is the realm of *unlimited possibilities*; imagine an infinite number of possibilities. For some people it may be impossible to fathom this concept.

The Impersonal God is the *Indomitable Mind* or *Universal Mind* aspect of the Godhead. The Impersonal God can be described as *all-knowing consciousness* without a vibratory element. It is *darkness*. When I make a reference to this aspect of the Godhead as darkness, I am simply making a statement that this portion of God is the unmanifested portion of God. It is not *light* because light implies possessing energetic properties and this aspect of God does not possess energetic properties. Light implies creation. The Impersonal God part of the Godhead is pure consciousness. The Impersonal God could also be considered *unmanifested thought*. Some religions and philosophies refer to this characteristic of God as the *Void* or the *Nothingness*.

The reason this portion of the Godhead is difficult to understand is because it's the unmanifested portion of God. Being unmanifested, the Impersonal God is without energy and of course without form. As an all-knowing all-conscious God, the magnitude of His being-ness is far greater than we could ever imagine. To understand the Impersonal God much beyond this is futile while in the human form at our current level of consciousness. The Impersonal God is much grander and expansive than our un-enlightened individual minds can begin to comprehend. For now we need to be satisfied with this superficial but workable understanding of the Impersonal God. Moving forward, the Trinity continues to be complicated, interrelated, and downright confusing at times.

CHAPTER 15

The Christ Body or Oversoul

❧

"All are but parts of one stupendous whole, Whose body Nature is, and God the soul." Alexander Pope

The *Christ Body* is a term that intuitively came to me as a way to describe the varying aspects and energies that comprise this portion of the Godhead. The Christ Body should not be defined as, or confused with, Jesus Christ. They are different. So then, what is the Christ Body? The Christ Body is *God Consciousness manifested into form*, also known as *Spirit-form*.

The Impersonal God gave birth to the Christ Body.

"He is in the image of the invisible God, the first born over all creation." Colossians 1:15

The invisible God referenced in the verse above is the Impersonal God. The Christ Body, as the first-born, is also then The Only Begotten Son of God and not Jesus as Christianity typically defines Him. The Impersonal God or unmanifested God, having inherent within it an infinite realm of possibilities, gave birth to one of those possibilities by creating the Christ Body. Take notice of the word *image* in the verse above. The word *image* implies *visibility*. Therefore we can take this verse to mean that the invisible God became visible; the unmanifested became manifested. In other words, the Impersonal God manifested a portion of Himself into the visible Christ Body. It follows that the Christ Body is then the *manifested singular soul body* of the Impersonal God.

"There is one body and one Spirit…." Ephesians 4:4

This singular soul body is also known as the *Oversoul* or the *Supersoul*. However, the Christ Body has a dual nature. In one sense the Christ Body is the *One Body* of God manifested in Spirit-form. In another sense, the Christ Body is also *the one collective body of all individual souls* that God created. What we are looking at is two differing facets of God that at first blush contradict what we think possible. How can the Christ Body be one soul and many individual souls at the same time?

> "The body is a unit, though it is made up of many parts; and though all its parts are many, they form one body. So it is with Christ." 1 Corinthians 12:12

Defining Christ as the Christ Body may be a new concept to some people. The concept of *one and many at the same time* may be difficult to understand as it's inconsistent with what we typically understand as a potential reality. How the Christ Body can be one body or Oversoul and also be many parts or many souls at the same time might be best explained by making a simple analogy. Consider an ocean. An ocean is one body of water and yet it's made up of billions of droplets of individual water. It is both one body of water and many parts or drops of water at the same time.

The Christ Body is referenced as one body and as many bodies in the Bible in several places.

> "…Christ is all, and is in all." Colossians 3:11

> "Let the peace of Christ rule in your hearts, since as members of one body you were called to peace." Colossians 3:15

> "Do you not know that you are members of Christ himself?" 1 Corinthians 6:15

The verses above make it quite clear that we are all members of the Christ Body. Included in the Christ Body is every prophet, every apostle, every saint, and every soul ever created, including yours and mine.

The Impersonal God as earlier discussed is the portion of the Trinity that has no form or energy and therefore does not have a vibratory element associated with it. The Impersonal God is pure God Consciousness only. However, everything created by the Impersonal God has form and energy and therefore vibrates. That is the Universal Law of Vibration. The Christ Body thus has form, energy, and a vibrational component to it. The Christ Body is still fully *God Conscious*, but as *Spirit in form*, it is more commonly referred to as being *Christ Conscious* (versus God Conscious). An individual soul that is enlightened is also considered to be *Christ Conscious* or *possessing Christ Consciousness*.

The greater the consciousness of anything, the higher the vibrational rate associated with it. Christ Consciousness is a very high level of spiritual development as one might imagine, and it carries a very high vibratory rate. Therefore high levels of consciousness, vibrational rate, and spiritual development go hand in hand when you refer to the Christ Body as a single entity or as an entity full of Christ Conscious souls.

The Christ Body in the aggregate sense is also called the *Supreme Personality of God* and as a result is considered to be the *Personal God*. The Personal God is what we would normally expect our God to be, nurturing, compassionate, loving, empathetic, generous, caring, and much more. God's personality, as expressed within the Christ Body, is all-encompassing facets of love.

As individual Christ Conscious beings or souls within the Christ Body, we all have a separate personality expressed within our own soul or state of being. We all have our own purpose for being that no other soul can fulfill. As individual souls within the Christ Body, we are all considered to be the children of God. We are all children of God existing within the Christ Body. Collectively, as the Christ Body, we are all a part of The Only Begotten Son of God; individually, we are the sons of God. Whether I use the term "sons of God" or "children of God," I am referencing all of us as humanity.

On one level we are in effect all fragments of the Christ Body. Because the individual soul is only a fragment of the Oversoul or Christ Body, we (as individual souls) are not equal to the collective consciousness of the Christ Body and should never think that we are, individually speaking, the collective Christ Body. We are less because we are only a part of the whole. However, at the highest level within the Christ Body, we are all equal in consciousness because we are all one Oversoul as stated in the Law of Unity. We are equal because as one fully conscious enlightened being, we are a singular soul vibrating as one. We are all equal in consciousness because we are one consciousness. As one fully enlightened Christ Conscious soul, we are all equal in stature within the Christ Body, even to Jesus, because there is only one Oversoul. At this level you could even go as far as to say that Jesus does not exist because there is no separation.

The term *Christ* is then a title for *any and all individual souls within the Christ Body* because they are all operating on a level of Christ Consciousness; they are all Christ Conscious or enlightened beings. Individually or collectively within the Christ Body, we function as a Christ because it is correct to think of Christ as a title or state of being. Another way of saying this is that there is a Christ in all of us. All of the Great Prophets such as John the Baptist, Elijah, Moses, Daniel, Sarah, Samuel, Abraham, Krishna, are part of the Christ Body and I believe, are Christ Conscious souls. Since all points of consciousness or souls within the Christ Body are equal in consciousness, I could just as easily say that as enlightened beings we are Buddha-Conscious or Krishna-Conscious. I think you get the point that as fully enlightened beings we are all equal in consciousness within the Christ Body. However, after the fall in man's consciousness not all souls were equally conscious.

Over mankind's history, enlightened masters from the Christ Body descended into the physical plane in order to remind us once again that we are all one within the Christ Body. Jesus, as well as the other prophets listed above, acted as one of God's intermediaries so that we would come to re-member God and re-member the god in us because only through the Christ Body can we know the Father as the Impersonal God. The Christ Body, The Only Begotten Son, is our connection to the Impersonal God.

> "Jesus answered, 'I am the way and the truth and the life. No one comes to the Father except through me. If you really knew me you would know the Father as well. From now on, you do know him and you have seen him.'" John 14:6-7

This verse suggests that Jesus Christ as an enlightened soul is the physical and visible manifestation and reflection of the Impersonal God. His words *if you really knew me* may be suggesting his symbolic representation of the Christ Body of which we are all a part.

I know this chapter on the Christ Body may overall sound confusing because it may contradict what we might have been taught. But when you embrace this new definition of the Trinity and compare it to original writings such as those in the Bible, you may now grasp, and maybe for the first time ever, what you are reading, because with this new awareness the verses now make sense. Even reading something as difficult and esoteric as the Bhagavad-Gita is now rendered comprehensible. Bhagavad-Gita is a summary of India's spiritual wisdom, as spoken by their savior Lord Krishna, whom the people of India consider their own Supreme Personality of the Godhead or their own Christ. At the very least, this new understanding of the Christ Body will infuse new meaning into the Bible.

> "Love your neighbor as yourself." Matthew 22:39

Understanding now that the Christ Body is really one collective soul, maybe we can better appreciate this commandment.

CHAPTER 16

The Holy Spirit

❦

The Holy Spirit is a manifested energy of the Impersonal God, just as the Christ Body is a manifested energy of the Impersonal God. The Holy Spirit in its own right seems to be multifaceted, which one might expect since the Holy Spirit is the creative force or creative energy of the Impersonal God. The Holy Spirit is the Impersonal God's intelligence or intellectual energy as *thought expressed*, which created the Christ Body.

The Christ Body in this case could be considered the form, while the Holy Spirit energy could be considered the energy that created the form. The Christ Body can be looked at or defined as *a point of God Consciousness as the Oversoul* or *points of God Consciousness as individual souls within the Oversoul* while the Holy Spirit may best be described as *a stream or river of God Consciousness pouring outward from the Impersonal God.*

> "Whoever believes in me, as the scripture has said, streams of living water will flow from within him. By this he meant the Spirit…" John 7:38-39

The phrase "streams of living water" is consistent with defining the Holy Spirit as a stream of God Consciousness. The Holy Spirit can also be defined as the *universal life force energy* of God as expressed here in John:

> "In him [Jesus] was life, and that life was the light of men. The light shines in the darkness, but the darkness has not understood it." John 1:4-5

In verse 4, the Holy Spirit is referred to as *life* or, more accurately, *life energy*, the universal life force in Jesus. In both verses above, the Holy Spirit is also referred to as *light*. Light suggests something manifested; it suggests form and energy. It is also clear in the latter verse that mankind does not understand the true nature of the Holy Spirit. Given the complexity of the Holy Spirit, it is easy to see why we do not understand it.

> "Do you not know that your body is a temple of the Holy Spirit, who is in you, whom you have received from God?" 1 Corinthians 6:19

Moreover, it becomes clearer and clearer to us that the Holy Spirit is the life force energy that lives in each one of us. I would further suggest that the Holy Spirit is the life force energy in all matter whether seen or unseen.

As the universal life force energy, the Holy Spirit has inherent within it three characteristics or sub-energies. The Holy Spirit is an energy that *creates*, just as it created the Christ Body. In this way the Holy Spirit is considered the feminine aspect of God, the creative force of God. The Holy Spirit has inherent within it the force that *destroys* or tears down, and finally, the Holy Spirit has inherent within it the force that *sustains* or upholds life. Thus the Holy Spirit can also be considered the glue of the universe; it is what holds creation together. The Holy Spirit is the life force energy that causes *the vibration in life itself* or is possibly the vibration *of* life itself, also known as the *AUM vibration*.

The AUM sound, inaudible to us at lower levels of consciousness, is a result of the cosmic creative vibration of the Holy Spirit. It is most often represented in the Eastern religions as AUM, commonly pronounced as *OH* with a long *O* sound followed by an *MMM* sound. The primordial sound of AUM (OHM) is most accurately recreated with the blending of the two sounds. So in other words, it takes at least two people to create the most correct sound of AUM. One person should be making the sound of *OH* while the other is making the sound of *MMM*.

It is easiest to create the sound properly if you have a larger group chanting it for a while. An accurate blending will then naturally occur. The minimum requirement of two people being present is consistent with what is stated in Matthew about Christ:

> "For where two or three come together in my name, there I am with them." Matthew 18:20

The meaning of AUM is *I AM*. It is the sound of God declaring who He is. The purpose of chanting AUM is to bring the body into the same resonance as God, to heighten our vibratory element in order to assist us with our transformation back to the Christ Body and Christ Consciousness.

Verses of the Bible also reference the Holy Spirit as a *Counselor* and as the *Spirit of Truth*. Jesus Christ promises to send the Counselor (Holy Spirit) to the apostles before He leaves earth.

> "And I will ask the Father, and he will give you another Counselor to be with you forever—the Spirit of Truth. The world cannot accept him, because it neither sees him nor knows him. But you know him, for he lives with you and will be in you." John 14:16-17

This verse describes the Holy Spirit as *another* counselor. Could Jesus be referencing Himself as the initial counselor?

The Holy Spirit exhibits a certain level of mysteriousness because *the world neither sees him nor knows him.* This sense of mystery is further exhibited in Acts:

> "When the day of Pentecost came, they were all together in one place. Suddenly a sound like the blowing of a violent wind came from Heaven and filled the whole house where they were sitting. They saw what seemed to be tongues of fire that separated and came to rest on each of them. All of them were filled with the Holy Spirit and began to speak in other tongues [or languages] as the Spirit enabled them." Acts 2:1-4

I personally believe that the term *speaking in tongues* represents the God-given ability to understand and speak any language once the soul becomes enlightened.

The mystery of the Holy Spirit is also witnessed in Matthew:

> "As soon as Jesus was baptized, he went up out of the water. At that moment heaven was opened, and he saw the Spirit of God descending like a dove and lighting on him." Matthew 3:16

Could the Spirit of God *descending like a dove* and *lighting on him* be a reference to an orb of white light? Either way, it is clear that the Holy Spirit has many interesting qualities.

The Holy Spirit in Eastern religions is referred to as *prana.*[1] Prana is a Sanskrit word meaning *breath.* Sanskrit is one of the many official languages of India. The Holy Spirit as prana is considered to be God's breath or the *Breath of God.* The Holy Spirit in the physical plane, as represented by the Law of Correspondence, is our own breath; without the Holy Spirit's universal life force energy within us we would not be alive.

> "...the Lord God formed the man from the dust of the ground and breathed into his nostrils the breath of life, and the man became a living being." Genesis 2:7

This verse in Genesis references the breath of life as the Holy Spirit entering man. Prana is but another descriptor of the Holy Spirit as the universal life force in man.

The Holy Spirit is also known as the *comforter.* This term once again expresses the feminine divine nature of the Holy Spirit versus the masculine nature of the Christ Body.

The Holy Spirit is also considered God's secret wisdom of the ages as referenced in Corinthians.

> "...we speak of God's secret wisdom, a wisdom that has been hidden and that God destined for our glory before time began." 1 Corinthians 2:7

The Holy Spirit knows God's thoughts as well as man's thoughts:

> "For who among men knows the thoughts of a man except the man's spirit within him? In the same way no one knows the thoughts of God except the Spirit of God." 1 Corinthians 2:11

Could the reference to *man's spirit* be the same as the *Spirit of God?*

The previous verses indicate that the Holy Spirit is in fact the wisdom of God and at the same time God's own thoughts. And the following verse indicates that this Holy Spirit wisdom is available to us so that we may have the mind of a Christ:

> "For who has known the mind of the Lord that he may instruct him? But we have the mind of Christ." 1 Corinthians 2:16

The unmanifested Impersonal God manifested Himself in form as the Christ Body, the result of His creative thought energies or wisdom, which is the Holy Spirit. The Christ Body is in effect the receptacle of God Consciousness manifested by the powers of the Holy Spirit as God's thought. The Holy Spirit, since it is God Consciousness, is omnipresent in all form, however in varying degrees.

Before we move onto the definition of the *Christ Principle* in the next chapter, it is important to remind you that the Christ Body and the Holy Spirit in reality are inseparable. How can one divide an ocean? They are both Spirit in form or Spirit-form. Only for the sake of this discussion did I attempt to separate them so that you may better understand the various energies of the Trinity. The Holy Spirit as God Consciousness is then in reality the same energy as Christ Consciousness. This is another definition of the Holy Spirit. The Holy Spirit is by definition Christ Consciousness. When the Holy Spirit enters a person and fills that person up, the Holy Spirit has in effect enlightened that person's soul. That person becomes Christ Conscious and may enter, or rather return to, the kingdom of heaven.

CHAPTER 17

The Christ Principle

⚜

As I was returning home from one of my almost daily walks, I received a very straightforward message from my higher self. My higher self, associated with that little intuitive voice I sometimes hear, I believe is my soul. I received the words *Christ Principle*. Until then I had never heard of the phrase Christ Principle. Upon reaching my home, I performed a quick Web search and discovered that the term Christ Principle actually exists. The Christ Principle is *the Spirit of God in material form.*

Material form is considered a manifested energy or extension of the Christ Body. It is not the Christ Body. It should not be confused with Spirit-form, which is the Christ Body and the Holy Spirit. The Christ Body is the Oversoul, and at the same time all souls; whereas the Christ Principle is *material form* created by the energies of the Holy Spirit through the Christ Body.

> "He is of the invisible God, the first born over all creation. For by him all things were created: things in heaven and on earth, visible and the invisible, whether thrones or powers or rulers and authorities; all things were created for him and by him." Colossians 1:15-20

Here the Bible clearly states that all things manifested in the creation of material form was made by the first-born, who is over all creation, which I have already explained is the Christ Body. It further states that all things outside of the Christ Body were not only made specifically by the Christ Body, but for the benefit of the Christ Body. These verses directly contradict Genesis where it states that God created the heavens and the earth, birds, animals and so on. However if Genesis is in reality referring to the Godhead (versus the Impersonal God), then there is no divergence in scripture. Another term for the Christ Principle beside material form is *material nature*. These two terms mean the same thing and can be used interchangeably.

The Christ Principle as referenced in the above passage is everything manifested seen and unseen, with the exception of the Christ Body and Holy Spirit, of course. Our human bodies are consequently members of the Christ Principle whereas our souls are members of the Christ Body. It is important to note that all material form (material nature) is a lesser form or energy of God while Spirit-form (the Christ Body and the Holy Spirit) is superior form and energy; Spirit-form in its original pure state operates at a level of Christ Consciousness while material form operates at various levels of consciousness below that of Christ Consciousness. Our souls are Spirit-form. Spirit-form, as I will propose later, can easily become polluted by human form and other material nature.

Therefore, the Christ Principle is all material form in various manifested levels of consciousness (less than that of Christ Consciousness) existing in vibratory creation. The Christ Principle could be considered the *material fabric* of the universe. Another way of saying this is that the entire manifestation of God in every way, meaning all physical planes, spiritual levels, and alternate realities or universes, and possibly even heaven itself, constitutes the Christ Principle. Let us now set our attention to *Jesus as man*.

CHAPTER 18

Jesus as Man

⚜

Yeshua ben Joseph, also known as *Jesus of Nazareth*, is believed by some to be the actual birth name of Jesus. However, on the surface this contradicts Luke:

> "On the eighth day, when it was time to circumcise him, he was named Jesus, the name the angel had given him before he had been conceived."
> Luke 2:21

That being said, it is very possible that since the Bible was not written in English, Jesus is somehow a transliteration (a phonetic translation) of *Yeshua*. The original languages of the Bible are Aramaic, Hebrew, and Greek. The Old Testament was written in mostly Hebrew with a few chapters or words written in Aramaic, while the New Testament was primarily written in Greek. The actual translation or transliteration from the original word (Jesus) to other names has been presented in many ways. Yeshua is quite possibly the original Aramaic proper name for Jesus.[1] Yeshua could have been originally *Yeshohua*. Or Yeshohua may have been the proper Hebrew name for Jesus.[2] The surname *ben Joseph* is much easier to translate. It means *son of Joseph*. Many people confuse the name Christ to be a surname for Jesus; it is not. As stated earlier, the word Christ is a title. Christ comes from the Greek word *Christos*, which means *anointed one*. In reality we do not know for sure exactly what Jesus' birth name was or how his name was actually pronounced that long ago. Either way it is irrelevant. The actual name of this man, pronounced correctly or otherwise, does not change the person, nor does it alter the acts of love or miracles performed by Jesus.

If you are familiar with the Bible, you will notice that there are large gaps in Jesus' life. Essentially the only reference to Him as a child is cited in Luke 2:41-51, where Luke depicts Jesus in the temple talking to the temple teachers. It has been suggested that *Jesus' lost years* were spent in the Orient studying the ancient Eastern religions and sacred texts preparing his mind, body, and soul for spiritual enlightenment.

Jesus, as man, is believed by many to be mankind's savior and is the central figure around which the Christian church was created, even though the term *Christian* wasn't used to describe His followers until after His death. Jesus as a single spiritual entity is a fragment, or a single soul, or an individual personality that descended from the Christ Body and became mortal man. In the physical sense he lived and breathed just like any other human being because He was fully human. He was *man and god*, just as we all are man and god.

You may find it shocking to hear there have been a number of spiritual figures born centuries before Jesus that reportedly share a number of highly significant similarities with Jesus. These spiritual figures were born of a virgin mother and considered to be "the word made flesh." They were born on December 25th, were visited at birth by wise men, and announced by angelic figures. They were baptized in a river, began preaching at thirty years of age, raised a man from the dead, and tempted by the devil. They restored sight to a blind man, cast out demons, healed a leper, and walked on water. Their adopted father was a carpenter. They were slain because of their beliefs and three days later rose from the dead. There are many more similarities than just the ones I mention above, including being crucified on a Friday, having had twelve disciples, and was considered a Christ as both man and god. Each was identified as the Good Shepherd, the Morning Star, a lion, and a lamb. And the similarities go on and on down the list.[3]

Mithra, Zoroaster, Horus, Osiris, Buddha, Attis, and Krishna are just some of the examples of deities that in part share the same life and death story of Jesus mentioned above.[4] There may even be others. These people may or may not have been mythological, just as Jesus may have had some myth surrounding His acts of love or miracles. In reality, Jesus may not have been born from a virgin mother. We have no proof of this. We live in faith that it occurred. For me, it really doesn't matter if it is true or not. It wouldn't alter the manner in which I am living my life if I discovered that it was not true.

What this says to me is that Jesus may not have been the first to die and rise from the dead. For that matter, it may be the very same soul coming back time and time again reenacting the same scenario to teach about love! If this is true, this incredibly loving soul suffers incredibly each time He returns to earth. It could be, in a way, considered to be His karma. Conversely, even if Jesus did not actually physically rise from the dead, the story of Jesus then metaphorically represents his conquest over sin and the rise of the Christ within him, from death in sin to life in God as an enlightened being. In truth, it doesn't matter, the story is the same. I bring this to your attention solely for the sake of your edification. I for one believe in the death and resurrection of Jesus, because I believe it is possible for all of us to do the same. Therefore I believe that Mithra, Zoroaster, Horus, Krishna, and the other deities mentioned above could without doubt have accomplished the same. As a human being, I believe that we all have a Christ in us. We are all both man and god.

I believe Jesus, as man and god, was tempted as all humans are tempted. That much is for certain as it is expressly stated in the Bible. However, I believe He also sinned or missed the mark as all humans do. Matthew 4:1-10 speaks to the various temptations Jesus endured, however only after his enlightenment. I believe that Jesus at birth and throughout the majority of His life was not a fully realized Christ. He was not born perfect, which means that He had not yet attained full enlightenment or Christ Consciousness. If that is true, then it should not come as a shock that Jesus may have been a sinner.

> "Although he was a son, he learned obedience from what he suffered and, once made perfect, he became the source of eternal salvation for all who obey him…" Hebrews 5:8

The above verse in Hebrews states that Jesus *learned obedience,* suggesting that he may have sinned initially and that later in life He was made perfect. Could the reference of learning obedience be learning as a consequence or the karma of His actions?

Jesus not having been born perfect is again echoed in the Gospel of Luke.

> "And Jesus grew in wisdom and stature, and in favor with God and men." Luke 2:52

It is clear to me that the phrase *grew in wisdom* means that Jesus as a child, teen, and young adult was not as yet enlightened. For if He had been enlightened, He would have by definition been filled with the wisdom of the Holy Spirit (God) and therefore could not have grown in wisdom. He would have been a fully realized enlightened being. In fact, it wasn't until John the Baptist baptized Jesus that Jesus became an enlightened being.

> "As Jesus was coming up out of the water, he saw heaven being torn open and the Spirit descending on him like a dove." Mark 1:10

Jesus' enlightenment—which I believe occurred during His baptism by John the Baptist—is once again verified in the Gospel of Luke.

> "Jesus, full of the Holy Spirit, returned from Jordan and was led by the Spirit into the desert…." Luke 4:1

Luke here describes Jesus as being *full of the Holy Spirit,* signaling His enlightenment and being made Christ Conscious. At the moment of His baptism, Jesus became full of the Holy Spirit (Christ Consciousness) and became a fully realized Christ (Christ Conscious).

Jesus was thirty years old at the time of His baptism (Luke 3:23). Shortly thereafter, John the Baptist was thrown into prison. Jesus then began to proselytize and perform miracles.

> "From that time on Jesus began to preach. 'Repent, for the kingdom of heaven is near.'" Matthew 4:17

The Bible does not make any references to Jesus performing miracles before Jesus' baptism. However, once baptized, at which time Jesus became enlightened, Jesus performed many miracles, although probably none greater than rising from the dead.

Jesus died at the age of thirty-three when He was crucified on the cross. Three days later He rose from the dead transcending His own death. Jesus was born again; this time of Spirit.

> "Flesh gives birth to flesh, but Spirit gives birth to Spirit. You should not be surprised by my saying, 'You must be born again.'" John 3:6-7

When Jesus said, *"You must be born again,"* He was referring to attaining a state of enlightenment and a return to immortality; for Him, this was being reborn in Spirit. This is somewhat contrary to what born-again Christians believe. At the age of eighteen, I was asked to accept Jesus into my heart and in doing so I was from then on supposedly saved. At eighteen, I was in effect reborn and could not go to hell no matter what I did. Nowadays, it is rather my contention that the concept of being reborn is more accurately defined as *growing in consciousness until we return to our fully conscious immortal body as enlightened souls*, which is quite different from what born-again Christians are suggesting.

I would also suggest that Jesus Christ upon rising from the dead returned in His immortal body. This is evident in the Bible in that the apostles did not immediately recognize Him. Jesus, having risen from the dead, had obviously been transformed or transfigured in some manner.

> "Afterward Jesus appeared in a different form to two of them while they were walking the country." Mark 16:12

The Gospel of Luke tells the same story slightly different:

> "As they talked and discussed these things with each other, Jesus himself came up and walked along with them, but they were kept from recognizing him." Luke 24:15-16

The Gospel of Matthew speaks of their initial reunion after the Resurrection.

> "Then the eleven disciples [the original twelve minus Judas] went to Galilee, to the mountain where Jesus told them to go. When they saw him, they worshiped him, but some doubted." Matthew 28:16-17

Remember, these apostles were constantly with Jesus for three straight years and yet they did not recognize Him. Some apostles even doubted that it was Him with Jesus standing right in front of them! It is clear to me that Jesus was transfigured due to Him returning to His immortal body.

Even Mary Magdalene didn't immediately recognize Jesus after reaching His tomb shortly after His Resurrection.

> "At this, she turned around and saw Jesus standing there, but she did not realize it was Jesus." John 20:14

This is not the first time Jesus was transfigured into another form of being:

> "After six days Jesus took with him Peter, James, and John, the brother of James, and led them up a mountain by themselves. There he was transfigured before them. His face shone like the sun, and his clothes became as white as the light." Matthew 17:1-2

The following verse in Corinthians further suggests that we, too, at some point in time will be resurrected into an immortal body.

> "So it will be with the resurrection of the dead. The body that is sown is perishable, it is raised imperishable; it is sown in dishonor, it is raised in glory; it is sown in weakness, it is raised in power; it is sown a natural body, it is raised a spiritual body. If there is a physical body, there is also a spiritual body." Corinthians 15:42-44

What did Jesus' birth, death, and resurrection accomplish? Jesus Christ showed us the way to Christ Consciousness when he completed his spiritual progression by fully receiving the Holy Spirit at the time of His baptism. By becoming Christ Conscious during His lifetime, Jesus regained His own immortality, allowing Him to later overcome His own physical death. Jesus showed us the way home back to heaven and immortality. Because of this, He should not be considered the *Great Exception* but rather the *Great Example*. He lived His life as an example for us. He was not the exception to the rule, but rather the rule that we all must eventually follow.

"I tell you the truth, anyone who has faith in me will do what I have been doing. He will do even greater things than these, because I am going to the Father." John 14:12

"He will do even greater things than these" clearly states that we are all god and man just as Jesus was god and man. In this way, He is like our big brother. Doesn't thinking of Jesus in this way bring Him closer to us? Doesn't this possibly even make Jesus seem more real because what He accomplished suddenly becomes attainable for all of us, and in reality necessary for us all to attain?

"In him we have redemption through his blood…" Ephesians 1:7

The verse above makes it clear that through Jesus we are redeemed of our sins. But what does redemption mean? One of several definitions of redemption includes *the act of being brought back.* So when Christ redeemed us of our sins, what he actually did was show us the way back home to the Christ Body by rising above sinful nature. Jesus showed us the way to everlasting life, not by dying for our sins, but rather by demonstrating what is possible for all men to achieve, that is, immortality by regaining the original state of Christ Consciousness. He did not die for our sins but rather died *because* of our sins.

It is important to understand that we are not guaranteed heaven simply because Jesus died on the cross as many Christians believe. Jesus as a Christ *only* showed us the way back home. Jesus regained Christ Consciousness because He personally overcame sin. Gradually, throughout Jesus' life, He prepared for and eventually attained a pure enough state for the Holy Spirit to fully enter Him. Jesus rose above the possibility of sin when He became Christ Conscious at the time of His baptism. When Jesus was later tempted in the desert, He did not succumb to sin because He had been filled with the Holy Spirit (Christ Consciousness).

"Then Jesus was led by the Spirit into the desert to be tempted by the devil." Matthew 4:1

It is impossible for us to enter into heaven while in a corrupted state. And while we continue to sin we are in a corrupted state. In Paul's letter to the Romans he writes about sin:

"For if you live according to the sinful nature, you will die; but if by the Spirit you put to death the misdeeds of the body, you will live, because those who are lead by the Spirit are sons of God." Romans 8:13-14

Paul did *not* say to the Romans, "Go ahead and sin because Jesus died for our sins as a sin offering so we are all going to heaven anyway." What he said was quite the reverse.

It is only through the power of the Holy Spirit that we can put to death our misdeeds and subsequently live above our sinful nature as Jesus illustrated for us.

The road to heaven is subsequently narrow.

> "But small is the gate and narrow is the road that leads to life, and only a few find it." Matthew 7:14

In this verse it appears that only a few will make it to heaven. So how then do we make it to heaven? Jesus answered this question to the apostles in the Gospel of Matthew.

> "Be perfect as your heavenly Father is perfect." Matthew 5:48

This is obviously easier said than done.

Later in Matthew, the apostles were concerned about *who* might actually make it to heaven. Jesus again answered them.

> "When the disciples heard this, they were greatly astonished and asked, 'Who then can be saved?' Jesus looked at them and said, 'With man this is impossible, but with God all things are possible.'" Matthew 19:25-26

These verses reflect how it is impossible for us to reach heaven if we try to do it alone without God. It is equally clear that only *through* God can we make it to heaven. This is consistent with an enlightened Jesus saying, *"No one comes to the Father, except through me."* The enlightened Jesus understood Himself to be one with God the Father.

Christ became an example for us by showing us the way to heaven by overcoming sin. Jesus taught us about love. The man Jesus embodied love. The way back to heaven was demonstrated by Jesus as sinful man returning to the status of an enlightened being.

In the Gospel of Matthew, John the Baptist is prophesying about the one to come, that being Jesus.

> "He will baptize you with the Holy Spirit and with fire." Matthew 3:11

That is how we will make it to heaven, through the power of the Holy Spirit. Just as Jesus prepared himself during His *lost years*, we too must prepare ourselves by moving closer to God, by gradually moving away from our sinful nature. And as we gradually move away from our sinful nature, the Holy Spirit will fill us up incrementally until we eventually become filled by the Holy Spirit, which is by definition the state of enlightenment. This is the *true baptism* Jesus spoke of and what Jesus' personal baptism represented. Baptism has nothing to do with being immersed in water, but rather being immersed in the consciousness of the Holy Spirit. Water is simply a metaphor representing the flowing consciousness of the Holy Spirit. Once we are fully conscious, at the time of our death, we will once again return to our immortal body and heaven as perfected beings free of the necessity to reincarnate. This is what Jesus showed us by His life, death, and subsequent resurrection. We will be born again, this time of Spirit.

The *National Geographic Explorer* series aired a program called the *Secret Lives of Jesus* on 12-12-09. Within this program the narrator spoke about a farmer who found the Nag Hammadi Library (religious texts) concealed in a large earthen jar in the year 1945. Written by unknown scribes between the third and fourth centuries, contained within these texts were previously untold stories surrounding the life of Jesus. The authenticity of the documents was not in question but rather what was written within the texts is considered by the Christian church to be heretical. In these texts the young Jesus was described as having a bad temper, was cruel at times and may have even caused the death of another child. Overall, the young Jesus was described as an immature child with supernatural powers. The texts go on to say that Jesus was a wild youth through His teen years and that He may have had a relationship with a woman. However, as Jesus grew older He began to better understand His own divinity and the responsibilities that came with it.

Later in the program it talks about a man named Issa. Issa traveled to India spending six years studying with high priests. Issa then went out to teach the Word of God to the people of India. It might surprise you that Issa translated means Jesus. Eventually, as the story goes, Issa (Jesus) left India under threat of death because He began to teach the Word of God to the people of a lesser social class. This strongly suggests that Jesus spent significant time in India educating Himself on eastern religions as previously speculated. Other stories revealed within the Nag Hammadi Library document the events surrounding the death and resurrection of Jesus in a substantially different way. Apparently, Jesus may have instructed Judas to turn Him over to the Pharisees so that the events that were meant to unfold would unfold in order to fulfill prophecy. This explanation for the betrayal of Jesus appears in the Gospel of Judas which clearly contradicts the Bible. One of the religious texts discovered near Nag Hammadi also states that Jesus rose from the dead as a giant, which I believe is another way of saying that Jesus resurrected in His immortal body. This also contradicts church doctrine.

As with the Bible many of the stories contained within the Nag Hammadi Library are outlandish if taken literally. Many of the texts found at Nag Hammadi are obviously meant to be symbolic representations of the life of Jesus. Some of the stories may have even been written to discredit his humanness placing Him above man and what man can eventually achieve; a return to enlightenment. To be honest, the truth about Jesus will never be entirely known to us at our present state of consciousness. I imagine if we found additional books detailing the life of Jesus, they would be equally discredited by one group or another. What is fundamentally important to realize is that we do not know with absolute certainty the truth behind the life and death of Jesus which consequently leaves a vast number of possibilities open. Minimally, His life on earth and His return to heaven remain open to interpretation.

CHAPTER 19

Summary of the Trinity

ॐ

The Trinity collectively represents all levels of consciousness. It is the light and the darkness, the unmanifested and the manifested, form and non-form, energy and non-energy, personal and impersonal.

The Father or the Impersonal God, the truest essence of God, is unmanifested; it is non-form and non-energy and pure consciousness. Inherent within the all-knowing Impersonal God is an infinite number of possibilities. Out of the unmanifested Impersonal God was born the Personal God as the Christ Body through the energy of the Holy Spirit as God's thought expressed into form.

The Christ Body is Spirit manifested in form or Spirit-form. The Christ Body is also considered the Supreme Personality of God or the Personal God. The Christ Body has a dual nature. As an undivided being or singular soul, it is one Oversoul. The Christ Body simultaneously is also all points of individual God Consciousness or souls. It is both one being and many beings at the same time. It is a point of God Consciousness and many points of God Consciousness concurrently. These Christ Body beings, collectively as one, and individually as many, in a state of perfection vibrate at the level of Christ Consciousness. It is only through the Christ Body that we come to know the Impersonal God.

The Holy Spirit is the Impersonal God's creative energy (God's thought expressed) and the universal life force that sustains all life. It is the life force within each of us. On the spiritual plane, it is considered the feminine aspect of God. On the physical plane, it's represented in form by Mother Earth and by Mother Nature. The Holy Spirit acts as a wave of consciousness, whereas the Christ Body acts as an ocean of consciousness as well as particles of individual consciousness. Again, how God is defined depends upon which facet or aspect of God you are referring to or focusing on. The Holy Spirit is also Christ Consciousness itself; a level of being or enlightenment. It is Christ Consciousness itself versus a being that is Christ Conscious; a small but noteworthy distinction.

The Christ Principle is material form, which is a creative product of the Christ Body made possible by the creative energies of the Holy Spirit. The Christ Principle has a lesser consciousness and is not considered a part of the Christ Body or Holy Spirit. However, in the truest sense, there is no separation between any one of these aspects; everything in reality is a part of one Universal God and everything else is a non-reality. Is not everything connected?

Now that I have hopefully summed up the various energies or aspects of the Trinity, I wish to present another concept that may have eluded you up to this point. Since Jesus is only one of the many personalities of the Supreme Personality of God, and all souls within the Christ Body are equal, then the Christ Body is for all religions. The Christ Body is not just about Christ and Christianity. The Christ Body encompasses all faiths and all philosophies. Jesus' message is therefore a message for everyone. Buddha's message is a message for everyone. Krishna's message is a message for everyone. God's true prophets taught us about love, kindness, compassion, and forgiveness. False prophets teach about hate, retribution, and other forms of evil. Hopefully, one day all people from all religions will wake up to the realization *it is only through love*, understanding that we are one acting as many, that we can put a stop to our evils ways once and for all.

All of the great true prophets came from the same loving entity referred to as the Christ Body. For that matter, they could have been the very same soul reincarnated, having suffered in the same way each and every lifetime! Either way, whether the same soul or not, they carried the same message about love from the One Universal God in miraculous ways to various cultures and times. All of the great prophets descended from the Christ Body onto earth within their own appointed time, place, and culture. The personalities or prophets that descended on our behalf throughout mankind's history attempted to raise the consciousness of humankind so that we could all re-member with God. Think of the wars that could have been avoided had we understood from the beginning that all of the great prophets were attempting to deliver the same message *about love* from the same God. Mankind has fought and killed and continues to do so over semantics, claiming that a specific religion and a particular saviour is superior to all others. Is it any wonder that in our ignorance we find the path back to heaven narrow and difficult?

Section IV

MERGING SCIENCE WITH GOD

CHAPTER 20

Quantum Theory and Thermodynamics

❦

Science versus God, are they necessarily at odds? Is it possible that *God is consistent with science* and *science is consistent with God?* Do they need to be necessarily adversarial? How might they be complimentary? Both science and God operate under certain laws of nature. Science works under certain principles such as the law of gravity. God reveals Himself to us via His own set of universal laws. Are they incompatible in any regard? My answer is a very adamant "No." The more science discovers, the closer we are to proving the existence of a universal intelligence. This intelligence is no different from God Himself. Science reflects the universal intelligence as consciousness behind the universe of form.

Based on previous chapters, we know that our soul as Spirit-form acts like a particle of consciousness within the Christ Body and at the same time acts like a wave of consciousness, i.e. the Holy Spirit. In quantum physics this phenomena is called *wave particle duality*.[1] Wave particle duality states that *light and matter act both like a particle of energy and as a wave of energy given the right circumstances, and that matter and light exhibit both properties of a wave and a particle.* Thus far, the English language does not contain the proper terminology to describe this phenomenon, nor does science have an explanation as to how both can be true at the same time. Neither do we have the exact terminology that describes the Holy Spirit as the same energy as our soul, which is also the same as Christ Consciousness. All of these energies have both the properties of a wave and a particle. In other words, there is not much difference to be found between God and science in terms of wave particle duality.

What about quantum physics' *Entanglement Theory?* Entanglement Theory states that *two separate particles from the same origin will affect the other particle's state when the first particle is measured in some fashion.*[2] More easily stated, *the two separate particles being measured are somehow interconnected.* Once again, Quantum Theory has not been as yet able to come up with a solution as to why this phenomenon occurs; it has only determined that it is an actuality. However, the solution is much simpler than science is willing to suggest or admit; the answer stems from the fact that *everything is made of the same spirit-matter from one original source, only various measures of it.* With regard to spirituality, it is similar to saying that *we are all connected*, since we all come from the same source which is God; we are all of the same Christ Body. We are all one. Similarly, we can say that *everything is God*. Another way of explaining *spiritual entanglement* is to say that what one person does affects the whole universe, because it does. Entanglement Theory is really *consciousness affecting consciousness*, and of course everything has consciousness. This is similar to the *Butterfly Effect* which states that a butterfly flapping its wings in the Amazon could cause an atmospheric disturbance somewhere else in the world because weather is all interconnected. Weather is in effect one organism or process and therefore weather in one location could be considered to be entangled with weather somewhere else in a completely different location.

Let's look at quantum physics' *Superposition Theory*. The principle of superposition states that *when we do not know the position of a particle at any point in time, it is actually in all possible positions at the same time, as long as we don't attempt to measure it*.[3] It is the measurement itself that limits the possibilities to the one reality. In truth, the observation itself affects or determines the outcome or location of the particle. In other words, on a subatomic level, *a particle is a wave of possibilities until such time the particle is measured* (i.e., by scientists). When it is measured, it becomes a particle of energy, whereas it had previously been acting as a wave of energy. Once you discontinue the act of measurement, the particle is potentially anywhere, consequently once again acting as a wave of possibilities.

This scenario not only happens in the subatomic world, it occurs in the spiritual world as well as our day-to-day world. Spiritually, the Impersonal God contains within it an endless realm of possibilities until it collapses into one quantifiable outcome. This universe is full of endless possibilities until time, space, and consciousness determine which outcome it will be, at which time it becomes measurable. Likewise, our individual lives are filled with these endless possibilities until we make a decision about something, at which time they suddenly collapse into one outcome.

Science is bit by bit proving that all possibilities are available to us at any time. In other words, all possibilities are available to us until we choose one possibility; and then it is no longer a possibility because it becomes a reality. The wave function in quantum physics represents the physical manifestation of the infinite world of possibilities within the scientific realm. The wave function relative to the realm of spirituality collapsing into a single point of consciousness is similar to us choosing one of the infinite possibilities as it becomes our physical reality. For example, I chose this job over that job.

For many, the most interesting and the most difficult to understand of all the quantum theories is *Superstring Theory*. Superstring Theory states that *everything created in our universe is a result of the interaction of one-dimensional particles that obey symmetry and have zero thickness*.[4] Superstring Theory unifies all energetic forces by reducing the essential building blocks of all matter to primal elements called *superstrings*.

The vibrational interaction of the superstrings is responsible for all matter. This in spirituality can be compared to the vibration of Spirit; vibration has zero thickness and is the primal cause of all matter. What is necessary to understand here is that *what happens in the spiritual realm has a counterpart in the physical world* in which we live. There has never been anything created without it first being a thought. This is the Law of Correspondence. What is true above is true below. What is created on a higher level of consciousness manifests in time on the physical plane.

A related theory that quantum physicists are working on developing is the *Unified Field Theory* or the *Theory of Everything*. In quantum physics, a unified field theory *would explain how everything in terms of particles, waves, and energies all relate to each other within one single theoretical framework.*[5] It would explain *the interrelatedness of everything in creation*. Actually in spiritual terms, I can do that for you now. It is called *consciousness*. What has been discovered thus far in the world of science follows the universal laws of the Creator. Science is only now discovering the laws of the Supreme Intelligence that created this universe. Science is proving itself to be nothing more than a physical reflection of the Creator's universal laws and of the Creator Himself as Supreme Consciousness within nature.

More recently scientists have come up with a new theory called *M-Theory*, where the M stands for *Membrane*. The gist of the theory states that *everything in our universe is connected together by an infinitesimal rippled membrane*.[6] In attempting to explain the weakness of gravity a scientist discovered that the force of gravity that affects our universe is actually being fed from another parallel universe. Gravity leaking into our universe from a parallel universe would explain why the force of gravity is so weak when compared to other forces found within our universe. Prior to this it was presumed that our gravitational force was leaking from our dimension into another dimension. Out of this scientific analysis, M-Theory was born.

M-Theory hypothesizes that there are eleven dimensions in this universe. In Superstring Theory there were purportedly only ten. However, mathematical calculations failed to support the existence of only ten dimensions, whereas eleven dimensions seem to approximate the truer number. Science has even suggested that an additional dimension may exist yet to be discovered. If this is so, there may be twelve dimensions in our universe versus the eleven suggested by M-Theory.

> "…Lisa Randall of Princeton University and Raman Sundrum, now of Stanford University, describe a scenario in which an extra, infinite dimension could have remained undetected thus far."[7]

M-Theory also supports the theory of a *multiverse, an infinite number of parallel universes*, each with its own set of universal laws of physics. This supports the notion that God was busy creating other universes before our universe was created. We are, then, one universal reality within an infinite field of universal realities; one universe of many universes. Some of these universes may have life in them and others may not. It is very possible that there exists a universe exactly like ours without human life. There may possibly be another universe that reflects ours in some dramatic way, maybe even with life on it. Maybe there exists an antimatter universe as well. Who is to say? What is important to note here is that parallel universes are not disputed by science; rather, the number and exact nature of parallel universes have yet to be resolved.

Parallel universes are not static. Because of this, M-Theory may explain the "big bang" in that it suggests two parallel universes, each with their own rippled membrane, collided. In colliding they created matter. This would seem to solve the singularity problem, that life was created from one singular point. However, what created the membranes or other parallel universes in the first place? We may have solved one problem and created another problem yet to be explained. What's more, if parallel universes do exist, then the concept of time may have existed before our universe was created.

I would further suggest that all universes may be interconnected in some way. It is possible that *black holes* actually take matter out of our universe and deliver it to another universe. *White holes* would then perform the opposite function; they would take matter from the opposing universe and deliver it into our universe. These are just some possibilities that have yet to be proven. Obviously, it is not possible for a human to travel from one universe to another, or so it seems. Possibly, we will one day be able to travel through space and time via *worm-holes*, i.e. hypothetical tunnels or shortcuts through space-time. Often the science-fiction programs we watch on television today become tomorrow's realities.

As I explored further the possibility of parallel universes, I came across an extremely interesting article entitled exactly that, *Parallel Universes*, written by Max Tegmark. In this article, Tegmark surveys physics theories concerning parallel universes that form a natural four-level hierarchy of multiverses allowing progressively greater diversity.[8]

In a Level 1 parallel universe, Tegmark explains that space is infinite and that the universe is uniformly filled with matter. This infinite space may in all probability encompass many other universes, some identical to ours in many ways. As a matter of fact, a Level 1 universe suggests that each parallel universe within this infinite space share the exact same laws of physics but had differing initial conditions. Since we are dealing with the infinite here, these differing initial conditions suggest an infinite number of possibilities all occurring at the same time; that there are a multitude of copies of *you and me* existing on a infinite number of earths identical to ours but divided by space. This of course means that we, by definition, would be multidimensional. In this model we could theoretically reach another dimension as long as we are capable of traveling faster than the rate of the expansion of the universe, which at our current level of technology is impossible. In short, in a Level 1 parallel universe, there exists an infinite number of universes in the same infinite space. Pretty mind-expanding, don't you think?

In a Level 2 parallel universe, Tegmark asks for the reader to imagine "an infinite set of distinct universes, some perhaps with different dimensionality and different physical constants."[9] In this model, infinite space includes within it an infinite number of universes as separate domains. Each universe is itself a bubble and is considered one bubble of an infinite number of bubbles. The *Theory of Chaotic Inflation* suggests that bubble universes are still being created emerging out of other inflationary bubbles in a never-ending chain reaction. It goes further to suggest what might be considered the impossible; that each bubble as a parallel universe is infinite in size. In other words, space is infinite within the bubble. This is obviously counterintuitive, but supported by current scientific research. If bubbles are continually being created, and have been created forever, there would consequently be an infinite number of parallel universes. If this is the case, then there can be no such thing as "the beginning of time" and no absolute "big bang" since another big bang occurs each time a new bubble is created. This second theory is *not* inconsistent with the first theory on parallel universes. There could still be a multitude of copies of *you and me,* an infinite number of us, in each of the infinite number of bubbles experiencing each and every infinite possibility.

The major difference between the first two levels is as follows. In a Level 1 parallel universe, we reside in a universe along with an infinite number of other universes in the same infinite space. In a Level 2 parallel universe, we reside in a bubble universe with our own infinite space among an infinite number of other bubble universes with their own infinite space.

In Level 3, quantum physics plays an important role in explaining parallel universes. Tegmark writes, "If the fundamental equations of physics are what mathematicians call unitary, as they so far appear to be, then the universe keeps branching into parallel universes…whenever a quantum event appears to have a random outcome, all outcomes in fact occur, one in each branch."[10]

In other words, rather than a multitude of possibilities collapsing into one reality, in a Level 3 parallel universe all possibilities are occurring at the same time in an infinite number of universes as alternate dimensions.

In 1957, Hugh Everett III postulated that during a quantum event, one reality would split into a superposition of many realities. Further, the observers (*you and me*) would individually experience this splitting merely as a slight randomness and would not perceive it as a splitting of realities into alternate dimensions. Let me give you a possible example. Recently I submitted this book to a publisher, which in my life I would consider a major event. In one reality (mine) it was rejected for publication. However, if this event was considered to be a quantum event, there would have been a split in this universe so that another universe was created (splitting off from this one) in which this book was in fact accepted by the same publisher. Instead of there being one dimension or universe where my book was rejected, there are now two dimensions or universes where one was rejected and one was accepted and I (or some form of me) would now reside in both.

Now take this concept and expand it until every possibility is occurring at the same time. What is suggested here is a superposition of every possible world as an infinite number of dimensions or universes. Thus far scientists have not been able to rule out this possibility, as it appears to be consistent with scientific research. Altogether, the Level 3 parallel universe theory of *infinite dimensional space* does not alter the number of universes or potentialities; rather it is consistent with Level 1 and Level 2 in that all of them suggest an infinite number of potentialities all occurring at the same time as infinite realities.

In a Level 4 parallel universe, all universes within the multiverse are based on a variety of mathematic principles. Level 4 parallel universes suggest that not only is our universe based on mathematics and our own corresponding laws of physics, there also exists alternate universes where every other mathematical possibility is occurring within their own set of rules, structures, and mathematical principles. If our physical world is a mathematical structure, an abstract immutable law existing outside of space and time, then mathematical equations would then describe all aspects of our physical world, not just some aspects of it. This would then be true for all universes; even their mathematical structures would vary to an infinite degree. This in no way negates the possibility that there is a *you and me* in every universe, but rather that each universe is based on its own set of mathematical principles with many of our own principles yet to be discovered in our universe. If our universe is based on mathematics, it just may be a mathematical formula that helps us formulate and eventually solve the Theory of Everything.

As a quick overview, in Level 1 parallel universes there is no clear demarcation between alternate universes. They all exist in one dimension of infinite space. In Level 2 parallel universes, they are considered to be separate bubbles, each with its own infinite space. In Level 3 parallel universes, universes are defined in terms of quantum physics in that they exist as separate dimensional realities within a superposition of many or an infinite number of realities. In Level 3 universes, when a major event occurs, defined as a quantum event, there is a split in the one reality to form additional realities in other dimensions so that all possibilities occur at the same time, not just the one we experience. In Level 4 parallel universes, all universes within the multiverse are based on mathematical systems and every possibility within the infinite number of possibilities and mathematical systems is occurring at the same time. What science is suggesting by the varying levels of parallel universes is that we cannot limit what we think to be true, that what we experience is not the only reality. Rather, what we think to be true is far from the complete truth when factoring in the concept of a multiverse. It is possible that *everything is true* within one universe or another as all possibilities may be occurring simultaneously within an infinite number of universes.

What may appear to be very nonsensical at first in terms of scientific hypotheses sometimes rises to the surface as the ultimate truth or gives birth to even greater truths. What's more, science seems to be explaining the processes of the Creator; but can science ever prove a Creator? Maybe one day they will acquiesce by admitting to the existence of an intelligent authority that cannot be scientifically proven. Either way, the concepts of science and God need not be incompatible with each other. It goes without saying that God is only partially revealed in nature.

> "Nature shows us only the tail of the lion. But I have no doubt that the lion belongs with it, even if he cannot reveal himself all at once. We see him only the way a louse that sits upon him would." Albert Einstein

In the early 1850s, James Prescott Joule made the observation that energy is conserved during chemical reactions.[11] It does not disappear as if destroyed or obliterated from existence. The overall level of energy is maintained even though it may be transferred to another object or released. His observation ultimately led to the science of thermodynamics, the study of the relationship between heat and the internal energy flow of a system. In the world of thermodynamics, there are two central laws. The first law states that the total energy of the universe is constant, versus being variable, and that energy can neither be created nor destroyed. Appropriate questions to ask then are as follows: *Who created energy in the first place?* and *How is consciousness related to energy in that neither can be destroyed?*

The second central law of thermodynamics says that the distribution of energy in the universe over time regresses from a state of order to a state of disorder.[12] The second law is of primary importance here. It states that over time things will become less complex rather than more complex. Now this flies in the face of Evolutionary Theory because the process of human development would then be rendered mathematically improbable, if not impossible. The human system is so complex it defies probability under the laws of thermodynamics as well as other laws. Therefore it is safe to assume that there is intelligence behind creation. This scientific finding could be considered an important argument for God. Some might consider it proof enough. Many highly educated people believe that science is slowly proving the existence of God as intelligent consciousness. Science may even one day suggest that parallel universes are alternate planes of consciousness or our heavens. Who knows? Remember, I asked you to keep your mind open to greater possibilities.

CHAPTER 21

Creation of the Universe

In 1929, Edwin Hubble, an American astronomer, discovered evidence that galaxies were moving apart from each other and thus inferred that the universe is expanding. [1] At the time this new evidence refuted the belief that the universe had been infinite and forever, which had been the prevailing theory until then. Albert Einstein's Theory of Relativity supported Hubble's conclusion that the universe is neither constant nor unchanging. Hubble later concluded that if the universe was expanding with time, then it would be logical to presume that if one could go back in time the universe would shrink; and as you continued backwards in time the universe would continue to shrink until it reached a single point of mass. This single point of mass would necessarily have to have a zero volume due to the intense gravitational force that exists.[2] As one might expect, zero volume implies nothingness. Zero volume further implies that the universe originated from nothing or nothingness. In other words, *if the universe originated from a big bang, it would have stemmed from a single point of nothingness.* Correspondingly, the big bang created matter that set time and space in motion. But how can science begin to suggest that the universe originated from nothing? How is that even possible?

Scientists do not agree on a precise date as to when the big bang occurred; and no wonder, because science suggests that it occurred sometime between thirteen and fifteen billion years ago, an unfathomable amount of time.[3] Life on earth began nearly four billion years ago[4]; some say slightly longer ago than that. Either way, the important questions really are *Who or what created the universe? What prompted the big bang? Where did the first atom come from? Where did the first breath of life come from? Where did the first protozoa come from? Did life spontaneously develop out of nothing as science suggests or did something exist before the big bang? How can something develop out of nothing?*

Logic would dictate that *some thing* had to exist before creation; otherwise our current existence could not be possible. But what was that some thing that existed before the big bang? Here is the answer. The some thing that existed was *intelligent consciousness.* The creation of the universe did not spontaneously create itself out of *no thing.* Logically then, there has to be a higher power. The intelligent consciousness of God is that power and the force behind the creation of this universe no matter how it might have actually occurred. How the existence of God can ˙ another matter. However, here is how I suggest the big bang ⸑ this universe.

What existed before time and space was intelliger this book as God the Father, that is, the Impersonal Gou. ˍ universe, we were a part of the unmanifested Impersonal God. We wɔ. of the infinite realm of possibilities. This universe before its creation was initiaₙₗᵧ ⱼ a *pre-thought* of God. God then within His thought created the Christ Body through the power of the Holy Spirit, God's creative energy. Form now existed as *light with consciousness*.

"And God said 'Let there be light…'" Genesis 1:3

This may be where the term "light beings" originated. As souls we are light beings or beings of light, the light of God manifested as energy within form.

Quite possibly then, the creation or manifestation of material form or matter (the Christ Principle, our universe) occurred when the Christ Body's own light, being of pure unadulterated God energy, exploded into fragments of itself. If so, the Christ Body's light in its original invisible form would have exploded into fragments of light forming the cosmos, later cooling into the much denser forms that exist today. This would include the sun, the earth, the moon, the planets, and of course the balance of this universe including all planes of consciousness, everything seen and unseen. Time, space, and relativity in addition to material form were created in that moment.

The Christ Body's light exploded or fragmented similarly to what occurs when natural light is refracted by a prism; it became colors visible to the human eye as represented by a rainbow. From this, all life emerged. Within this creation everything that was needed for future development was already included within all matter as *God DNA*, the conscious intelligence of the Impersonal God as the Holy Spirit. This original explosion of light that created our universe did not dilute the Christ Body's magnificence or strength. Rather it should be considered an extension of the Christ Body and a further manifestation of the Impersonal God's infinite realm of possibilities created through the Christ Body by the power of the Holy Spirit. Eventually, the God DNA within matter led to the evolution of mankind. As it stands, I believe this theory of creation is *not* inconsistent with any other type of creation theory and therefore cannot be disproven. However, as all theories, it cannot *as yet* be proven. Only time will tell.

CHAPTER 22

The Evolution of Mankind

Historically, there has been an ongoing debate regarding the evolution of mankind. That being the science-based *Theory of Evolution* (Evolutionary Theory) versus religion's *Intelligent Design Theory*. Intelligent Design proponents suggest that there is greater complexity within life than simple random mutations or natural selection suggests or would allow. Intelligent Design proponents suggest that there *has* to be a Creator that has intelligence and that this intelligence is behind the perceived complexity of creation. However, Intelligent Design on the surface seems to be based more on faith and religion than empirical evidence. How is it possible to prove beyond a reasonable doubt that the evolutionary process could not produce the same results as we have witnessed today without an intelligent consciousness behind it all? How is it possible to prove that a God exists? It really comes down to what you choose to believe. Once again it comes down to *science versus faith*.

Did we evolve, as British naturalist Charles Darwin (1809–1882) hypothesized in his book *The Origin of Species*, via natural selection? Or did a higher intelligence have its hand in it? Written originally in 1859, *The Origin of Species* (full title: *On the Origin of Species by Means of Natural Selection, or the Preservation of Favoured Races in the Struggle for Life*), Darwin explains the Theory of Natural Selection (Evolutionary Theory) as follows:

> "The theory of natural selection is grounded in the belief that each new variety, and ultimately each new species, is produced and maintained by having some advantage over those with which it comes from competition; and the consequent extinction of less favoured forms almost inevitably follows."[1]

Darwinists, also known as Evolutionists, believe that over time a species will mutate into a superior form and because of its superiority cause the lesser parent form to become extinct.[2] He additionally implied in his writings that man has a common ancestor with ape man, and that man descended from this apelike being. By his own definition then, monkeys or apes should be nonexistent today, because as Darwin writes,

"...for in all cases the new and improved forms of life will tend to supplant the old and unimproved." This is referred to as the *survival of the fittest*.[3]

Darwin's theory further states that it is possible that one of two living species may have descended from the other (one species split into two species) but that it would be unlikely in that one of the species would remain unaltered for a very long period of time while the other developed substantially. He then suggests, via the process of natural selection, that the weaker species should again have been eliminated. If man split from ape, then ape should have become extinct. However, this obviously did not happen; the ape form was never extinguished.

Another potential problem in Darwin's theory is a lack of fossil evidence. Darwin suggests that in time his *ape to man theory* will be proven correct. But time has not revealed the transitional links necessary to prove his theory correct, and consequently it remains a theory; the "missing link" is still missing. Even so, today the notion that apes and humans having descended from a common ancestor is readily accepted by many scholars without hesitation. Again, the exact date is unknown, but it is safe to say that the supposed split between ape and man occurred millions of years ago, an unfathomable amount of time as well, assuming it actually happened that way.

However, there are important aspects of Darwin's theory that should not be overlooked. One very important point he makes is as follows: "I am strongly inclined to suspect that the most frequent cause of variability may be attributed to the male and female reproductive elements having been affected prior to the act of conception."

This claim has been supported by more recent scientific research. A *Time Magazine* article dated October 9, 2006, entitled *What Makes Us Different*, makes an astounding claim: "Science figured out decades ago that chimps are our closest evolutionary cousins, roughly 98% to 99% identical to humans at the genetic level. When it comes to DNA, a human is closer to a chimp than a mouse is to a rat."[4]

The article goes on to say that a small variation in the FOXP2 gene within the human variant, which plays an important part in the development of speech and language, differs from that of the chimp in just two locations out of a total 715 locations. This could easily explain the emergence of human speech. Further, a tiny mutation in a gene on chromosome number seven could explain how our ancestors evolved smaller jaw muscles some two billion years ago. This loss in muscle strength may have allowed the braincase and the brain to increase in size. The article goes on to say that when an inversion, deletion, or duplication occurs in a gene or in a set of genes after conception, it is possible the change gives the new organism an advantage that can be passed on to future generations. There are several other striking discoveries that point to the evolution of man from ape. I use the term *ape* loosely here as it appears that we may have a common ancestor with the chimpanzee and not the ape.

The two other schools of thought competing with evolutionism are Intelligent Design and Creation Theory.

"Intelligent Design adherents believe only that the complexity of the natural world could not have occurred by chance. Some intelligent entity must have created the complexity, they reason, but that "designer" could in theory be anything or anyone. In 1802, William Paley used the "divine watchmaker" analogy to popularize the design argument: If we assume that a watch must have been fashioned by a watchmaker, then we should assume that an ordered universe must have been fashioned by a divine Creator. Many traditional Creationists have embraced this argument over the years, and most, if not all, modern advocates for Intelligent Design are Christians who believe that God is the designer.

Creationism comes in many varieties, from the strictest biblical literalism (according to which the Earth is only a few thousand years old, and flat) to the theistic evolutionism of the Catholic Church (which accepts evidence that the Earth is millions of years old, and that evolution can explain much of its history—but not the creation of the human soul)."[5]

For the sake of this discussion I will not delve into the differences between Creation Theory and Intelligent Design. Both theories come from the perspective of opposing Evolution Theory, and therefore, I will use them interchangeably.

In the Bible, Genesis claims creation occurred in six days.

"By the seventh day God had finished the work he had been doing; so on the seventh day he rested from all his work." Genesis 2:2

Having been raised Catholic, I thought Creation Theory seemed very plausible since I was taught that God could do anything. Surely God could create the heavens and the earth, Adam and Eve, and the Garden of Eden in less than seven days. However, if the Bible is taken literally, it flies in the face of Evolutionary Theory.

The scientific consensus is that life evolved over millions or billions of years. But is it possible that both Intelligent Design and the Theory of Evolution are correct? Can these two opposing theories be married into one presumably correct theory? If parts of Creation Theory, as stated in the Bible, are metaphors for something else, then it is very possible. Then by this line of reasoning, many other parts of the Bible could not or should not be taken literally either.

However, by marrying the two theories you create other problems, such as determining the point where science ends and religion begins. Additionally, empirical measurement becomes more of an issue when you add God to the equation because God is obviously immeasurable. And thus the debate continues: what role did God play in regards to creation, if any?

Genesis states that man was made in the image of God.

"So God created man in his own image…" Genesis 1:27

It is unlikely that God looks like an ape or what morphed into man as we know ourselves to be today. Therefore it would be obvious that *the soul*, as consciousness in form, is what was created in the likeness of God. But the question remains, *When did ape become man?*

I believe that the introduction of the soul is the key to marrying the diverging concepts of Evolutionary Theory and Intelligent Design. When the ape was physically developed enough for a soul to reside in the form of the ape, ape became man. The term *ape* here again is used loosely; *chimpanzee* may be more accurate. The main point I am trying to make here is that the addition of a soul's consciousness to ape form is what made man a man. This theory would explain how the divergence between ape and man occurred without the extinction of the parent organism. Before the introduction of the soul into ape, all ape forms were more or less soul-less beings, or rather beings without the superior God Consciousness aspect in them, similar to how they exist today. The ape, as is true for all animals, is not conscious to the level of man. Animals tend to operate more on instinct and do not have freedom of choice to the extent that man does.

The increased level of consciousness that occurred when individualized souls entered apes created a higher level of conscious being, immediately causing a split from the ape form. The *parent ape* continued as an ape because in effect it remained a completely distinct creature. The ape did not become extinct as Darwin suggests it should have because the higher level of consciousness created in ape-man was in essence a new type of being unrelated to the ape. With the addition of the soul, there was a split or divergence in the line of apes. Apes continued as the parent species virtually unaltered because the child species was born with a new consciousness. In this way, the unaffected parent species could continue its existence and even coexist with the new ape-man species, and did.

This theory might sound like Intelligent Design, but it is not only Intelligent Design at work here. Proponents of Intelligent Design suggest that aspects of our phenomenal world show signs of having been designed by an intelligent being rather than having developed naturally through evolution. However, I do concede that this theory may be considered a variant of Intelligent Design, as I am suggesting both Evolutionary and Creation Theories are true. It is a symbiotic hybrid of both theories; it is God's intelligence we witness within the process of evolution. Specifically I merge the two competing theories into one by introducing the concept of soul consciousness entering the form of the ape.

The final sentence in Darwin's introduction to *The Origin of Species* is quite revealing and may have opened the door to the concept of a higher intelligence: "Furthermore, I am convinced that Natural Selection has been the main but not exclusive means of modification."

It sounds like Darwin was keeping the door open to additional possibilities.

Borrowing from Darwin's notion of *eventuality*, I believe that all this one day may be proved. In combining both theories, Intelligent Design and Evolutionary Theory, there appears to be no violation of the universal laws. But how does all of this correlate with the story of Adam and Eve and the Garden of Eden?

CHAPTER 23

The Fall of Man and the Garden of Eden

❧

As I suggested earlier, the Bible should not be taken literally in all cases.

"He created them male and female and blessed them. And when they were created, he called them man." Genesis 5:1-2

What is interesting to note here is that the word for *man* in Hebrew is *Adam*. [1] I believe that the story of Adam and Eve is simply a metaphor for what occurred within the evolution of creation. In the beginning, God created the souls within the Christ Body and they were called man or Adam. God created Adam or man in His own image, which is actually God Consciousness as souls in form and energy. God did not make man in the image of God as a man. God does not look like an ape, nor does he look like a man. God is not an old man up in the clouds as I once thought as a child growing up in the Catholic Church. Again, I cannot emphasize this enough: the Impersonal God is everywhere as infinite unmanifested consciousness and therefore we are made in His likeness, which is the physical manifestation of God's consciousness as souls existing in form with energetic properties. We are the manifested physical reflection (form) of the unmanifested infinite all-encompassing ever-present consciousness (non-form).

And out of Adam's rib came Eve as the original woman. Adam in the aggregate sense represents the consciousness of man and the rational mind. Eve in the aggregate sense conversely represents the consciousness of woman and emotions. Man and woman as souls eventually entered the body of an ape and became *ape-man* or God Consciousness in physical form. However, there were many souls in the Garden of Eden, not just Adam and Eve. In one sense, Adam and Eve are simply metaphors or representations of the aggregate man and the aggregate woman. As such, many female-oriented and many male-oriented light beings (consciousness within the context of gendered souls) entered the physical bodies of many apes to experience form in a much denser state, not just the original man as Adam and the original woman as Eve.

I further believe that the Garden of Eden represented the earth in its original perfect state. It was not a specific place as the Bible suggests. However, it is curious to note that in Genesis, it states that the Garden of Eden was located in the east:

> "Now the Lord God had planted a garden in the east, in Eden; and there he put the man he had formed." Genesis 2:8

In the above passage it is not clear what constitutes "the east." An interesting question to ask is the following: *If Adam and Eve were the first original man and woman created by God as prescribed by many Christians, what would Eden be considered east of, since they were the main focal point of creation?* Of course, we can make a general reference today in terms of east and west, but what was the reference point being addressed back then at the point of creation? Eden was located in the east relative to what? It makes sense to me that Eden was the perfect state of earth at the point of creation until the fall in man's (and woman's) consciousness. Is the reference to east a spiritual metaphor for enlightenment since Adam and Eve were perfect beings? In the second chapter of Genesis it states that the Garden of Eden was located near four rivers: Pishon, Gihon, Tigris and Euphrates. This would place Eden in or near modern day Iraq. It is interesting, but not crucial for our understanding to know the location of Eden exactly, whether it was in fact the entire earth or simply a location upon earth, or why it is considered to have been located in the east.

Prior to entering the ape, perfect souls (as fully enlightened entities) had unlimited access to anything and everything on earth and to other planes of consciousness. For now, I am going to focus solely on the earth plane. Souls could enter a rock and experience the denseness of a rock. Or they could enter a plant and experience the life essence of a plant. They could fly through the ocean if they wished. They were not at all earthbound souls, but rather had unlimited access to everything on this physical plane of existence. The souls in this state of consciousness knew themselves to be children of God and were in constant contact with God. It might be easier to understand this if you think of souls as spiritual beings of light that initially were not as yet locked into any tangible or physical form. In this way, you might be able to better imagine their capabilities of entering objects and flitting around from here to there as enlightened souls.

As time progressed, God's science/intelligence-based evolutionary process for the planet had reached a point in time where souls could enter the ape form and spend significant time within the ape. Subsequently, souls could better experience the physical realm in a much denser state. Their experiences were much more tangible while in a physical form. However, the souls could still exit the ape form as they pleased. Upon entering the ape form, the consciousness of the ape was immediately changed, creating a being of higher consciousness, much higher than that of the previous animalistic nature of the ape. Upon exiting, the ape returned to its more unintelligible form.

Adam and Eve, as perfect conscious beings, were in constant communion with God in the Garden of Eden (the perfect earth) and understood themselves to be one with God until they violated God's authority through an act of sin, as the Bible suggests. Under God's authority they were forbidden to eat from the tree of knowledge of good and evil. But what was that original sin? And what constituted the tree of knowledge of good and evil? The Bible is not clear on either point.

> "And the Lord God commanded the man, 'You are free to eat from any tree in the garden; but you must not eat from the tree of the knowledge of good and evil, for when you eat of it you will surely die.'" Genesis 2:16

What does the tree of the knowledge of good and evil represent? Surely this story is a metaphor for something else. Certainly it is not a piece of fruit. What act could they have committed to cause them to suddenly *know* the difference between good and evil? What could an enlightened being in a physical form do to defy one of God's laws as original sin?

Little in the Bible points to the definition of the original sin. The Bible provides us only a hint:

> "…but God did say, 'You must not eat fruit from the tree that is in the middle of the garden, and you must not touch it, or you will die.'"
> Genesis 3:3

Often passages in the Bible have dual meanings or are metaphors for something else entirely. If this is true, the tree of the knowledge of good and evil may be referencing the physical body. The reference to the fruit on the tree that is located *in the middle of the garden* could be a reference to sexual organs, which are located in the middle of the physical body. By eating the fruit, this passage may be referencing *sexual intercourse*, while touching the fruit may be a reference to *masturbation*. If this is the case, then God may have been warning Adam and Eve that the act of sexual intercourse or masturbation would be a sin. The reason God would have considered sexual intercourse or masturbation to be a sin is because as enlightened souls sex would have been completely unnecessary. The souls were already in a state of enlightenment and could enter or exit the ape form as they pleased. As perfect souls, Adam and Eve would have never tasted death. In committing the original sin of sexual intercourse souls delved into the animalistic nature of the creature they inhabited. I realize defining sexual intercourse as original sin may sound somewhat mainstream, and even though my analogy of the Garden of Eden to the human body may seem a little farfetched to some people, no other scenario than intercourse has risen to the surface as a more likely explanation for original sin. There may be a perfectly valid reason for this.

If Adam and Eve experienced original sin as intercourse, they would have been sinning against their higher nature as perfect souls, and there would of course have been consequence as stated in the Law of Karma. As a consequence, their sins would cause them to be reverted back to the more animalistic nature of the entities they entered, that being the ape. As an additional consequence (karma), Adam and Eve were denied access to the tree of life. What this really means is that Adam and Eve would suffer pain, illness, and even death due to their fall in consciousness from perfect enlightened beings to unenlightened beings within ape-man. Adam and Eve took a step away from God and in doing so lost their immortality. Assuming that the story of Adam and Eve alternatively represents collective mankind at that stage of evolution, then many souls may have potentially committed the same sin.

Ironically, the phrase *original sin* does not exist in the Bible. Nor does it exist in the Jewish writings. Saint Augustine (354-430) was considered to be one the greatest theologians in the Western church. Although Saint Augustine did not create the concept of original sin, he was one of the first to preach that man is born into a state of original sin.[2] Saint Augustine taught that the original sin of sexual intercourse is transmitted from generation to generation.

> "Augustine's take on sex has also left a deep mark on our civilization. He, more than anyone else, was responsible for the idea that sex is inherently evil. He called it the most visible indication of man's fallen state."[3]

If you consider the consequence of original sin to be a fall in consciousness, then yes, we all carry the stain of original sin with us as we all continue to suffer the consequence of that sin, that being a lower consciousness.

I know the concept of original sin being defined as sexual intercourse will definitely turn some people off. However, I am *not* saying that in today's society sex is bad or evil, or that sex out of marriage is even a sin. As a matter of fact, I would feel comfortable suggesting the opposite; that sexual intercourse is a natural part of our evolutionary growth in consciousness. What I am saying is that for Adam and Eve, as perfect beings on a perfect earth, sex was unnecessary, and indulgence in this unnecessary act caused mankind's decrease in consciousness to a point of consciousness substantially less than that of enlightenment.

> "The official Catholic position harks back to Augustine's ideas about the Fall. The whole of humanity is marked by the original fault committed by our first parents, the latest Catholic catechism tells us. The church still says that human misery and inclination toward evil are transmitted to us as a result of Adam's sin."[4]

As I mentioned, many verses contained in the Bible have dual meanings. The serpent, assumed to be the devil in the story of Adam and Eve, could easily be a metaphor for the Kundalini energy that exists in the physical and spiritual body of mankind. Kundalini energy is at times considered to be the same energy as the sexual energy in us; our libido. It is also the creative energy of the universe and may be considered the power of the Holy Spirit, as I suggested in an earlier chapter. In an enlightened being, unadulterated Kundalini energy travels up and down the spine through the spiritual energy centers present in the physical body. Before the fall in consciousness, this energy was fully functioning in Adam and Eve because they were fully conscious enlightened beings. The body's spiritual energy centers (also known as chakras) which had been fully open previously, suddenly became corrupted by sexual desire and the unnecessary act of sexual intercourse. The act of sexual intercourse (having an orgasm) lowered Adam and Eve's Kundalini energy to that of being less than Christ Conscious due to an explosion of spiritual energy out of the second chakra, which is associated with the sexual organs. The act of sexual intercourse disrupted this natural flow of Holy Spirit Kundalini energy up and down the chakras. Again, the result was a drop in spiritual consciousness to that of being substantially less than enlightened.

If the original sin was indeed sexual intercourse, the Bible suggests that Eve was the first to be tempted by the serpent (Kundalini energy) as sexual desire. Eve tempted Adam, and Adam embraced Eve with the same sexual desire. In doing so, Adam came to know good and evil through sexual intercourse and fell along with Eve in consciousness from the ranks of an enlightened being to that of ordinary conscious man. Either way, it is not important who caused the other to fall in consciousness. What is important to realize is that by delving into their sexual nature, perfect man and perfect woman might have thought that they could be more like God, the source of all creation.

> "'You will not surely die,' the serpent said to the woman. 'For God knows when you eat of it your eyes will be opened, and you will be like God, knowing good and evil.'" Genesis 3:4-5

The consequence of their act was to be cast out of the Garden of Eden. The act of intercourse could be considered the first misuse of the Universal Law of Free Will. In their desire to be more like God, the consequence of sin was for souls to forget their own God-like nature. They in effect forgot they were God's children. The souls in human-like ape form from then on would experience illness and physical death. Souls were now captive within the ape form and now operated under the authority of their physical material nature and a lower reflection of the true nature of God. By tasting "the apple of their desire" as sexual intercourse, souls fell from a higher perfected consciousness to a much lower level of consciousness. The Holy Spirit energy that flowed freely throughout the spiritual soul body and the ape body had become corrupted, causing a decrease in consciousness. Now, as beings of a lower consciousness, they were fallible, knowing and experiencing both good and evil. In essence, the souls received what they sought after, knowledge of good and evil.

Their existence on earth as they knew it was no longer the perfect Garden of Eden. Their karma necessitated physical death and the need to return to another physical body until they regained their state of enlightenment. Thus began the cycle of reincarnation.

In sinning against their perfect immortal bodies, it is plausible that they became mortal, their spirits or souls from then on trapped in the flesh of ape; this is suggested in Genesis:

> "The Lord God made garments of skin for Adam and Eve and clothed them." Genesis 3:21

In this passage, man was given *garments of skin.* Apart from the obvious interpretation that man now needed to keep himself warm, this could be interpreted as immortal man was now trapped in the physical mortal body.

> "And the Lord God said, 'The man has now become like us, knowing good and evil. He must not be allowed to reach out his hand and take also from the tree of life and eat, and live forever.'" Genesis 3:22

The verse above details the consequence of their sin. Souls now trapped in the physical body must eventually experience a physical death in order to leave the physical body. Having committed the sin of sex, the consequence for man was mortality. Man's actions had a negative effect upon the consciousness of the planet. After the fall, the earth was transformed to a less than perfect place. The imperfect souls no longer had dominion over the weather of this earth. In a direct way, when we fell, the world fell as well. It became corrupted due to our decreased consciousness. It was no longer heaven on earth. The earth was no longer the Garden of Eden.

Also, notice the word *us* in the verse above referencing the Lord God. How can one singular God be referred to as *us?* Was God referencing the Trinity? Was He possibly referencing the Christ Body? Or was God referencing a greater hierarchy of Gods we have completely dismissed?

Some Christians believe that only through the acceptance of Jesus within your heart will God forgive you of sin. The Jewish faith finds the concept of original sin unacceptable. Jews believe that man enters this world free of sin, with a soul that is pure, innocent, and unadulterated. Hinduism does not buy into the concept of original sin either. Rather, Hindus believe that all living beings are divine. Hinduism uses the word *papa* to convey *any mistake committed by a soul,* or as creating bad karma. I like the word *papa* better than the word *sin* because it removes any religious dogma associated with any action that causes us to move away from God. The word *sin* has too much dogma attached to the word. It immediately brings up a lot of negativity and guilt for me, and I can only assume others. Sin is simply a choice we make to move away from God, of course with negative consequence.

Did God know Adam and Eve would sin in advance of the act since he is omniscient? I can only imagine that the answer is most definitely yes. This may be confirmed by a passage in Genesis.

> "For this reason a man will leave his father and mother and be united to his wife, and they will become one flesh." Genesis 2:25

Of course, since the Bible was written by man, this could simply be a reference based on the culture or level of spirituality at the time of its writing or simply an attempt to explain the authors' perception of history. Of course, it could have a variety of other meanings as well.

It is thought provoking to ask the following question: *Was the fall in consciousness purposeful or rather purpose-filled?* It's very possible that original sinned was preplanned. It was clearly a decision made by Adam and Eve. Minimally, it occurred because of their free-will choice to fulfill their desire for sexual intercourse. The potential reason(s) for a purpose-filled fall of consciousness is explored more thoroughly in the next chapter. But to satisfy your curiosity in this moment, let me say that without a fall in consciousness, this world as we know it would not seem real. As enlightened beings, we would have immediately understood our connectedness, our immortality, and heaven as our truest reality.

CHAPTER 24

The Meaning of Life

The meaning of life has been contemplated by many great minds such as Aristotle, Einstein, Plato, and Descartes. I can only suppose that it is something that has been contemplated over and over by millions of people at some point in time during their lives. Usually this happens during times of hardship or stress. The meaning of life is not a subject that should be taken lightly, even though it seems that the majority of people rarely give it much consideration during the good times. In good times, most people go through the day focusing on the things that immediately demand their attention. Some people actually seek to fill their days with mindless activities in order to avoid thinking about the meaning of life. Some people are so involved with making more money that they ignore that there must be some greater meaning to their existence.

For me, the meaning of life from my mid-teens to my early thirties was about being successful in the material world. However, one day I woke up to a frightening realization: *No matter how much money I made or material possessions I owned, I could never fill the void I felt in my life.* Since then, I have been on a profound quest to understand the meaning of life and the part I play in it. I have prayed about it. I have meditated on it. I've questioned gurus, spiritual mentors, pastors, and priests about the meaning of life. I have studied numerous religions and philosophies. After much contemplation and deliberation, I have come up with two explanations for the meaning of life; one primary purpose for life and one secondary purpose for life.

The primary purpose (as in original purpose) for our creation is this: *the Godhead or Trinity created this universe for souls to experience as one of the infinite realms of possibilities inherent within the Impersonal God.* The Godhead or Trinity created a material universe in which souls as the energetic consciousness of God can experience form. In other words, this *universe of matter* is meant to be a *material playground* for us to experience as souls of the Christ Body. The secondary purpose (meaning of life) is for us *to remember our divine nature,* that we as souls are a part of the Almighty God. In re-membering with God, we return to our original state of Christ Consciousness before our fall in consciousness.

As you may recall, within the Impersonal God there exists an infinite realm of possibilities. The universe we exist in is just one of an infinite number of possible universes. What do you think the Impersonal God was doing before He created our universe thirteen to fifteen billion years ago? Was God resting or simply stagnant? Of course He was not. But what was God doing then? I can only imagine that He was busy creating other universes besides our own, or ending them, or maintaining them. I have to assume that we are not the only game in town. We are just one of many universes. I personally believe that our universe is just one bubble of consciousness in a mega-universe of bubbles as quantum physicists suggests.

The next logical question would be concerning just how many other universes are coexisting with us, and then how many have existed before us, and how many will exist after us. I cannot even begin to answer these questions. And then one might question what will become of us? Will we eventually disappear as a universe? Will the Impersonal God reabsorb us? One question that keeps arising is whether or not the universe we exist in is simply an illusion or a projection of God's mind, as if a movie of some sort. Is this universe a physical reality, or are we in effect just figments of our own imagination, or God's imagination? Are we all just a thought of God and consequently this universe is not real? Is this one big cosmic joke? Some of the spiritual leaders in this world almost certainly would answer yes to a few of these questions. They might suggest that we do in fact live in an illusion, that we live in a mirage of sorts. Personally, I don't entirely agree with their assessment.

For me, this all seems too real to be a God-thought projection, or some other type of non-reality. I obviously agree that the human body is not the ultimate reality of who we really are, but I also believe that the physicality of this universe is real; that the things we see, taste, hear, smell, and touch are all very real. I believe that I have a physical body and that it is real. I do not believe this world is simply a thought of God as if a movie or projection. We are, however, God's thought projected into reality, into form, into matter, into material nature, and that is the primary purpose for our existence in this universe, to experience form. It is our playground. We came here in order to experience and through the experience become greater souls. In the experience we as souls grow. Minimally, we grow in experience. Is this not true for us as humans as well? We grow through our experiences, correct? Have you ever personally felt a sense of grandness after having completed a major task? Of course you have. We all have.

Some people might argue that this material world is all there is and accordingly there is no heaven and no hell, and no God. Given the hypocrisy and pain we often witness in our world, I can thoroughly understand why someone might balk at the notion of an unconditionally loving God. How can a caring person not question at least once in his or her life how a loving God would allow such horrific things to happen to His children? It is only human to question why we as souls, as a part of the Christ Body, need to experience such evil. Maybe more importantly, one might question why God through us needs to experience anything at all since God supposedly is everything. God knows all. He is perfect. But there is the argument that even though God is perfect in knowledge, He is lacking in experience. That somewhat makes sense to me, but I still question how God could lack anything; after all, He is God. So I pose the question *Did God create all of this for His experience or for us to experience it?*

In order to begin to answer this question, I decided to look up the meaning of the word *experience*. I wanted to make sure I understood the word completely. The website Hyperdictionary.com has two main definitions for *experience*.[1] The first definition reads: *the accumulation of a knowledge or skill that results from direct participation.* The second definition reads: *the content of direct participation or observation of an event.* These two meanings vary slightly but the distinction is important. The answer to the question *Did God create man for His experience or ours?* is not that simple—it can be rather complex.

According to the first definition, whether or not God accumulates knowledge based on the experience, I would have to answer *no*. God does not experience by that definition, because I believe that God does not learn from the experience. God does not accumulate knowledge or increase his skill level by experiencing anything. God is already all-knowing. By the second definition regarding the direct participation or observation of an event, the answer is *yes*. God does experience by this definition. God does directly participate and observe in this universe. Actually, God is the *Ultimate Observer*, and at the same time the *Ultimate Participant* over all of His creation. He participates in his creation as the observer through our individual souls and collectively through the Christ Body.

Let's look at this in a slightly different context. Did God create this universe for His own evolution or progression? Again, here are two similar words with different meanings. Hyperdictionary.com defines *progression* as *the act of moving forward toward a goal.* The Merriam-Webster Dictionary defines the word *evolve* as *to develop or change by or as if by evolution.*[2] I assume by the distinctions I made in the last paragraph that you may already have a more thorough understanding of the difference I am about to make between these two words.

God does progress toward a goal in that He is moving toward fulfillment of His own great plan. However, God does not evolve in the sense that He changes or develops. So here the answer is *yes to progression* and *no to evolution* by strict adherence to the definitions as stated above. I hope you see the difference. God is infinite and unchanging in terms of His own divine nature. He does not learn, evolve, or develop. He does, however, participate in and observe creation, and in this way He progresses via the experience. What God progresses toward is the realization of His great plan. I have mentioned God's great plan a couple of times now without really saying specifically what it is. God's great plan is to continually manifest universes for an eternity in order to experience every possibility within the infinite realm of possibilities. This is a lot to consider in terms of God's immenseness of purpose.

But why did God create anything in the first place? Did God have a desire or need? The answer is that God created because that is what God does, God creates. God birthed us and everything else in this universe. Just as humans birth babies, God births mini-gods. What is true above is true below. This is the Universal Law of Correspondence at work here. Therefore, we as souls are an extension of His glory, the unmanifested God within His infinite world of possibilities, manifested into being-ness. However, if in reality there is no such thing as time, as some metaphysicists and scientists suggest, then by definition all possibilities are occurring at the same time and everything is occurring simultaneously within the present moment. All universes, all things past and present, all our countless reincarnations are occurring within the *now*, the present moment. In effect, God is experiencing everything all at the same time in the ever present moment. To disagree with this is to suggest that God lives within the dimension of time. Rather, I believe we as souls created the illusion of time.

But why did we create the illusion of time? The answer is that we created the illusion of time to better recognize, define, and understand the experience.

"Time is God's way of keeping everything from happening at once."
Unknown

Time is like a book. Everything contained within the book is occurring all at the same time. It isn't until you begin reading the book does it appear to come alive, but again, it takes time to read the book. And so is the experience of life, it takes the concept of time to experience it. And all our experiences are recorded in the Book of Life (the wisdom of the Holy Spirit) held within the mind of God.

Do we simply *experience* or do we *evolve* as souls? I believe we do *experience* as souls. As individual souls we are not all-knowing beings given our current state of consciousness. We do experience life and all it has to offer. We learn, progress, and *evolve* to the state of remembrance of our own divinity. The secondary explanation for the meaning of life is to remember our own divinity and that we are an aspect or facet of God. So yes, souls do experience and evolve.

However, the progression of a fully conscious soul working its way back to a state of remembrance implies first a regression in consciousness. This regression of consciousness would then be followed by an evolution of consciousness. Previously, before the Fall of Man, all souls were fully conscious, inhabiting the form universe and the various planes of consciousness. We knew who and what we were: children of God (mini-gods). The universe of form was our playground. We enjoyed the earth and its form in many ways. We eventually entered the ape, spending considerable time within the ape form. When the Fall of Man occurred as a result of sexual intercourse, we lowered our consciousness to that of something less than a fully realized being. We also set karma in motion. By committing the original sin, we fell from grace, which is another way of saying *falling from remembrance*. We fell in consciousness and therefore forgot our true essence. In effect, the material nature of this universe corrupted our divine nature.

The only question not answered here is *Why? Why did man make the decision to fall? Why did the Christ Body fall? What was the purpose? Was it a test for Adam? Would God test us? Why would God test us? And could a Christ Conscious being such as Adam fail a test?* The answers are surprisingly straightforward.

First, I believe that God did *not* test us; rather, as children of God we have freedom of choice. We have freedom of choice each and every second of the day. Freedom of choice is an ongoing test we humans face every day, a choice between good and evil. In a way it is our test for our-selves. We set the parameters and we set the boundaries in which we play our game. It is not God doing the testing. God doesn't test us. We create the tests for ourselves. If this is true, then Adam may have failed in his own test. He made a conscious decision along with Eve to indulge in the desires of the physical body through sexual intercourse. Together they engaged in the energies of the second chakra, a specific spiritual energy center of the body associated with the sexual organs. In doing so, they fell in consciousness. Our goal now is to increase in consciousness until we regain our original state of Christ Consciousness, which is verified in Ephesians.

> "…to prepare God's people for works of service, so that the body of Christ may be built up until we all reach unity in the faith and in the knowledge of the Son of God and become mature, attaining to the whole measure of the fullness of Christ. Then we will no longer be infants tossed back and forth by the waves, and blown here and there by every wind of teaching and by the cunning and craftiness of men in their deceitful scheming. Instead, speaking the truth in love, we will in all things grow up into him who is the Head, that is, Christ. From him the whole body, joined and held together by every supporting ligament, grows and builds itself up in love, as each part does its work." Ephesians 4:12-16

This verse talks about reaching *maturity in Christ* (as a title, not Jesus) which is another way of saying Christ Consciousness. As an individual aspect of the Christ Body, we are referred to here as being held together by *ligaments*. Ligaments suggest connectivity. We are all one. As a part of the Christ Body, we each have our own specific type of service to perform that only we can do, each of us individually. We each serve an important role. No other individual soul can fulfill our life's purpose. We each have a specific purpose for our creation. We all play an important function for the Christ Body as an integral part of the Christ Body. Through service to others, we build ourselves up in God's loving consciousness. To give meaning to life is to serve God and man. Without service to others, we lack meaning to life. When we selfishly seek for ourselves, we can never fulfill our destiny or fill the void in ourselves, no matter how much wealth we accumulate.

The real you is your soul, which is forever immortal implying beyond illness, death, time, and space. To once again know or remember that our truest self exists as fully Christ Conscious beings in an immortal body is today our more immediate goal. Had we not experienced a fall from grace, we would not have to rise again in consciousness. We had freedom of choice and we made a choice. We violated God's only law for us; that is, not to eat the fruit from the tree of the knowledge of good and evil (Genesis 2:17). Adam and Eve's fall from grace is simply a metaphor for what we may have purposely decided so that we may more fully experience this universe of form and God's love for us and each other.

Whether the fall was purposeful or not, we will continually reincarnate to the experience of this physical world until we reach a state of enlightenment once again. Now you can see why I call our return to Christ Consciousness the secondary purpose or reason for our existence. The primary reason for our existence is to experience form within a form universe. The secondary reason or purpose for our existence is to return to our original state of enlightenment and heaven; but to become as we were once before, we must serve. Serving others increases the richness of life.

What happens to this universe after we have completed our mission or purpose? Eventually we will all return to the Godhead as the Christ Body within heaven, at which time we may have several options from which to choose. As a first option, we may return to the nothingness in which we were originally, Supreme Consciousness void of energy and form. In that case, we would return to the realm of potentialities within infinite consciousness. The God-thought manifestation of this universe would be ultimately just a memory. We would simply be stored away in the Impersonal God's memory as consciousness. The second option we might have is to create another universe manifesting yet another one of the infinite realm of possibilities. As a third option, we could travel throughout this universe indefinitely, or infinitely enjoying our physicality of Spirit in form as once again fully conscious beings, possibly evolving into something greater beyond our human imagination.

Another possibility is that we create a brand-new drama within the various planes of this form universe, perhaps with another planned fall in consciousness initiating a brand-new story yet to unfold. The last possibility that I can think of is that we are spun off as a separate God. Why not? Anything is possible. Since earth is a reflection of heaven, maybe we are merely mini-gods in training. When we complete our mission, we could be spun off like larger corporations spin off subsidiaries when they have reached a certain level of maturity. Maybe as souls we are evolving into something we might consider another form (or non-form) of God. Maybe eventually we will birth baby gods ourselves just as the Father birthed us. Any one of these scenarios is possible. God is all-powerful, and as children of God so are we. As enlightened children of God, we may even create new expressions of heaven even beyond our own soul's imagination.

Maybe the best and simplest explanation of the meaning of life is expressed by the parable of the prodigal son (Luke 15:11-31). In short, a father had two sons. His youngest son left home venturing out into the world eventually squandering his wealth on wild living. The older (oldest) son stayed home never disobeying his father's orders. Upon the return of the younger son, the father rejoiced and celebrated by killing a fattened calf. Angry, and refusing to participate in the celebration, the older son questioned his father as to why he was never given as much as a young goat to celebrate with his friends. Here is his father's reply:

"'My son,' the father said, 'you are always with me, and everything I have is yours. But we had to celebrate and be glad, because this brother of yours was dead and is alive again; he was lost and is found.'" Luke 15:31

As the story goes, we are the errant children of the Father that have left home venturing out into the material world, having wronged the Father. And one day we will return home having become richer for our experience because in the experience we become grander souls.

And with God in heaven *we* will celebrate!

CHAPTER 25

Marriage and the Science of Procreation

oﬔo

If Saint Augustine was correct in that sexual intercourse is the original sin, then is it permissible for mankind to marry? Is it permissible for us to have sexual relations of any type, or will it cost us eternal life in heaven? In an attempt to answer these questions, let us turn to the Bible to see what it says.

> "Flee from sexual immorality. All other sins a man commits are outside his body, but he who sins sexually sins against his own body." 1 Corinthians 6:18

Here is an additional biblical verse that addresses inappropriate sexual relationships:

> "But among you there must not be even a hint of sexual immorality, or any kind of impurity, or of greed, because these are improper for God's holy people. Nor should there be obscenity, foolish talk or coarse joking, which are out of place. For this you can be sure: No immoral, impure or greedy person—such a man is an idolater—has any inheritance in the kingdom of Christ and of God." Ephesians 5:3-5

It seems clear from these verses that immoral sex, along with a laundry list of other sins, is not going to get us to heaven. But is heterosexual intercourse in marriage okay? Is heterosexual intercourse with someone you love outside of marriage permissible? For that matter, is homosexual intercourse permissible?

Let's look once again to the Bible for clues. In a letter Paul writes to the Corinthians:

> "Now for the matters you wrote about: it is good for a man not to marry. But since there is so much immorality, each man should have his own wife, and each woman her own husband. The husband should fulfill his marital duty to his wife, and likewise the wife to her husband. The wife's body does not belong to her alone but also to her husband. In the same way, the husband's body does not belong to him alone, but also to his

wife. Do not deprive each other except by mutual consent and for a time, so that you may devote yourselves to prayer. Then come together again so that Satan will not tempt you because of your lack of self-control. I say this as a concession, not as a command. I wish that all men were as I am. But each man has his own gift from God; one has this gift; another has that." 1 Corinthians 7:1-7

It seems here that sex in marriage between a husband and a wife is permitted as a concession, but it does not seem as if it is the highest path we can take. When Paul says, "I wish that all men were as I am," I can only assume that Paul is suggesting that it is better for us to be celibate. But why does he suggest this? Let's look at additional Bible verses where Jesus addresses a question from the Pharisees that came to test Him regarding whether or not it is best to marry.

"Jesus replied, 'Not everyone can accept this word, but only those to whom it has been given. For some are eunuchs because they were born that way; others were made that way by men; and others have renounced marriage because of the kingdom of heaven. The one who can accept this should accept it.'" Matthew 19:11-12

Jesus is suggesting here that eunuchs (defined as a castrated man), whether born that way, made by man to be that way, or others that are destined for celibacy or minimally have the strength to be celibate, should be celibate or remain celibate and unmarried to another human being. Eunuchs and other celibate individuals should then look to find their mate in God. They are in effect married to God as their truest divine mate because they renounced the concept of an earthly marriage to seek the kingdom of God above all else.

For those of us not capable or not wishing to be celibate, Paul in his letter to the Corinthians gives us hope. He states to the Corinthians that "it is better to marry than to burn with passion."

"Now to the unmarried and the widows I say: it is good for them to stay unmarried, as I am. But if they cannot control themselves, they should marry, for it is better to marry than to burn with passion." 1 Corinthians 7:8-9

Paul makes it clear above that the lesser state of marriage, versus remaining single, is preferable to unbridled passion.

Paul suggests that whether married or unmarried when the Lord calls you, it is best to stay as you are and not to change your marital status. I can only *hope* that when we are called by the Lord we will possess the wisdom, strength, and clarity to make the right choice.

"Each one should remain in the situation which he was when God called him." 1 Corinthians 7:20

However, Paul confirms once again that marriage is better than burning with desire.

"But if you marry, you have not sinned; and if a virgin marries, she has not sinned." 1 Corinthians 7:28

This seems pretty straightforward that sex within marriage is not a sin. What appears to be a sin is the unfulfilled burning desire (lust) to have sexual relations. Remember sin is defined as anything that takes us away from God. Therefore a lust-filled burning desire to have sexual relations with another person is not consistent with God-mind; therefore marriage, as suggested by Paul, is a better circumstance in which to be.

However, even though marriage has become a longstanding institution, today more than half of all marriages end in divorce. What does the Bible say about divorce? When the Pharisees asked Jesus whether or not it is ever lawful for a man to divorce his wife, Jesus answered them.

"'Haven't you read,' he replied, 'that at the beginning the Creator made them male and female, and said, for this reason a man will leave his father and mother and be united to his wife, and the two shall become one flesh? So they are no longer two, but one. Therefore what God had joined together, let man not separate.'" Matthew 19:4-6

It is made clear by the passage above that no one should come between married couples. Adultery is surely a sin under any condition or circumstance.

In 1 Corinthians, chapter 7 discusses the dynamics of marriage in some detail.

"I would like you to be free from concern. An unmarried man is concerned about the Lord's affairs—how he can please the Lord. But a married man is concerned about the affairs of the world—how he can please his wife…" 1 Corinthians 7:32

An unmarried person may be better positioned to dedicate his or her life to God. Moreover, those who give up any member of their family to serve the Lord will be rewarded heavily, according to the Gospel of Matthew.

"And everyone who has left houses or brothers or sisters or father or mother or children for my sake will receive a hundred times as much and will inherit eternal life." Matthew 19:29

Again, this verse is indicative of the importance to serve God first and foremost. Of course, if you are married, this may seem a lot easier said than done, given the demands sometimes placed upon a married person or couple.

Did Jesus always serve God first and foremost? Is it possible that Jesus had sexual relations? It has been suggested by some religious scholars that Jesus may have been married to Mary Magdalene and may even have had children with her. The church today refutes this claim, declaring that Jesus was divine from the beginning and therefore would not have had sexual relations with any woman. However, if Jesus did not become enlightened until His baptism at the age of thirty, this would effectively eliminate the church's argument. Either way, I believe that once Jesus became enlightened He did not have sex, because if He had, He would have fallen in consciousness once again as Adam had previously in the Garden of Eden. In reaching or regaining His enlightenment, Jesus rose above everything that might have kept Him separate from God, including all sexual relations. He in effect became like a eunuch. In other words, as an enlightened soul Jesus' vibrational energy was above that of desiring to engage in sexual relations.

The same holds true for mankind. As a soul progresses in consciousness to a point of enlightenment, he/she will no longer feel the desire to engage in sexual relations. Until then, souls in human form that continue to have sexual relations (or masturbate) cannot become enlightened. They are by strict definition committing the same sin as Adam and Eve. We must first rise above the point of all sexual desire. Of course, coming to this point of consciousness may take many more lifetimes.

There are perhaps hundreds of sacred texts that were not included in the Bible due to their controversial nature or conflicting viewpoints on sexuality. One such text is called *The Acts of Paul and Thecla*. This story primarily revolves around Thecla, an aristocrat, and how upon hearing Paul's teachings renounced family, wealth, fully embracing chastity.

In this sacred text, Paul is reported to have preached sexual purity in the following manner:

> "Blessed are they who keep their flesh undefiled...Blessed are they who have wives, as though they had them not, for they shall be made angels of God...Blessed are the bodies and souls of virgins, for they are acceptable to God and shall not lose the reward of their virginity, for the word of their Father shall prove effectual to their salvation in the day of his Son, and they shall enjoy rest forevermore."[1]

When Paul's companions were questioned about Paul and his teachings, they responded with this answer:

"...We cannot so exactly tell who he is, but we know that he deprives young men of their intended wives, and virgins of their intended husbands, by teaching, 'There can be no future resurrection, unless you continue in chastity and do not defile your flesh.'"[2]

This, of course, did not sit well with the men whose wives or intended wives decided to become chaste. Both Thecla, because of her decision to remain an unmarried virgin, and Paul, due to his teachings concerning the necessity of chastity, came under threat of execution. *The Acts of Paul and Thecla* as a sacred text makes it clear that chastity is a prerequisite for attaining heaven, at least as far as Paul the Apostle was concerned. And who would know better than Paul what Jesus was preaching? I can only imagine that Paul's message was the same as Jesus' message. However, the message of chastity was obviously divisive for the early church and understandably squelched by the majority of church leaders. Who would follow a religious sect where sexual intercourse was not permitted? How could a church increase its membership base if none of its members were producing offspring?

By delving into the sacred texts and "lost gospels" not included in the Bible, you might get a better sense on how hugely diverse the Christian beliefs were for centuries following Christ's death and resurrection. There appears to have been an incredible amount of divergence in the sacred writings, much more than the Christian church would ever like to admit. Could this be the reason why much of what is hidden in the Vatican library is not shared with the general public, and anything that conflicts with currently accepted doctrine is quickly denounced by Rome as sacrilege?

This comes from the Gospel of Mary:

"The Savior said, 'Sin as such does not exist, but you make sin when you do what is of the nature of fornication, which is called sin. For this reason the Good came into your midst, to the essence of each nature, to restore it to its root.' He went on to say, 'For this reason you come into existence and die [...] whoever knows may know [...] a suffering which has nothing like itself, which has arisen out of what is contrary to nature. Then there arises a disturbance in the whole body.'"[3]

It is obvious why the messages contained within *The Acts of Paul and Thecla* and the *Gospel of Mary* are not clearly delineated in the Bible as we know it today. Most, if not all religions, would surely steer clear of the notion that sexual intercourse in any form is a sin contrary to nature that necessitates physical death and potentially condemns a soul to an eternity of suffering.

"We are punished justly, for we are getting what our deeds deserve" may indicate that at least one of the criminals repented and in dying fulfilled his karmic debt. Subsequently, he will be with Jesus in paradise because he had complete faith, he believed without doubt.

Contrary to what many religions suggest, I do not believe that we go to hell for an eternity because of our sins. Neither do I believe that we are redeemed of our sins because Christ died on the cross. He died *because* of our sins, not *for* our sins. We have already determined that the consequence of sin is rebirth. However, only by giving up sexual relations and orgasms can a person become Christ Conscious again while in a mortal body. Possibly, a more accurate way of saying this is to state that once a person reaches enlightenment, he or she will no longer require or desire sexual union. The vibration of his/her soul is above that point of consciousness. Sexual intercourse or masturbation lowers the vibrational consciousness of the soul closer to that of our animal nature. Again, that is not to say that sexual union is necessarily bad or evil or a sin, per se. It is not. Immorality is a sin. Sexuality and sexual relations are a part of our evolutionary consciousness back to our original state of enlightenment. It is an interim step in our spiritual development. Eventually we will all grow in consciousness beyond the desire for sexual relations at which time we would have discovered something much more fulfilling, a higher vibrational consciousness.

Does the church address masturbation as being sinful or minimally undesirable while in the priesthood? The original concept of Catholic priests being celibate could have been a move in the direction of seeking a higher vibrational consciousness. They were not allowed to marry because they dedicated their lives to God and consequently were not supposed to have sexual intercourse. They in effect were supposed to be like eunuchs, as Jesus and His apostles were presumed to be. Within the Catholic Catechism it states that *masturbation is an intrinsically and gravely disordered action.*[4] However, it appears that attempts at celibacy within the Catholic Church have lead to instances of sexual immorality and misconduct with young children which is most certainly an intrinsically and gravely disordered action far surpassing the act of masturbation itself. Herein lies proof enough that this creative sexual (Kundalini) energy, if not properly channeled, can lead to improper, even hideous behavior. I will let the evidence of misconduct within the church speak for itself and not delve into this further.

I personally believe that giving up all orgasms is very difficult at our current state of consciousness and is presently not the intended path for most of us. Most of us are not called to be celibate at this point in time in our conscious development. However, we can incrementally move in that direction with the power of the Holy Spirit, intention, willpower, and intense spiritual desire to rejoin with God. Eventually, after additional reincarnations and as we progress in our consciousness, I believe that we will all over additional lifetimes aggregately achieve this state of true celibacy and raise our consciousness back to the point of enlightenment. More simply stated, as humanity consciously moves toward reunion with God, the Holy Spirit will continually fill us up with Her goodness, and we will grow in spiritual strength. This in the short term (within this lifetime) is only possible if we are able to dedicate ourselves to a high level of spiritual discipline and align our lives and vibration with the Holy Spirit. The alternative is that we move forward in our consciousness at the relatively slow current state of evolutionary growth as we have been doing over eons of time.

Again, please understand what I am attempting to present here: at this time in mankind's evolutionary process, making love to someone you love is beautiful and definitely an integral part of life. Eventually, however, the mass consciousness of humanity will move into an advanced level of spiritual evolution, channeling their sexual energy upwards to the higher chakras in order to reach higher spiritual levels of existence. Relatively few individuals thus far have been successful in properly channeling and redirecting this highly volatile powerful sexual energy upwards in order to reach their own personal spiritual enlightenment. Jesus and His apostles did. Buddha did. Krishna did. And I can only imagine that other very spiritual prophets did as well and a few others not as renowned.

So, if we were to stop having sex, wouldn't the human race become extinct? At our current level of consciousness, it is necessary to continue our species. For those who are married or in a committed loving relationship, sexual intercourse appears then to be a necessary concession. Please remember that possibly even Jesus wasn't born enlightened and subsequently may have had children. Therefore it is possible that some souls may reach enlightenment even after having had children. But remain ever mindful that immoral sex may be damaging to the body and harmful to the soul's progression as it may increase karma.

Overall, a few of us may become enlightened by successfully raising this energy, while most of us will take the slower evolutionary route to heaven along with the majority of mankind and will not stop having sexual intercourse. To be perfectly honest, I thoroughly question whether or not I am ready to give up the idea of a loving partner and sexual intercourse with her. However, I do realize that I have a number of options. I can still have a loving partner even if I give up sexual intercourse with her altogether, all the while channeling the Kundalini energies up my spine and achieving higher levels of desired consciousness. Alternatively, I can intermittently practice channeling these energies up my spine and occasionally have sex with my partner while realizing that continued intercourse may necessitate my return to experience another lifetime. Similar to the concept that Mozart may have become a master of the piano over several lifetimes, I could become a master at raising my Kundalini energy to my higher chakras over a number of lifetimes, eventually reaching enlightenment.

To further address the previous question about the possibility of the human race becoming extinct, those who do not reach enlightenment will continue to have babies or may reach enlightenment after they have had children. When we collectively reach a level of consciousness where we no longer desire sexual union with another human being, that being the state of enlightenment, we will once again be immortal as we were in our original state. Reincarnation will become a thing of the past. We will once again be experiencing this universe of form as immortal beings. There will no longer be sickness, disease, or death, or the need to procreate. Sexual relationships will be nonexistent because we will have rediscovered a consciousness much greater than we could even imagine as humans. Sexual union will be replaced by an incredible level of never-ending bliss. It will be greater than living in a constant state of orgasm. That, my friends, sounds like heaven to me.

Taking a more practical look at the current state of marriage, I believe that sex plays too important of a role in most relationships. Often we meet someone and we are immediately attracted to him or her. Sooner rather than later, the couple is in bed enjoying each other in a primarily sexual capacity. The relationship then has immediately changed. What we need to do first and foremost in regards to human relationships is to determine whether or not there is a sturdy foundation for the relationship. A sturdy foundation is necessary for happiness within marriage. Why do you think we have over a fifty percent divorce rate? Is the primary reason for divorce because someone within the relationship changed? No, I believe most marriages fail because the person they married is not the person they were intended to marry! Having sex way too soon in a relationship will mask the level of incompatibility that exists between a man and a woman. Too many marriages are initially based on sexual desire and not compatibility. Too often, the couple discovers this all too late.

Marriage needs to be based on the following tenets or areas of compatibility:

<u>Spirituality</u>: God must come first in our lives and above our relationships with others, even our spouse. Without a belief in a higher power, we often will fail because we lack a moral compass with which to navigate through life. Without a belief in a higher power, we may choose to negate or disregard the Law of Karma (i.e. what comes around, goes around). Subsequently, if we cheat, we will be cheated. Possessing a belief in an intelligence above our own is important for any long-term relationship. Belief in a higher power means that we must treat others as we wish to be treated. Only by being a faithful mate will we be able to attract and maintain a relationship with another faithful mate. Ironically, many of our relationships with other souls in human form are based on previous karma, and when the karma has been worked through, the relationship will terminate.

<u>Emotional compatibility</u>: We need to be emotionally connected, not just connected; sex will accomplish the latter, but not the former. We need to be emotionally connected

with a minimum level of emotional compatibility. For a successful relationship, the couple needs to have similar levels of emotional intelligence. If you or your significant other possesses significantly less emotional intelligence, the relationship will not typically survive unless there is some sort of intervention such as counseling. Otherwise jealousy, anger, or some other negative emotion will eventually poison the relationship, and the relationship will terminate.

Mental compatibility: If the other person you are involved with does not stimulate your mind, nor has the ability to engage you on a level somewhat equal to your level of intelligence, then the two of you will have little to share on a mental level, much less have the ability to hold a stimulating conversation with each other. A successful relationship is more than just sharing the same interests; rather, it is about possessing a cognitive ability to effectively communicate shared interests.

Physical compatibility: This often receives the most attention, though it may be the least important of the four areas of compatibility. Sex with someone you love is wonderful, but if you don't share enough in common to form a successful relational foundation, what initially attracted you to your partner (or vice versa) will soon fade into a distant memory. You might even suggest that it is your partner who changed for the worse. But what really changed is your awareness of the other person. So after years of marriage you may now find yourself in a relationship with children and huge financial commitments. Possibly these financial concerns and/or the children make you feel trapped in a marriage you no longer find pleasurable. You may decide to stay married no matter how unhappy you feel. This unhappiness may eventually lead to an extramarital affair. The statistics state that more than half of all married men have had an extramarital affair. While the percentage of married women involved in extramarital affairs is less than half, they are quickly closing the gap.

Spiritual, emotional, mental, and physical compatibility concerns disintegrate when we attract our *true intended soul mate* for this lifetime, or as I like to call this person, our *companion soul mate*. A companion soul mate is a very special soul. We all have one. Our companion mate will most often, if not always, reincarnate with us each lifetime. They are often our truest companion lifetime after lifetime. This special soul serves the function of our truest mate in that they aid us in our greatest spiritual growth since they most accurately reflect back to us who we are and where we still need to grow spiritually. They serve as a near perfect mirror for us, and therefore we will often *not* attract this person until we are spiritually ready for that person. That is just one of the reasons why it is important that we lead a life that places our spirituality first. When we put sex into proper perspective, we create the greatest opportunity to attract our companion mate. Sex is a second chakra issue, as I will discuss in a later chapter. In a nutshell, we as the human race need to gain greater control over our sexual energies.

In first seeking a deeper more loving relationship with God, we can then seek a deeper more loving relationship with our companion mate. But how will we know if the person we met is our companion mate for this lifetime? In getting to know another person mentally, emotionally, and spiritually *before* having sex with him or her, we discover compatibilities, and conversely, incompatibilities. In getting to know the person first, and then making an intelligent choice about sex, we greatly increase our chances for creating a longstanding union with the companion mate we are spiritually contracted to be with this lifetime. When we place our primary emphasis on our second chakra-based sexual energies, we will most likely *not* attract our companion mate. However, when we are willing and able to begin the process of purifying our hearts and minds along with our thoughts and desires, we will naturally draw our companion mate to us within divine timing. This is the Law of Attraction at its best! Until we make conscious steps in this direction, we will attract mates based on sexual desire and suffer the consequences attached with that occurring. For me, it has led to two divorces, even though I am certain that the second marriage was with a soul mate but just not my true companion soul mate for this lifetime. To be honest, looking back in time, I was not yet ready for my true companion mate. I was too spiritually immature.

The union of two individuals in a sexual relationship should never be underestimated. Many things occur besides the exchange of bodily fluids and possibly infectious diseases. Souls touch. There is an instantaneous exchange of spiritual energy. A lower vibrational being lowers the energetic vibration of a higher vibrational being. Emotional cords between the souls are created that are sometimes difficult to cut. At times a partner may actually feel as if he or she lost a piece of themselves. A person may be left feeling less than whole. The positive side of sexual relationships between two companion mates is the incredible sharing of love. For that matter, homosexual couples may be companion mates and consequently their sexual union as their expression of love for each other would not be a sin as far as God is concerned. When companion mates unite as one, it represents the actual union of the male and the female aspects; Adam and Eve in the aggregate sense. Sex is one of the moments in life when we should feel ecstasy and bliss, not just a sexual release. Sexual union in our current level of consciousness is an integral part of life and needs to be celebrated in a spiritually, emotionally, mentally, and physically healthy manner.

However, sex as the union of two incompatible souls should not be taken lightly. Sex with an inappropriate partner can create greater karma for us and others. Before we unite with another soul sexually, we need to open our heart, mind, and soul to that person to determine long-term compatibility and the intended purpose of the relationship. Until we each meet our intended companion mate for this lifetime, possibly abstinence is best. In this way, you are telling the universe that you are willing to wait for the right person to come into your life. Too many times we operate from need and desire, not balancing our head with our heart, and we subsequently enter a relationship out of neediness versus balance. It can be quite troubling and painful for all concerned if we are with the *wrong person* when the *right person* comes along, or if the right person doesn't come along because we are with the wrong person.

Either way, by staying unattached (sexually speaking) we keep our options open, giving us time to make the right decision. When we take our time to get to really know the other person, we do not make our decision solely based on sexual attraction even though it is most often what initially brings two people together. Alternatively, when we meet that special person (companion soul mate) that stimulates us spiritually, mentally, emotionally, and physically, we may feel like we have created a *heaven on earth*.

"The Lord God said, 'It is not good for the man to be alone. I will make a helper suitable for him.'" Genesis 2:18

It is clearly stated in the verse above that God created woman to be man's companion or at least a *helper*, but a helper in what regard? To address this question, let me take you one step further.

As mentioned, Paul said it is better to marry than to burn with desire. Paul also stated that marriage is a concession for those that are either not spiritually, emotionally, or mentally capable of celibacy. However, it is also clear that marriage with the wrong partner often occurs due to our inability or lack of desire to refrain from sexual relations with another soul; the unintended incompatible soul. Herein lies the sin as missing the mark. Marriage, as a concession, is meant to be between two true companion mates intended to come together, not between incompatible souls. Much too often we are drawn to another soul because of sexual attraction. Marriage is meant to be a vehicle in which two companion mates come together in mutual support of each other combining the rationale mind of man and the emotional nature of woman toward obtaining greater balanced levels of spirituality. That is what I believe is meant by woman being man's helper. Paul also said, "Do not deprive each other except by mutual consent and for a time, so that you may devote yourselves to prayer." In this way, a companion soul couple comes together in sexual union, but when not in sexual union substantial energy is expended helping each other with their combined spiritual growth; the rational mind of man helps the emotional nature of woman, while the emotional side of woman aids the rational mind of man.

Sadly, I believe that too often our hearts and minds are not pure enough to draw our companion mate. Rather, what happens today is we marry someone to whom we were initially sexually attracted. Divorce is the natural consequence of a mismatch between souls, especially when the couple focuses on this dimension's materialistic nature and not on things related to God and spiritual development. Divorce under these conditions would not be a sin. Divorce would then be a correction to a previous sin, i.e. missing the mark of not waiting for the true companion mate. Divorce is a karmic consequence of either being with the wrong person or not being spiritually aware enough that the divorcing couple is already with their intended companion mate. In the latter case, the divorce is most likely a consequence of not seeking things of a spiritual nature, but rather seeking material things of this world. Adultery in the truest sense would occur when we cheat on our companion mate this lifetime. Obviously, believing that you are currently with the wrong person is not an excuse for cheating on your current partner. There is no integrity in cheating and would most likely increase karma.

We all need to focus more on growing spiritually, understanding that marriage between true companion soul mates is a vehicle for managing our sexual desires given our current level of consciousness. As Paul suggests, "Then come together again so that Satan will not tempt you because of your lack of self control." When companion soul mates make love, they become one and they become whole. As a couple learns to manage their sexual desires, they have the opportunity to engage their minds and hearts in a balanced fashion, mutually supporting each other until they reach a point in their consciousness of total devotion to God, at which time their ultimate mate becomes God. This does not mean that they then need to divorce, but rather sexual desire has essentially become extinguished for the higher purpose of service to God and man. They have reached a level of spiritual maturity together and now can more fully operate independently of one another, if desired. They have in effect filled the lower nature in their lives with the higher nature of God. Until a couple reaches this point, they should attempt to strike an appropriate balance between sexual intercourse and attempts at raising their Kundalini energies. Kundalini energy is discussed thoroughly in a later chapter.

Together companion soul mates seek liberation from the cycle of reincarnation. Together they support each other in their search for enlightenment. Together they seek God and the god within themselves. The more energy and focus they place in their search for God and enlightenment, the less focused they will become in sexual union. In effect, they are jointly replacing their desire for sexual union with their partner with a more fulfilling union with God. This is what marriage is intended to be, the coming together of two companion soul mates based on an opportunity for greater spiritual growth, not sexual attraction. Together, as companion soul mates seeking spiritual progression, they maintain the option of procreation. Later, if they have children, they teach their children about God and the science of procreation. Supporting each other's efforts in spiritual growth is the truest intent of earthly marriage. It aids us in our journey back to heaven.

In heaven, as enlightened beings, we no longer feel unfulfilled in any way, so marriage is no longer necessary or desirable, as is stated in the Bible.

> "At the resurrection people will neither marry or be given in marriage; they will be like the angels in heaven." Matthew 22:3

CHAPTER 26

Everything Is Connected

❧

One night around 2:30 a.m., I found myself in that middle point of consciousness between awaked-ness and sleep, what I often refer to as the *middle realm*. While in that special place, I received an incredible vision. No, actually it seemed much more than that. It was a moment of absolute clarity. It was an insight of a greater magnitude than I had ever received before. It felt as if it came from the source of all, from God Himself. It was awe-inspiring. I wasn't sure exactly what had occurred at first. It felt like an incredible download of spiritual information occurring within a nanosecond (one billionth of a second). I soon understood that my third eye, my Christ Center, had completely opened. I had tapped into Christ Consciousness for a brief moment in time. I experienced enlightenment! Following this spiritual download, I felt completely overwhelmed. And now I almost find it too difficult to explain the magnitude of the experience, but I will do the best I can.

At first I thought I had been shown a graph or a formula for something. Then I realized what I had witnessed in that instant was a *matrix*. The matrix appeared to me as a network of interlocking systematic grids full of dark lines intersecting other dark lines. I believe these interlocking systematic grids represent the math-based systems we have on this earth that we don't quite fully understand as yet. Later, I came to the conclusion that the universal laws of God, and all of God's creation for that matter, are based on mathematics. My vision in effect showed me the interconnection of all things in our universe. After receiving the download I awoke. Now maybe you can understand why I might have thought it to be quite overwhelming and subsequently difficult to explain. Once completely awake, I received several words describing the fundamental nature of the matrix. I received the words *white, gold,* and *alchemist,* and I kept getting the word *brilliance* over and over.

I immediately knew that the portion of the message concerning the colors of white and gold were descriptive in nature of the Divine Trinity and that the word *alchemist* was referencing the creative aspect of God. Then another word came to me that I have never heard before. It was the word *pre-mordial,* which really isn't a word at all. What that non-word meant to me was that God was not just primordial, existing from the beginning of time; God was *pre-mordial*, existing before time. And latent within God lay the *unmanifested alchemist* in that *pre-mordial* state. The hidden meanings behind the words given to me were beginning to unfold. It wasn't until later in the day when I received an encrypted message within the earth plane (within form) that I began to more fully comprehend the spiritual download.

As I was returning from Sunday worship, I noticed a truck in front of me. The truck was not anything special; rather it was the license plate that struck me as peculiar. The license plate number had three 7s and three 1s and one letter. It struck me as a little peculiar, nothing more, until I glanced at the time on my car clock. The time was 11:17 a.m. Now I was a little more than curious regarding this *coincidence*, especially having just received an incredible download earlier that day. I immediately wondered what the numbers 7 and 1 meant in numerology and if the universe was trying to relay some important message to me. I believed that I was experiencing a moment of *synchronicity*, or what I like to call a *God-wink*. Synchronicity is the opposite of randomness or coincidence. Synchronicity is a sign that we are in the right place at the right time and on the right path. Synchronicity is a sign that we are in the flow of the universe and on our return back to our original state of enlightenment and heaven. Some people reject the idea of coincidence and state that nothing is a coincidence. We simply can't comprehend the hidden meaning behind the synchronistic event in that particular moment. It's almost as if God is winking at us to see if we catch His humor.

As I contemplated the download, I recalled that the color gold is associated with or represents the color of God the Father, if it were possible for God to be identified by or associated with a color. Notice that the word "gold" has God contained within it. Could this be just a coincidence, or rather another God-wink? Often as humans we speak God's truth without even realizing it, we speak of higher truths unconsciously. I like to call these unconscious soul memories that reflect higher spiritual realities *soul truisms*. Continuing on, the color white represents *the light of the Son* as the Christ Body. The actual color of the sun is white even though it appears yellow. It is the color white when broken down by refraction that gives us the colored rays of light energy found in a rainbow.

Then a much greater depth of understanding came to me. Since the word "sun" sounds the same as the word "son," could this be another soul truism that we as human speak? Could our universe's sun be the actual physical manifestation of The Only Begotten Son, the Christ Body? Is this another example of the Law of Correspondence, what is true in the spiritual realm manifests somehow in the physical realm as a reflection of God? In other words, is the spiritual energy of the Son manifesting as the physical energy of the Sun? The answer, as far as I am concerned, is most definitely *yes*. Remember, what is true above is true below. Further, if we are all made in the image of God, why would it be so difficult to believe that all of creation is simply a physical reflection of God's powers and diverse interwoven energies sometimes referred to as a matrix? This would be especially true if everything is God, wouldn't it?

A short time later I conducted an internet search and discovered a vast amount of information on numerology. I was astonished. The number 7 in Eastern Indian numerology symbolizes wisdom, discrimination, and spiritual knowledge, and is associated with the color white. It is also associated with the karmic lesson of practicalness, the metal white-gold, the ruling planet Ketu in the zodiac (astrology), and the gem cat's eye.[1] The number 1 is associated with our sun and the color gold as well as the element of gold. The karmic lesson of 1 is renunciation as in renunciation of materialism and things of this world. That would correspond to an end of all attachments to this plane of existence, which of course would lead to a spiritual liberation from reincarnation since earthly desires necessitate a return to the earth plane.

Suddenly this all made sense to me. I was grasping an even greater understanding of my spiritual download; Spirit was unveiling part of the *Great Mystery* to me. Spirit was showing me how absolutely everything has meaning and how everything is interconnected and reflects the Divine. Here specifically in this world of physicality, what I already knew about the colors white and gold was being confirmed by various websites, that is, Gold is the color associated with God the Father (Impersonal God) while white is the color associated with the Christ Body (The Only Begotten Son). The planet Ketu, upon further investigation, was described as a *headless planet* possessing the qualities of wisdom, discrimination, and spiritual knowledge, the same qualities as the number 7 in numerology. The negative qualities (or lower nature) of the planet Ketu are obsessive-compulsive and animalistic behaviors.[2]

Remember, there is always a dark or opposite side to all nature in the world of duality. This is the Universal Law of Relativity. Ketu is also considered to be the source of emancipation from the cycle of reincarnation. Does this not describe the positive nature of the Christ Body? The Christ Body is the source of our emancipation from reincarnation. The light of the Christ Body could also be considered *headless* in that we descended down onto earth and seemingly separated from the Father, separating from the Godhead (the Son without the Father). Interestingly enough, in Hinduism, one of the sun's names is Aditya, which means *first-born*. In Vedic Astrology the sun has another name, Bhutasya-Jatah, which means the *Father or Creator of all objects*.[3] I imagine if I continued my investigation of the various names of the sun, as I did for God, I would find a seemingly never-ending list. All of this supports my hypothesis of the interrelatedness of the spiritual realm with the physical realm and that there are many roads to heaven, not just through religion.

To my delight Spirit's *Great Mystery* continued to unfold as I further investigated the interrelatedness of astrology, numerology, metallurgy, and gemology to the Godhead.

The metal associated with the number 7 is white gold, a blend of colors associated with the Father (gold) and the Son (white), possibly illustrating the intertwined nature of the Godhead. The gem is the cat's eye. I can't help but make the reference of the gem cat's eye to the *All-Seeing Eye of the Christ Center*, the point of conscious enlightenment associated with the third-eye or the sixth chakra (discussed in greater detail in the next chapter). The karmic lesson of practical-ness is obvious. Is there a more practical example of achieving God Consciousness than that of Jesus, or any of the other great prophets for that matter? The cat's eye is believed to assist in healing disorders such as nerve-related illnesses, joint pain, anxiety, skin diseases, and much more. Just as numerology, astrology, and religion reflect differing roads to heaven, so are gemstones another avenue of developing wholeness and spiritual health.

The gemstone associated with the number 1 is the ruby. The ruby when used for healing purposes addresses issues relating to impotence. The ruby also assists with healing heart troubles as well as indigestion, fever, diabetes, and more. The sun's higher nature is associated with creativity, affection, and generosity. The sun's positive properties include willpower, wealth, bliss, success, wisdom, and *brilliance*. Brilliance was one of the words I received within my consciousness immediately following my spiritual download. The negative traits of the number 1, the sun, and the gemstone ruby are laziness, arrogance, jealousy, and nervousness. It should be somewhat clearer by now that the stars and planets (astrology) represent the various natures, energies, or personalities of God, and contained within each planet or star is higher God nature and lower human nature. Likewise it should be clearer that gemstones, as elements in nature, are available to us to heal the physical manifestations of the lower human nature, specifically our dis-ease. Does it really surprise you that God created everything we need on this earth to heal us in its most basic form? Maybe this is the underlying reason we are drawn to wearing certain gemstones on our bodies. Maybe this is a prime reason to better protect Mother Nature from the harm we humans inflict upon Her.

To better understand God I wanted to understand more about alchemy and what it truly means to be an *alchemist*. I was pleased with the definition I found on Hyperdictionary.com. It means *one who was versed in the practice of alchemy and who sought an elixir of life and a panacea and an alkahest and the philosopher's stone.* Let's pick this definition apart to get a better understanding about what we are talking about here. Alchemy was apparently a magical power or chemical philosophy thought to exist in medieval times that would convert base metals into gold. A *panacea* is a cure-all remedy for all diseases, illnesses, or difficulties once sought by alchemists. An *alkahest* is a universal solvent. The *philosopher's stone* is a legendary substance capable of turning base metals into gold. Of course this is all a metaphor for something much greater, whether or not true alchemists ever existed or not. What alchemy and alchemists represent is man's search for enlightenment, which is the greatest form of all wealth. It is reminiscent of King Arthur and the Knights of the Round Table's search for the Holy

Grail. Both the search for the Holy Grail and the myth of alchemy symbolizes man's search for Christ Consciousness and a return to the Creator.

In addition I looked into the study of astrology to see if I could discover any further interconnectedness between God and nature. Astrology is defined as *the study of the stars and their effect on human behavior.* Personally, I believe that each of the seven planets in our solar system possesses an aspect of God's loving Consciousness; that is, each planet possesses one of God's seven primary energies related to our seven chakras. In direct opposition to God's seven primary energies each planet has the potential to echo or reflect back to us our lower human nature referred to as the Seven Deadly Sins. For example, Mars is considered the *Angry Red Planet.* Anger is a feeling which by default would be associated with the third chakra. Astrology can be looked at as the physical manifestation or mapping of our spiritual progression back to the Godhead through developing or re-membering our God Consciousness and overcoming our lower dysfunctional human consciousness.

> "These are the words of him who holds the seven spirits of God and the seven stars." Revelation 3:1

The Biblical reference to the *seven stars* I believe are the seven planets of our solar system. These seven planets emit positive energies, *the seven spirits of God,* and send these energies to the earth, as suggested in Revelation:

> "...which are the seven spirits of God sent out into all the earth." Revelation 5:6

Could these seven spirits be God's seven archangels? Remember that all is energy in this universe of form, and the spiritual realm is reflected or possibly even projected into the physical realm as form.

> "The mystery of the seven stars that you saw in my right hand and of the seven golden lampshades is this: The seven stars are the angels...." Revelation 1:20

Assuming I am correct in my assumptions, these seven God energies would correspond to the seven chakra energies positively influencing all beings on this earth further illustrating the interconnectedness of everything.

Let me give you another reference in the Bible that supports this claim.

> "I, Jesus, have sent my angel to give you this testimony for the churches. I am the Root and the offspring of David, and the bright Morning Star." Revelation 22:16

Jesus declares that He is *the bright Morning Star*. The planet Venus is often called the bright morning star. Jesus here possibly claims to be the energy associated with Venus. Venus is considered the planet of love, and consistent with this claim is the fact that Jesus' message is all about love. Love is also the primary emotion associated with the fourth chakra. Is Jesus himself one of the positive planetary energies that influence this universe? What I am suggesting here is simply a physical manifestation of a very potent spiritual energy. Again, the Universal Law of Correspondence is definitely at work here, expounding once again that what exists in the spiritual realm manifests in the physical realm.

Look at our physical brain. It is the physical manifestation of the spiritual energy of the mind. Look at our body. It is the physical manifestation of our soul. It is also possible that Jesus' energy may be physically manifesting as the energies of Venus. If true, we should not be surprised that planets have a energetic influence on our earth and people. As an example, look at how the moon affects the tides and how a full moon can affect people's thoughts, emotions and actions overall. And isn't our body mostly made up of water? It should also not come as a shock to suggest that the planets are the physical manifestation of the spiritual energies associated with the Godhead. Believing that the sun, stars and planets are deities is not a new concept. The Mayan and the Egyptian cultures are some of the more notable civilizations that believed that the planets are the physical manifestations of deities. It appears that they may have been correct.

Are you beginning to understand that everything is connected, including the zodiac? Do we not as humans refer to the stars as *the heavens above?* Is this possibly another soul truism? Is it possible that the seven energies of God are not only the seven archangels but also interconnected to the seven planets, the seven chakras associated with the human body, and that there may be as many as seven heavens manifested into form? Are you beginning to open up to the possibility that this form universe is simply a highly complex matrix disguising the spiritual realm and that we within our current level of consciousness are simply not yet fully attune to this fact?

And how do specific stars interplay with the planets?

The zodiac has been referred to as the *Wheel of Karma*.[4] As such, the zodiac is considered the physical manifestation of our spiritual path back to enlightenment and can be used as a guidepost for our eventual return to the Godhead. If this assumption is correct, we all must learn and experience and sufficiently master each facet of each sign of the zodiac before we ultimately break free from the wheel of karma and reincarnation. In this regard, karma and the zodiac are the same. They are the pathways of the soul. Therefore, we can look to the stars to see our destiny. Scientists suggest that when we gaze into the night sky we are actually witnessing the past because the light of another reality has not yet reached the earth. Knowing that we are looking into the past, is it that much more of a stretch to consider the star constellations a map of our growing evolutionary consciousness? If this is true, then the zodiac could potentially map out our karma and the future yet to come. Space then represents the past and future *all at the same time.* This would indicate that time is *not a reality* as they coexist within the only time that is real which is the present moment. Can you begin to see that absolutely everything is connected and that even the seemingly mundane has much deeper meaning than we may have ever previously considered?

In my endeavor to understand my vision, I came to realize that it is not just religion or spirituality pointing the way to a return to Christ Consciousness or God Consciousness. Numerology points to the way back to the divine source as well. What's more, I decided that the spiritual download was a message that there are many paths to heaven, including yoga, astrology, numerology, science and what some people might consider the occult. It is important to realize that even an occult science has a higher and lower nature associated with it, just as religion does. It is what we choose that makes all the difference, be it the good or evil within each system. My spiritual download showed me without a doubt that, indeed, everything is connected. As a result, I knew in my heart that there are many paths to heaven or maybe even better yet, all paths lead to heaven, even New Age principles.

Section V

MERGING NEW AGE WITH GOD

CHAPTER 27

Chakras and the Development of Consciousness

The word *chakra* is a Sanskrit word meaning *wheels of light*.[1] Chakras are *spinning wheel-like energy centers* that are an integral part of our spiritual anatomy associated with various points within our spine and head. However, they cannot be x-rayed or dissected because they are spiritual in nature. Chakras connect to and feed the subtle energy bodies that surround the physical body as well as feeding the physical body itself by providing a pathway for the Holy Spirit, the universal life force energy. A s*ubtle body* is defined as *a nonphysical energetic spiritual body or light field that surrounds the physical body*. Collectively, the subtle bodies are a human energy shield commonly referred to as an *aura*. An aura is *the physical manifestation of the light of God or Holy Spirit within us*. It is the rainbow of our soul's energy. Each individual chakra is associated with a color of the rainbow. Blended all together they form the color of white, which spiritually represents Christ Consciousness. The greater the physical health of the body and consciousness of the soul, the greater is the size and strength of the aura. Chakras, subtle bodies, and auras are intricately connected yet invisible to the naked eye.

Stress and disharmony negatively affect the chakras and consequently negatively affect the overall health of the physical, emotional, mental, and spiritual body by creating a potential blockage in the chakra or, in more extreme cases, causing it to completely close. If a certain chakra is blocked, partially closed, or not properly functioning for whatever reason, it will eventually cause an illness or dis-ease within the body. If the causal factor is not rectified, over the long term a dis-ease will most likely evolve into a disease within the body. Some psychics can look at a person's aura to determine a person's level of spiritual evolvement. Some psychics can actually intuit physical injuries or illnesses by scanning a person's aura. When the soul is able to accept greater levels of life force energy from the Holy Spirit, the aura consequently becomes larger. This of course is indicative of a healthier mind, body, and soul, as well as higher levels of consciousness.

The consciousness of the soul directly affects the physical development of the human body. A more advanced soul may have a more active and healthier endocrine system as well as a more highly functioning brain. This may make the person much more psychic or intelligent than the average person. In other instances, the soul may chose a physical body that has certain abnormalities due to previous karma or lessons it wishes to learn or teach others this lifetime. A less developed soul whose brain did not fully develop may be more prone to evil influences and doing evil if raised in a traumatic family environment. Of course, there are potentially an infinite number of reasons we appear as we do and make the choices we make.

The color of an aura depends upon which chakras we are primarily operating out of at any given time which can change quickly with each situation. The color of our auras also very much depends upon our level of spiritual development. Normally auras will contain several colors within them, as we normally operate within the energetic realm of several chakras at any one given time. A person principally operating out of a lower chakra located at a lower part of the spine most likely is a less advanced soul than a soul that consistently operates out of a higher chakra located higher up the spinal column. However, it is important to remember that we may operate out of any one of the chakras at any time depending upon the situation in which we find ourselves.

There are seven main chakras associated with the physical body. There is an eighth chakra that exists eight to ten inches above the head of the physical body that may or may not have a corresponding subtle body (see illustration). The chakras are connected inwardly to certain portions of the physical body, assisting in the performance of our body's organs and physiological functions located within the endocrine system. The endocrine system is a multifarious part of the human body and is still not entirely understood. However, we do know that the endocrine system provides a chemical communication network that controls a vast array of physiological processes. Theosophist writers [Theosophy] were the first to observe that the position of the chakras on the body parallels that of the glands of the endocrine system.[2] Beyond the endocrine system, each of the seven chakras additionally supports the life function of the area of the body in which they are located.

Outwardly, each of the main seven chakras is connected to a specific spiritual subtle energy body. The seven main chakras run from the base of the spine to the top of the head and serve to regulate the physical, emotional, mental, and spiritual health of the body by connecting to the prana or universal life force energy of the Holy Spirit. This Holy Spirit energy, which flows up and down our spine feeding each chakra, is again referred to as Kundalini energy.

The eighth chakra, the *transcendental chakra*, is not directly affiliated with the physical body and represents a very high level of spiritual development as you will see later. Before I begin explaining the eighth chakra in depth, let's explore the seven main chakras associated with the physical body.

The first chakra, which is part of the spiritual body located within the physical body, is called the *base chakra* or *root chakra*. It is located at the base of the spine near the coccyx. The Holy Spirit energy first enters the body through the perineum and travels to the base chakra and then up the spine to the balance of the chakras associated with the body. After this life force energy has reached the top of the head, the Kundalini energy begins the descent back down the spine.

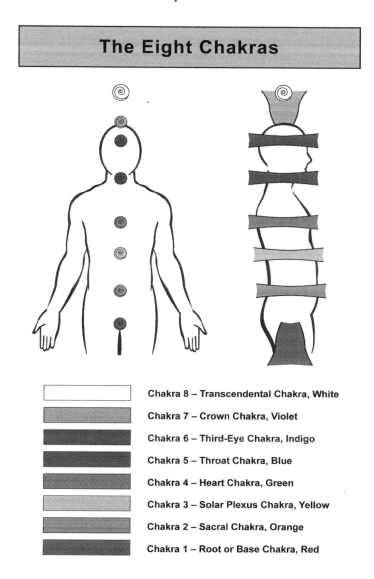

The Eight Chakras

Chakra 8 – Transcendental Chakra, White

Chakra 7 – Crown Chakra, Violet

Chakra 6 – Third-Eye Chakra, Indigo

Chakra 5 – Throat Chakra, Blue

Chakra 4 – Heart Chakra, Green

Chakra 3 – Solar Plexus Chakra, Yellow

Chakra 2 – Sacral Chakra, Orange

Chakra 1 – Root or Base Chakra, Red

This first chakra feeds the organs located in the lower area of the physical body, such as the lower intestinal tract. This chakra additionally provides life force energy to the adrenal glands within the endocrine system, which are responsible for the production of adrenaline and consequently linked to the *fight or flight response*. The root chakra is representative of the greatest level of physicality of a soul within a human body. The root chakra is also considered to be our connection to Mother Earth.

In regard to the spiritual evolution of mankind, the first chakra is all about survival and security. There is nothing more fundamental than that. The first chakra is connected to the subtle body that is closest to the physical body. The energy related to the base chakra is said to vibrate at the lowest frequency of all the chakras and is associated with the color red and is therefore responsible for the color red within the aura.

The next chakra as you travel up the spine is the second chakra or *sacral chakra*. The sacral chakra is located a couple of inches below the navel and is associated with the gonads. The gonads are the group of embryonic cells that serve as the fundamental base for future sexual development. In males, they eventually become the testes. In females, they eventually develop into the ovaries. This chakra is also associated with the genitals. This second chakra additionally feeds the bodily organs in the area of the chakra such as the upper intestines.

The second chakra within the evolutionary scheme of things represents sexual energy, procreation, and creativity. The color as it manifests in the aura or auric field is orange. Please note that the chakras numbering two through six are horizontal in nature and, as such, have a front and back component to each chakra. The first and seventh chakras are vertical in nature and have a top and bottom component to them. In this discussion of chakras, I will be primarily focusing on an overall description of the chakras and their related function without getting into too much extraneous detail.

The third chakra is located two or three inches above the navel and is referred to as the *solar plexus chakra*. The solar plexus chakra provides life force energy to the pancreas and organs connected to the digestive process such as the stomach, liver, and the kidneys, which in turn convert food into energy for the physical body. Specifically, the pancreas helps digest food by producing insulin.

The third chakra is linked to feelings such as happiness, anxiety, anger, resentment, and sadness. In terms of the evolutional development of consciousness, the solar plexus chakra is associated with personal power, self-esteem, and intuition. Here we often use the soul truism *feelings of intuition*. Please note that this is not the chakra for *emotions*. This chakra is associated with feelings, which are different than emotions. Emotions are very intense or exaggerated feelings and are overall much stronger than feelings. Yellow is the color associated with this chakra found within our aura.

The fourth chakra is called the *heart chakra*. This is the chakra associated with emotions and the emotional subtle body and is of course located near the heart muscle. Life force energy here supports the functions of the thymus situated just behind the breastbone. The thymus relates to and supports our immune system by creating T-cells. A T-cell is a type of white blood cell critical to our immune system. When functioning properly, T-cells attach themselves to invader cells within our body and destroy them. The life force energy associated with the fourth chakra naturally supports the functions of the heart and lungs.

The fourth chakra in the evolutionary process of mankind is associated with developing sufficient mastery over the emotions such as hate, fear, and love. The fourth chakra is primarily associated with the heart, emotional well-being, and spiritual healing. The heart chakra is located at the center of the seven body chakras. The color associated with this chakra is green. Spiritual healers are believed to have a lot of green in their aura. As the heart chakra continues to open, the individual will become increasingly *psychic*.

The fifth chakra is located in the throat and is often called simply the *throat chakra*. This chakra channels life force energy to the thyroid. Specifically, the thyroid is located in the middle of the lower neck, below the larynx, and regulates the metabolism in your body. Life force energy associated with this chakra feeds the medulla oblongata as well. The medulla oblongata is the lower portion of the brain stem that controls the automatic functions of the body and relays nerve impulses between the spinal cord and the brain.

The throat chakra, as one might imagine, is associated with sound, communication, expression, and speaking the truth. This chakra is also associated with the concrete mind. The spiritual evolutionary development of this particular chakra aids us in finding our individual voice, and in doing so, we create a deeper connection to the expression of our soul's desires and spiritual truth. The color of this particular chakra within the aura is blue.

The sixth chakra is referred to as the *third-eye chakra. The forward and sometimes visible portion of this chakra* is located slightly above the center of the eyes between the two eyebrows. The third-eye chakra is linked to the pineal gland. The pineal gland produces melatonin, which regulates many hormones in the body. The third-eye chakra, in terms of the evolutionary consciousness of mankind, is associated with the abstract mind and the elements of time and space. For the third-eye chakra to be fully functioning, a soul would have achieved pure awareness and the ability to perceive the absolute. At this point of evolutionary consciousness we know the Impersonal God but still consider Him to be separate. An individual soul, whether in its physical body or not, operating at the level of enlightenment understands his or her connection to God as being a part of the Trinity, knows the unknown, and understands the transcendental meaning to life.

This chakra when fully functioning is considered the All-Seeing Eye. All six senses, which include the sixth sense associated with psychic abilities, have been perfected. A person operating at this level of consciousness would have achieved the level of Christ

Consciousness because his or her mind would be in alignment with God's mind. A person at this level is said to be filled with the Holy Spirit, which again is just another way of saying that he or she is an enlightened being. Paintings of saints where there is an aura surrounding the person's head exemplified as a ring of light may be indicative of the attainment of Christ Consciousness or enlightenment. The color of this chakra as it appears in the aura is indigo.

The seventh chakra is called the *crown chakra* because it is located on the top of the head. In the physical body, it is associated with the pituitary gland and cerebral cortex. The pituitary gland is located at the base of the brain and is attached to the hypothalamus. The pituitary gland secretes hormones that regulate homeostasis. It is sometimes considered the master gland of the human body because it controls the functions of the other endocrine glands. The cerebral cortex is involved with complex brain functions such as language development. Spiritually speaking, there doesn't appear to be much of a difference between the sixth and seventh chakras because a person operating at either level is fully enlightened, and for the most part this is true. However, as it relates to the development of consciousness, the seventh chakra represents a higher degree of consciousness and is associated with a higher plane of consciousness. When the crown chakra is fully open, the white light of the Christ Body pours into our consciousness through this chakra. The color associated with this particular chakra is violet.

The next chakra, and the final chakra in this model of evolutionary consciousness for the soul, is the *transcendental chakra*. The transcendental chakra is the eighth chakra and represents Cosmic Consciousness, a state of unmanifested pure consciousness.

Some metaphysicists describe the human body as having many more chakras than just the eight I mention, which may be very true. However, if there are more than the basic eight chakras I mention it is not important, because what I am attempting to do here is explain the process of man's return to Christ Consciousness or God Consciousness through the development of the individual consciousness. Whether there are eight, ten, twelve, a hundred, or more, the evolution of consciousness of man remains the same. The process to the end result, as well as the end result, remains the same. I do not wish to get bogged down by semantics. That is already happening way too much in the world in our religion, politics, and relationships.

Overall the evolution of consciousness in mankind is consistent with and can be witnessed within these eight chakras. Generally speaking, by studying the chakras we can foretell how mankind will develop spiritually because each chakra corresponds to a spiritual plane of existence as well as the overall evolution back to God Consciousness. In the chapter on Planes of Consciousness, I will explain in more detail how the eight chakras are intrinsically related to the eight planes of consciousness and *heaven*.

CHAPTER 28

Kundalini Energy

❧

Kundalini is a Sanskrit word meaning *coil* or *serpent*.[1] The serpent is an ancient symbol for Kundalini energy. As serpent energy, the Kundalini energy enters the base chakra and is constantly moving through the body in an up and down flow that follows our central nervous system, primarily located in the spinal column. From there the life force energy stems out into the peripheral nervous system. One of the ways in which Kundalini energy manifests itself physically is as electrical currents (nerve impulses) that feed the body and its automatic systems, such as breathing and heart function. It also feeds the brain, which triggers the non-automatic functions of the body, such as walking and talking. As previously mentioned, Kundalini energy is also the universal life force energy that feeds the organs and other critical functions of the body. Without this life force energy, the body would be dead.

Kundalini energy is the same life force energy as the Holy Spirit and as such can be looked upon as Christ Consciousness when in its original state. It is also referred to as *prana*, which is, as stated previously, a Sanskrit work for *breath* or *breath of life*, much like the Holy Spirit is referred to as the *breath of God*. Kundalini energy, when raised up the spine, activates and opens the chakras. When the energy of the serpent completely opens the third-eye chakra, the individual has reached a point of Christ Consciousness. When the Kundalini energy completely opens the crown chakra, the individual has reached a point of God Consciousness. It is impossible to reach enlightenment while in a physical body without raising the Kundalini energy. In fact, enlightenment is closely tied to the process of raising the Kundalini energy in the body minimally to the sixth chakra.

As man evolves, his or her consciousness rises and the chakras open up, beginning with the base chakra upwards to the crown chakra. As mankind evolves, our spiritual consciousness rises over time; with it, the Kundalini energy naturally rises to the higher chakras and opens them as we sufficiently master the energies associated with each chakra. This is an integral part of the evolutionary process of individual man and collective mankind, from ape-man to enlightened man.

Life force energy enters either through the crown chakra or the base chakra because these two chakras are both vertical in nature. However, it is rare that we bring in any substantial amounts of life force energy into the body through the crown chakra because it's barely or rarely open. When this energy enters through the crown chakra, it is considered Christ Conscious energy. If it enters through the base chakra, it is considered Holy Spirit energy. When the energy enters through the crown chakra, it represents our connection to the Christ Body. As a reminder, there is no real difference between the Christ Body energies and Holy Spirit energies just as there is no real difference between the Christ Body and the Holy Spirit. The difference is fundamentally semantics. Kundalini energy, whether derived from the Holy Spirit or the Christ Body, is the universal life force energy that keeps us alive. It is as necessary as the air we breathe. Just as the Holy Spirit is the breath of God in us, it is the breath of life for us manifested literally in physicality. This is yet another example of the Law of Correspondence.

Once the first chakra accepts the universal life force from the Holy Spirit, the Holy Spirit energy or Kundalini energy travels up the spine and down the spine until it is used within the physical body or expended out one of the chakras. Kundalini energy is expended out of the chakras according to the function of the chakra. For example, if energy is expended out of the first chakra it is used as basic energy or base energy. If it is expended out of the second it is used as creative energy or sexual energy. If expended out the third chakra, it is expended as a feeling. If energy is expended out of the fourth chakra, it is expended as an emotion, and correspondingly up the chakras. The fifth chakra expends concrete thought energy, while the sixth chakra expends abstract thought energy.

The amount of energy that is expended out of each chakra further depends upon how open the chakra is. The openness of the chakra is based on the development of the soul as well as the situation the person is operating within. A soul that has the first through third chakras wide open will not expend much energy out of the chakras above the third chakra if the fourth through the seventh are partially or completely closed. Kundalini energy will intermittently be expended out of the chakras above that which we have sufficiently mastered because we are all working towards mastery of those chakras. For example, if a person has mastered their feelings (third chakra), they would necessarily be working on mastering the next chakra up which is the fourth chakra or the chakra dealing with the emotions. There will be some energy being expended out of the fifth or sixth chakras as well even though the energies associated with the fourth chakra may not have been sufficiently mastered.

Kundalini energy, as it rises up the spine and upon crossing each chakra, becomes adulterated due to the negative energies we hold within those chakras. The Kundalini energy, as it rises to the brain, is affected by faulty thoughts and belief systems contained within the mind. In addition, each cell in the physical body has a cellular memory that can affect the Kundalini energy, negatively or positively depending upon the body's past experiences. This now-corrupted life force energy travels up the spine and eventually reaches the crown chakra, at which time the corrupted energy makes a U-turn and begins to travel back down the spine.

The corrupted energy continues to cycle through the body via the spine and brain until it is then expended out of one of the chakras or used internally to sustain the life of the physical body. Because there is no lower nature to the Holy Spirit, as imperfect beings, we corrupt the Holy Spirit energy as it travels through us. If we were once again perfect Christ Conscious beings, we would have all seven chakras fully open and functioning. At the point when we become Christ Conscious, there is no longer corruption of the Kundalini energy. However, until we reach that point, the life force energy we expend out of the chakras as negative energy may be partially held as a memory within the corresponding cells. The cells' energetic properties then remain corrupted until they are somehow purified via a physical or spiritual cleansing process.

A gradual buildup of negative energy within the cells will negatively affect the body parts associated with that chakra. An organ affiliated with a certain chakra will begin to fail if sufficient negative energy is stored in the cellular memory of that organ. As an example, if an individual has a closed heart chakra and cannot open to the emotion of love then most likely the heart will eventually begin to suffer heart disease. Anger stored in the body may show up as some sort of cancer. Anger eats you up inside, doesn't it? It is the same as cancer. *What is true above is true below*. This is another reason why forgiveness of self and others is so vitally important because it directly affects a person's quality of life.

As mentioned, I believe that one of the fastest ways to raise the Kundalini energy, and consequently spiritual consciousness, is to stop or intermittently withdraw from having orgasms. I am referring to the two primary ways to orgasm; masturbation and sexual intercourse. There are obviously more than these two types of orgasms, for example, sneezing is a type of orgasm. For the sake of this topic, I will limit my discussion to these two primary methods of orgasms. I would never ask you to give up sneezing which, interestingly enough, on the spiritual realm represents rejection of an idea or circumstance. Anyway, by giving up intercourse and masturbation, the Kundalini energy is not expended from the physical body via the second chakra and therefore is maintained within the physical body. This can cause great discomfort for any person withholding the energy who is not familiar with any of the spiritual techniques for redirecting this energy up the chakras. For those familiar with the techniques, once these energies are directed up the spinal column to the higher chakras, there are substantial spiritual benefits. The higher chakras begin to open, increasing the level of spiritual and physical consciousness of the individual. The spiritual mind in essence awakens. However, the energy must remain uncorrupted from lower nature thoughts and desires.

This is accomplished by maintaining a constant vigilance over your thought patterns and changing them when inappropriate or inconsistent with spiritual growth.

There are several ways in which to redirect this energy away from the lower nature thoughts of sexual fantasy and material desire to the upper chakras. The first way to redirect this energy is to immediately change your focus by changing your thought. Focus your mind on something positive. Think of someone you love in a non-sexual way or a place you love to be. The second way in which to redirect your thought is to repeat something positive over and over in your mind until the tension is relieved, preferably a spiritual mantra. By chanting something positive in your mind over and over, you may redirect your energy upwards. Prayer will redirect the energy up the spine, assuming that you are praying for something spiritually beneficial. It is also possible to raise the Kundalini energy through various breathing techniques, meditation, and yoga. Another potentially easier method that works well is to change what you are doing. Go for a long walk or exercise. You may be surprised by the extra energy you have. By altering your activity to something more positive, you will redirect the energy up your spine, virtually eliminating the lower nature fantasy or desire. I personally lost ten pounds in one month by holding this energy within my body. With the increased Kundalini energy I found that I had more energy and more self-control, and consequently ate less. If these techniques should fail, you are probably not tapping into your willpower or using the power of intention.

To redirect the Kundalini energy up your spine to a higher chakra, it is often helpful to focus on the third-eye chakra. To focus on the third-eye chakra you do not necessarily need to close your eyes. Simply place your attention between your eyebrows *within your mind* and the energy should be redirected to the third-eye chakra (or up to the crown chakra) if that is where you are focusing your attention. By redirecting energy to the third-eye chakra or crown chakra, you create opportunities for them to open. Please note that you should not be focusing on your third-eye chakra (or crown chakra) when your attention needs to be directed elsewhere, such as driving a car or crossing the street. I have found focusing on my inner third-eye chakra or crown chakra to be most effective when in meditation coupled with chanting. In my mind, I will sometimes chant a mantra such as *right thought, right mind* over and over while focusing on the third-eye (or crown chakra) until the sexual tension is gone. Feel free to make up your own mantra. Whichever mantra you feel most comfortable with, use it to your advantage.

The second chant I at times use is *Ohm Mani Padme Hum* (pronounced ohm-mah-nee-pahd-me-hum). It is a chant widely used in Tibetan Buddhism meaning the *Jewel of the Lotus* referring to the thousand-petaled lotus flower that symbolizes the mind's enlightenment in Eastern religions.[2] With either chant it is very helpful to visualize the Kundalini energy moving up your spinal column from the base chakra to the third-eye or the crown chakra. It is also helpful to visualize a lotus flower in your mind opening its petals as the energy reaches your crown chakra. A word of warning: If your heart chakra is not substantially open, meaning that you carry negativity within it, or are selfish or self-centered, then it would be advantageous to focus on your heart chakra first before attempting to raise the Kundalini energy to the third-eye chakra or crown chakra. It is dangerous to bypass the heart chakra if the heart chakra is not significantly open. It may lead to devastating results. Open your heart first. For most of us, mastering our emotions is the next step in our spiritual progression anyway.

Visualization during meditation is probably the most powerful technique for raising the Kundalini energy. During meditation, imagine the energy within your spine moving up your spinal column. If you can, imagine in your mind pulling this energy up, literally pulling it up. For me, the power of intent is crucial in pulling up the energy. I visualize Kundalini energy moving up my spine from the point associated with the base chakra to the higher chakras. My mind focuses on the intent of this action, which is to fully open my upper chakras. At times I can actually feel the energy move up my spinal column. I continue to use the power of intention to pull it up. At times I have difficulty pulling the Kundalini energy up to my throat chakra because of the limitations I have set for myself within my mind. Other times I can feel the energy reach the back of my throat chakra. Sometimes I feel it reach my third-eye chakra or even my crown chakra.

When the Kundalini energy reaches these chakras I often feel a tingling in the chakra area. I then imagine the chakra bursting open, fully accepting this glorious Holy Spirit or Christ Conscious energy. With continued practice I am sure I will experience more successes. It is like riding a bike. The more I rode my bike as a child the better I got at riding it; didn't you? And did you give up after falling down a couple of times? Hopefully not, because the reward of riding the bike was greater than the pain we experienced or the effort we expended. The same is true here. The incredible spiritual growth we will experience when we are successful is well worth the effort and discomfort of temporarily withdrawing from sexual orgasms.

By intentionally channeling the energies up my spine, I experienced miraculous events and received invaluable insights. However, I do not suggest trying to raise your Kundalini energy simply from reading this book alone. Raising your energy too fast may cause instability if you are not spiritually ready for it. To properly raise your consciousness, you must integrate the mind, body, and soul together. If your mind or body is polluted with anything substantially negative, such as negative thinking, raising your spiritual consciousness will be much more difficult. Even something as simple as changing your diet will make a huge difference in how fast you progress spiritually. I suggest becoming vegetarian or minimally eating more organic fruits and vegetables while cutting back on eating animal flesh. You should consult a doctor or nutritionist first just to be on the safe side.

Permanently withdrawing from all sexual activity in order to raise the Kundalini energies may not be beneficial or even possible for some people. As a matter of fact, only a select few should consider becoming *like a eunuch*. Withdrawing from all sexual activity in order to raise the Kundalini energies, without making a corresponding concerted effort toward spiritual growth, may jeopardize one's own wellbeing or the wellbeing of others. Abstinence will not lead to enlightenment in and of itself. This change in behavior must be accompanied by a change in thinking. If we attempt to raise the Kundalini energies through abstinence, but do not adequately prepare ourselves spiritually, these energies may become adulterated by sexual fantasies or inappropriate sexual actions. Having sex without an orgasm can lead to poor results as well. Correspondingly, lustful sex with no orgasm is simply lustful sex with no orgasm. In these cases, the increased energy often felt within the body will not lead to enlightenment due to the corruption of the spiritual energy. So it is necessary to understand that in raising the Kundalini energy we must also shift our perspective to one of integrated spirituality. We must channel this energy in positive ways. The final chapter in this book entitled *Immortal Life Yoga* will help you more fully integrate spirituality into your life whether or not you decide you are ready to raise your Kundalini energy temporarily or permanently by withdrawing from sexual orgasms.

Just as reincarnation is hinted within the Bible, so is the concept of Kundalini energy.

> "No one has ever gone to heaven except for the one who came down from heaven—the Son of Man. Just as Moses lifted up the snake in the desert, so the Son of Man must be lifted up, that everyone that believes in him may have eternal life." John 3:13-15

Is the phrase *Just as Moses lifted up the snake* referencing the rising Kundalini energy of Moses? If this is so, then the phrase *the Son of Man must be lifted up* is not only referencing His ascension, it symbolizes the rise in consciousness by abstaining from sexual relations! Just as Moses raised his Kundalini energy in the desert, we too must raise our Kundalini energies.

In Exodus, Moses warns his people while at Mount Sinai.

> "Then he said to the people 'Prepare yourselves for the third day. Abstain from sexual relations.'" Exodus 19:15

It is clear here that abstaining from sexual relations is particularly important for their spirituality.

Practicing techniques to raise the Kundalini energy in your body this lifetime will not guarantee enlightenment this lifetime. It may take lifetimes of practice. As mentioned earlier, how is it possible that Mozart was a child prodigy on the piano? Mozart most likely played the piano over a number of previous lifetimes, and it was this soul memory that allowed him to be an incredible piano player at such a young age. In other words, it took lifetimes of practice, and so it is for each of us.

Practically speaking, it may be nearly impossible to stop having orgasms. If you are in a committed relationship, your partner will surely put up a fuss. In such a case, I would not recommend giving up intercourse with your mate altogether, as that may lead to serious implications or worse, divorce. What I do recommend, however, is to practice the techniques for raising the Kundalini energy while intermittently suspending sexual relations. In other words, I recommend continuing your relationship with your significant other balancing both the sexual and spiritual energies within the body. Over time, you may discover a gradual increase in the spiritual energy in your body as you raise your sexual energy up your spine to higher chakras while correspondingly discovering a gradual decrease in the need or desire for sexual intercourse.

I would also recommend practicing the techniques of raising the sexual energies in your body to the higher chakras with your partner or you risk growing apart. Tantric sex may or may not help you in this regard. Tantric sex could possibly raise the Kundalini energy or simply lead to better sex. Alternatively, tantric sex without an orgasm may lead to unfilled desires, which then lead to frustration and fixation in the area of the genitals. You may even begin to feel physical pain in that area. The chapter on "Marriage and the Science of Procreation" discussed in detail how a committed couple of true intended companion soul mates can best work together with Kundalini energy, sexual union, and spiritual progression.

I would venture to say that most of us are not spiritually ready to give up having sexual orgasms altogether. Not everyone's consciousness is at a level where they can tolerate the intense increase in spiritual energy, or be ready and willing to give up sex. Some people's minds are much too polluted with desires for material nature (materialism) and sexuality. Withholding this energy in any person who possesses a lower consciousness would be like giving a young child a loaded gun or the keys to the car...not a good idea. Equally, when a person is in the throes of sexual desire, it is very difficult to remove one's self from that level of desire into a higher level of consciousness. It may be best to release the energy via an orgasm and begin again. You should not consider it a failure to have an orgasm while intermittently attempting to raise the Kundalini energies. Was it a failure to fall off your bike when you were just beginning to learn how to ride? No, it was not; it was an opportunity to try again. It may be best to simply take prolonged breaks from sexual union, with mutual consent, to concentrate on spiritual matters. It is vital for any successful Spirit-based relationship to assist each other as companion mates with emphasis on each other's spiritual progression.

As mankind evolves spiritually, the less we will have a need for lower energy chakra fulfillment. Mankind will eventually move up the ladder of consciousness to a place of consciousness where we will not have such intense desires for sexual pleasures. We will experience greater control over our emotions and sexual desires. At the same time we will experience a greater level of fulfillment with the energies associated with the higher chakras. Most importantly, we will experience a greater sense of love for all of mankind. Eventually we will rise above the need for sexual union as we progress toward enlightenment. This often occurs as we age and mature physically as well as spiritually. What is true in the spiritual realm is again reflected in the physical realm.

Personally, abstaining from all types of orgasms may be one of the hardest things I have ever tried to do in my lifetime. I find these energies to be extremely powerful with advantages and disadvantages. The advantages include a sense of heightened awareness, power, and greater levels of joy. The pitfalls on occasion may include a seemingly never-relenting need to have sexual intercourse or to masturbate. At times, I may have even been slightly inappropriate in my speech or actions; at the very least, my thoughts and desires were from time to time inconsistent with the intentions surrounding my desire for rapid spiritual development. Over time, as I gain additional control of these energies, I work with them in more spiritually balanced ways.

The first rule in working with Kundalini energy is to *do no harm*. Actually, the first rule in life should be to do no harm. If you are interested in beginning this process of withdrawing from all types of orgasms, I would suggest studying spiritually-based materials on Kundalini energy. I would also suggest working with a qualified Kundalini yoga instructor or a spiritual teacher you trust. Any instructor or teacher that suggests having sexual relations with you in order to master these energies is not a trustworthy person.

Once again, if you choose to use visualization techniques during meditation, the principal way to lift the Kundalini energy from the lower chakras (first and second) to your higher chakras is to visualize a channel of upward flowing energy from the base of your spine to the crown of your head. Alternatively you can visualize the spine within your back; it is your spinal column that carries the Kundalini or Holy Spirit energy up the spine and through the brain stem to the top of your head. Imagine pulling this energy up the spine using the power of intention traveling to the top of your head to your crown chakra. On the way up the spine, imagine the Kundalini energy opening the fourth, fifth, sixth, and finally the seventh chakras. I typically pass on visualizing the first, second and third chakras opening because they have already been mastered and consequently are already open. When you are finished, resume focusing on your third-eye chakra, which again is your Christ Center. If you have difficulty focusing on the third-eye and visualizing pulling up the Kundalini energy to your crown at the same time, then alternate between the two visualizations.

At times, when there is a great deal of sexual tension in your body, you may wish to focus more on pulling up the energy than focusing on the third-eye. Remember, to master a lower chakra, you must naturally be working on the energies of the next higher chakra. By this I mean for a soul to become enlightened, the third-eye chakra center energies must be mastered, and to do so the individual must also work with the energies associated with the next higher chakra, the crown chakra. That is why the Kundalini energy must eventually be pulled up to the crown chakra. However, you should not attempt to fully open your third-eye chakra or crown chakra until your heart chakra is open because it is vital that we come from a place of love when we work with the Kundalini energy. Without love, we cannot enter heaven as enlightened beings; we cannot possibly reach the state of enlightenment without love. Mastering the various emotions surrounding love is the next step in our evolutionary process in our eventual return to heaven.

CHAPTER 29

Planes of Consciousness

✧

A plane of consciousness is another level or dimension of reality. When the Godhead created the universe through the Christ Body, He created more than just the physical plane of existence. God created a multitude of universes, alternate spiritual dimensions, levels of existence, or realities. Heaven and hell are two primary examples of these planes of existence. Planes of consciousness may also include an infinite number of parallel universes, physical dimensions, or worlds.

> "According to Vedic cosmology, there are countless universes, which are clustered together like foam on the surface of a Casual Ocean. The universes are separated from each other by the shell that envelopes each universe. Although the universes are clustered together, interactions between the universes are impossible. Each universe is completely protected by an enormous shell. Thus, each universe has a boundary. The universe is ball-shaped and surrounded by an eight-fold shell. This shell is composed of primeval material elements in their most subtle manifestation. The shell consists of eight spherical layers in which each successive material element is manifested and stored. If we penetrate the universal shell consisting of the eight spherical layers, we will enter the universal globe and find a hollow region containing all of the inhabited planets."[1]

I believe that there are a minimum of eight planes of consciousness or planes of existence in our universe, one associated with each of the eight chakras presented earlier. The eight planes of consciousness in all likelihood correlate to the eight spherical layers noted above in Vedic cosmology. Either way, the names of the eight planes of consciousness important to our spiritual evolution are as follows, cited here in order of greatest density to least density: physical plane, etheric plane, psychic plane, emotional plane, mental plane, spirit plane, Plane of Logos, and the transcendental plane. Each plane of consciousness within our universe has particular energies associated with them that our souls must master before we can graduate to the next plane of consciousness, similar to how educational institutions operate. Each plane represents a grade or class that we must pass before we can move to the next higher grade or class.

In the physical form, we exist in the densest plane of physicality; earth. However, even though we live on the earth plane we simultaneously live in an alternative dimensional reality connected to our spiritual nature. Overall, I believe that we currently live in the fourth dimension in terms of our spiritual consciousness and awareness. We are then operating in the fourth dimensional reality within the densest physical realm of earth. Since spiritually speaking we are in the fourth dimension, we must consequently live in a four-dimensional physical world. The four dimensions within physicality that we are consciously aware of given our spiritual awareness are height, width, depth, and time. As a result, in the physical sense, we are in a space-time dimensional reality. When we enter the fifth dimension associated with the mind, we will physically (while on earth) discover a new additional dimensional reality.

Once in the fifth dimension of this earth plane, we will have opened our hearts more fully, and will be utilizing our hearts and minds to a greater extent than we are currently utilizing them. In opening our hearts and minds we will become more psychic. I believe that this is the new fifth dimensional reality. So, when we are in a physical body, we exist in the lowest dimensional realm of physicality, but simultaneously we exist within the spiritual dimension correlating to our level of conscious development. As we continue to grow in consciousness, we move into higher dimensions of consciousness whether in body on earth, or elsewhere.

It's not that higher dimensional realities are not already present around us, we are simply not aware of them. As we grow in consciousness we become consciously aware of them. In this way growing in consciousness could predominantly be defined as growing in awareness. As we grow in awareness, our souls vibrate at a higher rate. The souls on earth that already vibrate at higher levels of consciousness than that of the fourth dimension we consider to be advanced souls or older souls. They really are not older in terms of age but rather in terms of their spiritual development. Even though they are more advanced, in all likelihood they are here to assist us as we transition to the next dimension. Their presence here serves to raise the overall vibration of the planet and may make our overall transition to the fifth dimension more bearable.

Once a soul leaves the body and the physical dimension of earth, the soul returns to the spiritual dimension consistent to where the soul currently vibrates as represented by its own spiritual consciousness. Each plane of existence or consciousness is an alternative or parallel dimension that has a corresponding level of spiritual vibration or development. As an obvious example, heaven would be associated with a much higher plane of spiritual consciousness than hell would be. In the aggregate sense, within the physical plane we as human beings can progress into the higher spiritual dimensions as humanity progresses spiritually. We grow in consciousness aggregately as well as individually as souls within this physical plane, obviously some much faster than others. The aggregate consciousness is called *group consciousness.*

The development of soul consciousness and group consciousness does not occur in concrete steps. The soul does not need to necessarily complete the lessons related to one particular chakra (one dimension) before it can begin another lesson associated with a higher chakra and a higher dimension. Generally speaking, there is an overall mastery of the energies associated with each chakra from the first chakra to the seventh chakra and the spiritual lessons associated with each plane of existence as the soul develops spiritually. Spiritual development occurs gradually as *a rising stream of consciousness* which is also one of the definitions for the Holy Spirit and Kundalini energy.

Our soul is a point of consciousness that acts like a stream of consciousness; therefore, I believe that every soul has a specific body, whether it is a physical body, subtle body, or an immortal body that exists in all planes of consciousness simultaneously. In this way, the soul may be working on perfecting the energies associated with any chakra within the physical body while at the same time coexisting in another dimension of reality or multiple dimensions of reality. One might even say that every soul exists everywhere and is omnipresent because of the Universal Law of Unity or All is One. However, the soul is seemingly unaware of this fact due to a lack of consciousness and is only aware of the one dimension he or she resides in at the moment.

Because of this ability for multidimensionality, a soul may be learning one particular lesson about love, which is associated with the fourth chakra, while simultaneously learning a lesson about speaking the truth, which is a lesson associated with the fifth chakra. Assuming this is true, an aspect of each soul could be existing in the fourth dimension and the fifth dimension at the same time, not to mention all of the other dimensions. In this way, the soul is making strides in several dimensions at the same time. In fact, it is necessary for a soul to be working on mastering the next highest chakra in order to perfect the energies of the chakra just below it. For example, the concrete mind function associated with the fifth chakra is necessary to perfect the chakra energies associated with that of the heart, that of the fourth chakra. In all cases, the next higher level of consciousness assists with perfecting the energies associated with a lower level of consciousness.

"We can't solve a problem at the same level of thinking that created it."
Albert Einstein

Again, we must rise above the problem to see the problem, to understand the problem, and then to solve the problem. Now let's look at each specific plane of consciousness in order from lowest to highest.

The lowest plane of existence is the *physical world*. Not surprisingly, you might have assumed hell was the lowest plane, but in reality it is the physical world. The physical world is the lowest plane not because it is hell but because it is the densest of all the planes of consciousness. The physical plane of earth is also considered to be the elemental world or the nature world. The physical plane of consciousness is what we experience every day. Living in the physical world we often assume it to be our only reality, but it is obviously not. In this world, as in all planes of consciousness, we create initially by our thoughts; these thoughts then lead to an emotion; emotions lead to an action; and by action we create results.

In the physical world, the amount of time and energy expended between an initial thought and the end result is greatest due to the level of density in this plane as compared to the other planes of existence. It is because of this denseness that the physical plane is the most grueling and arduous plane of all and seemingly the most real. This denseness of the physical plane is also the reason that souls learn their greatest spiritual lessons here. The other planes of existence (where souls are not in a physical body) are less dense, and consequently the lessons learned there are not as quickly absorbed into the soul memory as an experience. It would be like playing a video game versus actually experiencing it in the reality of this earth plane. In this instance, the experience of form is the key. It is as if the earth is our testing ground or school to learn the lessons we wish to learn. Because this is the densest of all the form worlds, it can be quite wearisome at times to be here on earth, as I am sure you will agree.

The physical realm on the surface seems to be primarily about survival of the fittest. I believe it is the only plane of consciousness in which we require the elements of air, fire, water, and earth (food) to survive. On the physical plane, lesser developed souls will most often seek to satisfy the material desires of their five senses through their thoughts, emotions, and actions. Less advanced souls are only conscious of this dimension and therefore they do not give other dimensions as much as a second thought. Conversely, spiritually developed souls will often have thoughts and feelings associated with a sense of a greater reality and a deeper purpose to life because on a soul level they are more in touch with their inner god.

The next higher level or plane of consciousness is called the *etheric plane*. Some people refer to this as *the other side*. The etheric plane is a very interesting plane of existence. This plane of consciousness is the closest to the physical plane. The energetic barrier between the physical world and the etheric world is commonly referred to as a *thin veil*. This thin veil is frequently pierced by intuitive or psychic people. The etheric plane is associated with our etheric subtle body. A subtle body is an actual body and you should think of it in that way, although it is much less dense than the physical body. The etheric body aspect of a soul has its presence on the etheric plane. When we see ghosts (trapped spirits), we are seeing their etheric body.

The etheric plane is associated with creativity. The etheric body desires to create, and due to its connectivity to the physical body, it is able to relay these desires to the physical body. Once the desire to create is received by the physical body through the second chakra, it is converted into creative energy. This energy can be expressed in numerous ways: art, music, writing, etc. It can also lead to a desire for intercourse and/or procreation. Likewise the creative energy we desire to express, if polluted by negative desires, can be used for destructive purposes such as graffiti, or even rape, which is a horribly negative misuse of the creative energies that are inherent within each of us.

The etheric plane also includes the fascinating world of imagination. Everything that exists on this earth plane was first created on a higher plane of consciousness. The etheric plane is accordingly the place of mythological creatures. Through the imagination, a soul can create a unicorn or a gremlin or a fairy or any other mystical creature it would like. While in the physical realm, we tap into this creative imagery and bring these creatures into being through stories, radio, and television. In reality, we are simply tapping into another reality or dimension where they really do exist, but here on the earth plane we call it our imagination.

The etheric plane is also where our dreams exist. When we dream, our soul is actually experiencing an alternative dimension within the etheric plane of consciousness, because when we sleep our consciousness slips into a higher dimension. Our soul then creates whatever scenario it wishes because it can do so. The soul can bring anything it saw during its awake time into its dream time whether the mind was consciously aware of it or not. Dreaming on the etheric plane is just as real as the awake world of earth; again, all planes of consciousness are real worlds. Dreams are real worlds created by our soul within the etheric plane that can be shared with other souls whether alive on earth or otherwise existing on other realms or planes of consciousness. Therefore, in our dreams we can once again be rejoined with our deceased loved ones. In this plane they are as real as they were on this plane of consciousness. However, they may take alternate forms. In whatever form they choose, they may be assisting us in some very specific way; or they may be possibly notifying us that they are content on the other side. Only by interpreting the dream can we begin to figure out the intended message of the dream.

The etheric plane is sometimes called the *underworld* even though it is not really under our world. The underworld is also not hell, as one might immediately assume, but could be if the soul creates it. On the etheric plane we can recreate our previous life on earth and all its activities, pleasures, and conversely pain if that is what we feel we deserve, but of course only in etheric form. It would be more like a hologram we created, or like a dream. It would be *real*, but not as dense as the reality we create on this earth plane of consciousness. We can also recreate our addictions if we desire or need to recreate them to serve some purpose. Of course, there are limitations to what we can create in the etheric plane because what we create is constrained by the level of the soul's spiritual development. If we were enlightened, we could create any reality we wish to create on any plane of consciousness. As we progress beyond the etheric plane, the planes of consciousness are much more difficult to explain as they become more esoteric and consequently less solid in terms of form and energy.

The next plane of existence beyond the etheric plane is the *psychic plane*. Here the *feeling subtle body*, which is simply another aspect of our soul in an alternate plane of existence, works in conjunction with the third chakra so that the physical body can experience feelings. The third plane of consciousness is also associated with the lower psychic energies. This is where we receive feelings of intuition. Have you ever noticed certain people feeling sad without them having given you any indication they are sad? What happened was you tapped into their thoughts or feelings of sadness in a general way via a psychic awareness. This is possible because we are all connected.

The feeling subtle body desires to experience feelings and sends these desires to the physical body. Once the desire to experience feelings is received in the physical body through the third chakra, the physical body seeks to satiate these desires. This energy leads to action, which in turn results in feelings. Feelings such as sadness, gladness, affection, and anger are created by this subtle body as a result of the actions of the physical body and are transferred back to the physical body via the third chakra. As you might be discovering here, there is a constant interactive process between the physical body and the subtle bodies. Overall, feelings represent a higher level of conscious evolvement than that of creativity, but not as high as emotions, which are experienced on the *emotional plane* of consciousness.

The *emotional plane* of consciousness is tied to the fourth chakra. Here, the *emotional subtle body* in this plane of existence works in conjunction with the physical body to experience emotions. This plane of consciousness is also associated with the higher psychic energies such as telepathy and telekinesis. I believe that this is also where we receive visions. Many people today have visions but do not recognize them as such, much less understand them. They consider them to be just vivid dreams and ignore their significance. The more open the heart chakra, the more psychic we become. The heart chakra should be open before opening the chakras located above the heart chakra, otherwise we will have psychic powers not entrenched in love. If the heart is not open, the psychic powers we will have developed will more than likely be used for negative, self-serving purposes.

The emotional subtle body desires to experience emotions and sends these desires to the physical body. Once the desire to experience emotions is received in the physical body through the fourth chakra, the physical body seeks to satisfy these desires. This energy leads to some type of action that in turn results in the creation of emotions. Emotions such as love and compassion and conversely negative emotions such as hate, fear, and depression are created by the emotional subtle body as a result of the actions taken by the physical body. These emotions are then transferred back to the physical body via the fourth chakra.

The fifth plane of consciousness is the level of consciousness associated with the *concrete mind*. This plane of consciousness is called the *mental plane* and is tied to the fifth chakra. This plane of existence works in conjunction with the physical body to experience lower mental functions versus higher mental functions, which are experienced on the sixth plane of consciousness. The subtle body on this level desires to experience mental functions consistent with the concrete mind and sends these desires to the physical body. Once this desire is received in the physical body through the fifth chakra, the physical body seeks to satisfy the desire. This desire leads to physical action (or thought processes), which in turn results in concrete thoughts. Concrete thoughts are created by this subtle body as a result of the actions of the physical body and are transferred back to the physical body via the fifth chakra. What is important to remember here is the interactive play between the physical body and subtle bodies. The chakras are the conduits that connect the physical body with the spiritual subtle bodies.

The fifth plane of consciousness deals with thoughtful expression and communication. In the fifth dimension of consciousness we will learn to master the lesson of truthfulness. In this plane of consciousness, we will develop a deeper relationship with our divine self and soul (sole) purpose. In the fifth plane, as mental and psychic awareness increases, we will have increased contact with spirits on the other side of the veil. As our minds expand, we will become more and more conscious. Our spiritual memory will increase as unconscious thoughts become more and more conscious. Some of these thoughts will include past life memories making the concept of time seem less real. Because our intuition will be much more developed we will know when people lie to us. As our fifth chakra continues to open more and more, our sixth chakra will increasingly open as well.

The sixth chakra is associated with the *spirit plane* in terms of a soul's increasing level of consciousness. This plane of consciousness is associated with the *abstract* mind. Here the corresponding subtle body in this plane of existence works in conjunction with the physical body to experience higher mental function. The subtle body desires to experience higher mental functions consistent with the abstract mind and sends these desires to the physical body. Once the desire to experience abstract thoughts is received in the physical body through the sixth chakra, the physical body seeks to satisfy these desires. This higher form of desire leads to mental action (or physical action), which in turn results in abstract thoughts. Abstract thoughts are created by the corresponding subtle body and are transferred back to the physical body via the sixth chakra. Many of the great discoveries originated on this plane of consciousness and were then shared with the souls on the physical plane through the use of their own sixth sense.

An individual that has mastered the sixth plane of consciousness, having been completely filled by the Holy Spirit, is considered Christ Conscious. This again is the All-Seeing Eye level of consciousness. In fact, all of the senses have been perfected at this level of consciousness, including all psychic abilities. At this level, souls in their immortal bodies maintain their separate identity and separate personality even though they understand in reality there is no true separation. This could also be referred to as Buddha-Consciousness or Krishna-Consciousness because at this level of consciousness all enlightened souls vibrate at the same rate. They are all equal in their spiritual development. I believe that all enlightened beings are consequently equal in their level of consciousness and therefore equal in stature as fully realized Christs.

As fully realized Christs, full memory as *divine knowledge* has been restored to the soul. As enlightened souls we understand everything. There is no longer an unconscious mind as everything has been made conscious by the Holy Spirit, God's divine memory. Within the spirit plane, souls are consciously aware of God, but because they have retained their individuated conscious identity they are still considered separate from the Impersonal God. The soul in the sixth plane, since it is still separate, may not be fully experiencing its own omnipresence. Either way, what is created on this level of consciousness is beauty beyond explanation. There are only two higher levels of consciousness that I am aware of beyond that of an individualized Christ Conscious being.

The seventh chakra is associated with the *Plane of Logos*. Here, souls that have elected to give up their personal identity completely merge back into the Christ Body. They are no longer separate individualized souls. They surrendered their soul and personality so that they could fully return to the one Christ Body. The soul is once again completely immersed in the Supreme Personality of God as the Oversoul and is hence omnipresent. The senses no longer exist because they are unnecessary. Here exists only a constant state of bliss. Here the Christ Body directly knows the Impersonal God because it is the Personal God. It is form and energy in its own perfection as part of the one Trinity. To explain this plane of consciousness beyond what I explained previously in the chapter on the Trinity would be like trying to describe the unimaginable. As a side note, I originally had another name for this plane of consciousness; however I changed it to the Plane of Logos because I was directed to do so in a dream. It is also the reason I capitalize this plane of consciousness.

The eighth chakra is linked to the *transcendental plane* of consciousness. To reach this level of consciousness, all form and energy must be relinquished by the soul or rather collectively by the Oversoul. If or when this occurs, the Oversoul's consciousness (Spirit) is reabsorbed back into the Impersonal God (as pure consciousness). The Christ Body would no longer exist, as this aspect of the Trinity represents energy and form. The Christ Principle would also be gone. This may occur within physicality as a collapsing universe. The only *Being* remaining would be darkness as unmanifested pure consciousness, which is the original state of God. The Oversoul would have merged back into the infinite Nothingness or Void, back to the realm of absolute consciousness and infinite possibilities. The Holy Spirit in this plane exists as a possibility only and is therefore latent within the Impersonal God because absolutely *no thing* exists, literally and figuratively. It is the plane of *no-thing-ness*. It represents the complete extinction of the Personal God or Oversoul as form and energy. There no longer is any division or separation from the Impersonal God. The Christ Body would have been reabsorbed back into the unmanifested Impersonal God and no longer exists on any spiritual plane of existence of form and energy. It has rejoined itself into the infinite world of possibilities as God the Father.

So the rise of the individual consciousness of a soul is witnessed through the development of the chakras and the individual planes of consciousness. For example, a soul in physical form first seeks to master the basic energies of the body and is primarily concerned about survival (first chakra energies). When those energies are mastered and satisfied, the soul moves up the chakra ladder to the next chakra. In the second chakra, mankind is concerned about creativity and the act of procreation, from which sexual pleasure is derived. In the third chakra or plane of consciousness, we witness in mankind an attempt to master his/her feelings. In the fourth plane of consciousness, mankind attempts to master the emotional body, i.e. emotions. In the fifth plane of consciousness, mankind attempts to master lower thought forms within the concrete mind. In the sixth plane of consciousness, which is directly connected to the energies of the sixth chakra, mankind attempts to master the abstract mind. Upon accomplishing this, we become Christ Conscious. In the seventh plane we reunite with the Christ Body as one body of consciousness still in form but surrendering our separateness as individual souls. In the eighth plane, we surrender all form and energy and return to the Infinite Supreme Consciousness.

Thus far I have made the assumption that there are only eight dimensions or planes of consciousness with the eighth plane of consciousness representing the Father as absolute pure consciousness, the Impersonal God. The eighth plane of consciousness is not a plane of form. However, if quantum physics is truly representative of the spiritual realm and if I am correct about there in reality being twelve dimensions (science has postulated eleven dimensions thus far, and possibly a twelfth dimension), then there may perfectly well be twelve dimensions and I must revise my model hypothesizing the existence of only eight dimensions. These additional realms would be beyond anyone's comprehension, beyond our wildest imagination, due to our lack of conscious development. The additional dimensions may be a part of the current form universe or they may be additional dimensions of form yet to be created. The additional universes may also be dimensions of consciousness without form. Either way, rest assured one day all these things will be known and we will know the number of dimensions that exist in our universe as well as the number of dimensions that exist in the multitude of other universes God created (other heavens).

CHAPTER 30

Dreams and Out-of-Body Travel

֍

In sleep or in *dreamtime* as the Aboriginal people call it, souls will travel to other planes of creation or dimensions. While asleep, we can travel to substantially higher planes of consciousness based on how spiritually advanced we are as souls. A soul, or that portion of the soul that is traveling, can be spiritually locked out of a higher plane of consciousness if the soul is not conscious enough to be allowed entrance. If a soul is *soul conscious* consistent to the third dimension, the soul would not be able to travel to the fourth dimension while traveling out-of-body. Dreaming, as stated in the previous chapter, occurs in the second plane or etheric plane of consciousness. Consequently, dreaming is very similar to out-of-body travel in that our soul leaves the physical body and enters the etheric plane of consciousness.

Visions and out-of-body travel typically occur in higher planes of consciousness than that of the physical plane. After a soul has traveled to these higher dimensions while the physical body sleeps, it is possible to awake with an acute awareness or insight of substantial magnitude. It is possible to problem solve or learn valuable lessons at any level when we travel outside of our physical body. Our *spirit guides* have immediate access to us on the other side of the veil. Some people call them guardian angels, but they are really our soul family that has decided to stay back on the other side to support us. We can also have conversations with them in other dimensions. We can have conversations with other souls traveling out-of-body as well when the physical body is asleep. I have on a number of occasions awakened with a memory of a conversation with a friend or loved one also traveling out-of-body. Oddly enough, upon awakening, they too recall having had a conversation with me while they slept.

Our *spiritual teachers* are usually more advanced beings than our guides and they can also come down to assist us if called upon. I say "come down" because they reside on a plane of consciousness higher than our own. They come from a much higher plane, typically not lower than the sixth plane of consciousness, because they are enlightened beings. They come down to us because we are energetically locked out from their plane of consciousness and cannot rise up to them. They are genuinely willing to assist us with anything that involves the development of our consciousness. Some mornings I will awake feeling completely exhausted, as if I never slept, which is a clue that I have been traveling out-of-body. Also, I will not remember dreams because while traveling out-of-body a soul will not dream.

Sleep is generally a time for the body to rest and rebuild its energy levels. The soul as consciousness does not need to rest. When we fall asleep we gradually lose our sense of physical self. Sleep is a form of death to our five senses. We then enter the middle realm between waking and sleep. I call it the middle realm because there is no sense of self and no thing seems to exist. I liken it to experiencing the Void or existing within a state of nothingness. The middle realm is where we can receive visions because our sixth sense is fully activated. Visions are similar in form to, but not the same as, dreams. Visions are very vivid and are messages much like an abbreviated dream would be. Visions are usually brief and often come to us symbolically like dreams.

Out-of-body experiences occur in real time, whereas dreams are not sequential in terms of time. When you have an out-of-body experience, it means that have you passed into a higher plane of consciousness beyond the middle realm and beyond dreamtime. Those people who recall out-of-body experiences would typically be considered an elevated, spiritually conscious, more receptive soul. Some individuals have elected to shut out all out-of-body memories either because they are fearful of the experience or because memory of such an event would create a form of *spiritual ego*.

Recurring dreams may be memories of a past lifetime. As a child I dreamed of being a prisoner of war. In my dream, I was being held prisoner in a chicken coop. The coop had previously served as a farmer's chicken coop and the barbed wire fence that surrounded the coop was the original fencing. In the dream, I dug a hole with a board I broke off from the coop and eventually crawled out. I escaped only to be later caught and killed by an Asian platoon of soldiers out on patrol. I believe that this is a memory of a former life. I also believe that previous to being captured, I had fallen in love with an Asian woman and had a baby with her. The baby was eventually murdered by its own people because it was biracial. I believe that I have met this same woman and daughter from the previous lifetime already in this lifetime. They too concur that is an actual past life memory that we all shared together.

In the dream world, our soul creates any scenario our soul wishes to create. Our soul is the ultimate creator of our dreams. Dreams in which people are aware that they are sleeping and consciously create within the dream are referred to as *lucid dreams*. Lucid dreaming is a higher more conscious form of dreaming. We can also use the dreamtime to sort out our personal problems or disturbing events of the day. Maybe most importantly, we may also use dreamtime to receive messages from our soul. The problem is that there are many types of dreams. It is up to each individual person to figure out which dreams are which. A heavy meal before bedtime may also affect the quality of our dreams. Disturbances within the physical body may affect our dreamtime. Overall, I believe our dreams are tools for us to utilize if we choose to use them as such. They can also help us sort and file our daily thoughts into our conscious or subconscious memory.

Some dreams are fear dreams, representing our fears associated with our awake life. Fear in this respect could contribute to the negative dreams that we manifest in the etheric plane, much like the fear we manifest in our awake life contributes to the negativity we experience on the earthly plane. Some dreams contain warnings. Some dreams simply help us process the day's events. Some dreams provide guidance. Sometimes I will even ask my higher self (my soul) a specific question before I go to bed, and subsequently my dreams will provide me guidance. Because we dream in symbols, it is rare to receive a straightforward message. If you ever receive a straightforward message, chances are it was not a dream. It may have been a vision or an out-of-body experience. If this is the case, it would be wise to follow the advice. Further, dreams may provide you with a warning about your health. At times, deceased family members may visit you in a dream to put you at ease about their recent transition to the other side. Other dreams may be prophetic.

However, dream analysis can often lead to misinterpretation. Rarely do we have only one issue at a time in our life. Therefore dreams that attempt to provide direction to us on an issue may actually be providing direction to us on some other issue altogether. When this occurs, I will ask another question to test the answer I previously interpreted from a dream. In this way I can better determine if the dream is really addressing the question I asked or if it is addressing some other concern I have in my life. Analyzing dreams is a lot of work. However, I look at them as messages from my higher self. At this point in my life I feel it would be inconceivable for me not to at least attempt to understand what message my soul is trying to get across to me. It would be like not opening a letter I received from God. Encrypted or not, I am going to open it. Many of the premises I make in this book were derived from an awareness I received while in the sleep state, a vision, or an out-of-body experience. Often I would take these revelations and verify them by asking a question before I went back to sleep. I would nearly always receive some additional clarification or verification. Sometimes I would have to ask the same question over and over until I reached a point of certainty about the answer.

Let me explain how I analyze my dreams. The first thing I do is keep a notebook and pen next to my bed. I write down my dreams immediately upon waking up, even if it is in the middle of the night. I don't wait until the morning because I will often forget them. I avoid turning on the light even if I am writing in the middle of the night and have subsequently become accustomed to writing in darkness. I find it is best for me not to stir too much upon waking, as movement hampers the process of remembering my dreams. It is easiest for me to recollect my dreams if I relax for a brief time while remaining in the same position I was in when I first awoke. Taking vitamin B complex stimulates memory and helps me to remember my dreams. When I am ready, I write down all of the symbols, the story as it unfolds in the order as I dream it, and how I felt and how others felt in the dream. In the morning, I look up each symbol and feeling in my dream interpretation book and associate them all back to me. Carl Jung suggested that every person in our dream is a different aspect of our own self and should be interpreted as such. How profound is that? Given that we are really one Oversoul, Jung may not have realized just how right he was.

There are numerous dream interpretation books available at book stores. I use *The Dreamer's Dictionary* by Lady Stearn Robinson & Tom Corbett.[1] Sometimes the symbol interpretations in this book are not very accurate or the dream symbol is too complex for the book. Sometimes the dream symbol is so bizarre that I would be surprised to see any interpretation for the symbol in any book. I occasionally use Hyperdictionary.com to interpret my dreams. This website will often have a dream interpretation in addition to the standard definition. Dream symbols for the most part are universal. In other words, if I dream the same symbol as you, chances are that the symbol will have the same meaning for you as it does for me. However, different dream books may have different interpretations for the same symbol, further complicating the process.

When looking up the dream symbol in the book, I consider which meaning best fits what is transpiring in my life at that moment, as sometimes there are alternative meanings to choose from. Sometimes I am forced to use my intuition to choose which meaning is correct for me regardless what the book suggests is correct. Some symbols serve as prophetic warnings about my future. Sometimes I dream about some event that occurred during the day, and my mind is simply processing it. Overall I try not to worry too much if I don't understand the meaning of my dream right away. Occasionally I will receive an insight much later on that helps put my dream into perspective, or subsequent dreams that provide additional information. Sometimes it will take two or three dreams before I can figure out the message my soul was attempting to send me. If I am unclear about a dream upon first awakening, I will ask myself, "What is this dream trying to tell me?" and then pay particular attention to the first thought that comes to mind. Sometimes I am not able to accurately interpret a dream until an additional event occurs in my life. Then I am able to go back and in retrospect understand the dream a little better based on what just happened. Keeping a dream journal allows me to review my overall success in correctly interpreting my dreams.

However, taking dream interpretation too seriously can be risky. It is far from an exact science. Further, the future is not predetermined, and it is our free will that reigns. Recurring dreams can be either past life memories or they could be issues we are refusing to address or some fear we can't seem to get beyond. Although it is rare, it is not unheard of to have dreams that are warnings for other people. By analyzing your dreams every day, you will get much better at it over time and subsequently they will become more and more useful.

Nightmares are typically fear dreams but should not be ignored because they at times are prophetic warnings. I once canceled a vacation to Hawaii because I had recurring dreams about car accidents while my girlfriend (at the time) continually dreamed of planes crashing. Days before our vacation, a motorcycle ran into me on the highway. My dreams continued to warn me of yet another car accident to come. In addition, I turned on the news just in time to hear about a man mourning the death of his wife; she had fallen off a cliff while vacationing in Maui. Was it just a coincidence?

On the same day we cancelled our trip, two owls flew over our heads while we sat in a hot tub. I thought this very strange because I rarely if ever see owls flying inside the city limits. However, we both immediately recognized its significance. We believed that God was sending us a symbolic message; that we were wise to cancel our trip. Of course, we are not sure if there would have actually been a plane crash or not, but we were confident that something very negative would have happened to one of us had we decided to go on our vacation. We decided *better safe than sorry*.

I believe that God sends us cryptic messages all the time. What we see or hear during the day may hold within it an important message. If something happens that is quite out of the ordinary, take heed of it. If you hear the same message repeated over and over, pay attention to it. You may hear something on the radio or on television similar to the message I heard about the man who lost his wife in Hawaii. You may see something completely out of the ordinary and that may be a symbolic message. You may see an exceptionally large quantity of one particular thing, something very peculiar, or out of season, and it could be a message sent to you from Spirit. They say if you hear something said three times in a short period of time, it may be a message from Spirit. Of course I am not suggesting that everything we see is necessarily a sign or a message from Spirit; rather that we can receive messages from Spirit in the strangest of ways and that being open to these messages might be advantageous. I call these obscure messages from Spirit *day-dreams*. I call them day-dreams because these messages are presented to us in the form of symbolism identical to our dreamtime symbols; so use the dream book symbols to interpret these daytime messages as well.

Just as an urgent message may be delivered to you by means of a symbol, an *earth angel* may come to you in a time of significant need to point you in the right direction. An earth angel is a term I made up to describe an incarnated soul (on this physical plane of existence) that pops into our lives at just the right time to give us just the right advice. An earth angel typically aids us by pointing us in the right direction for our continued conscious development. Sometimes they give us advice. Other times they may act on our behalf. They may or may not be in our soul family, though more than likely they are a member. It is crucial that we remain open to these messages from God; but remember, they can come in some pretty strange packages and in some pretty extraordinary ways. When we remain open to these messages we tap into synchronicity.

While writing this book, I had another incredible out-of-body experience. I remember it vividly. I was once again in the middle realm between sleep and wakefulness when I left my body. In all of my previous out-of-body experiences, I do not recall actually leaving my body, but this time it was different. I felt my soul leave my body through my third-eye chakra associated with the sixth plane of consciousness. It was like passing through a portal. Once through the portal, I found myself suspended in air. It was dark, but I had no problem seeing the magnitude of what lay in front of me. It was sort of like being in outer space. I saw in the distance what appeared to be stars. I could also sense a presence behind me or maybe even multiple entities. What was most amazing was what I felt and said. I said in complete awe, "Time has stopped. There is no time here!" And that was it. I then returned to my body.

Now when I say that was all there was to it, I am not including how the out-of-body experience affected me afterwards. To be honest, it created a significant disturbance in my thought processes. I had a difficult time functioning in a world that no longer felt like reality. The earth plane no longer felt like the real thing. The dimension I had just visited was to me a truer reality. The dimension I had visited felt more like heaven than I had ever felt before! As a direct result, I felt less motivated to participate in the physical world and all of its associated activities. This lasted for a number of weeks before I was able to re-acclimate and get re-motivated in this plane of consciousness.

This experience caused me an additional dilemma. I stated in the previous chapter that a soul can be spiritually locked out of a higher plane of consciousness if the soul is not spiritually evolved enough to be allowed entrance. Since the sixth plane of consciousness is consistent with being enlightened, I theoretically should not have been allowed entrance to this particular plane of consciousness because I do not believe that I am an enlightened soul. I have since come up with a couple of possible explanations as to why I was allowed to enter this plane. First, I could actually be an enlightened soul that came to earth to assist mankind in the spiritual transition to the fifth dimension. If this is the case, I would necessarily have agreed to not remember that I am a fully conscious enlightened being on the other side. As an enlightened soul, I would have access to all planes of consciousness whether in physical form or not. I doubt that this possibility is the correct explanation, even though it would be nice to think it true.

The second possibility is that I was wrong about a lower vibrational soul being locked out of higher planes of consciousness on the other side. Maybe in reality all souls have access to all planes but feel most comfortable with the plane in which they resonate in terms of their own soul's vibration. In other words, we *do* have access to all planes, but feel out of place in planes in which we do not resonate. Less developed souls born into higher dimensional planes would feel technologically, emotionally, spiritually, and maybe even physically out of touch with that reality. The soul may feel completely lost, as if it was taking a calculus class before it understood basic mathematics. Much higher developed souls in lower dimensions may also feel out of place or bored and suffer all sorts of abnormalities such as ADD (Attention Deficit Disorder) or Autism. They may become hostile and may turn inward due to an inability to cope with the lower dimensional frequencies.

Conversely, more advanced beings born into a much lower dimension such as ours may take on key roles in the world as our political, social, religious, or spiritual leaders. Their mere presence in our dimension raises our overall vibrational rate, making our transition to the next dimension hopefully a little less problematic. Finally, it is possible that I was allowed temporary entrance into the sixth plane of consciousness by exiting my third-eye chakra as a gift so that I could see firsthand that there are planes of consciousness directly tied to the chakras. Any way you look at it, I am without doubt that the chakras are directly tied to the various planes of consciousness within this universe. However, it is our ego that limits our expansive thinking and consequently our spiritual growth. Why is it that so often we allow our ego to limit what we believe to be possible with God and further delay the time it takes for us to return to heaven?

CHAPTER 31

Mind, Body, Soul, and Ego

The Holy Spirit can present itself in many forms. Let's look at water as an analogy. When a body of water is frozen, or in cubes, it's called ice while water in the form of vapor is often referred to as mist or fog. Water in a narrow flowing channel is called a river or a stream. Water collectively, as in a large body, is called a lake, sea, or ocean. Water falling from the sky is generally called rain while frozen water falling from the sky is called snow or hail. Water flowing over an embankment is called a waterfall. In one sense, water is our lifeblood. We cannot go more than a week or so without water before perishing. It also serves many functions. We wash with water. We cleanse our body of impurities by drinking it. It is clear that water comes in many forms and has many names and functions. This is equally true for the Holy Spirit.

As mentioned by me a couple of times now, the Holy Spirit is the universal life force that keeps us alive. However, if we limit our focus to the universal life force found within the spinal column that supports the organ functions of the physical body, it is called Kundalini or Chi energy. You can also look at the Holy Spirit as the creative energy of the Christ Body or the Impersonal God. As such, it is the energy that breaks down form and creates form. In this instance you might refer to the feminine nature of the Holy Spirit as Mother Nature, Mother Earth, or the Divine Mother. As a point of consciousness, the individual soul is the Christ in us. As a point of collective consciousness, the aggregate soul is the Christ Body. However, when you consider the soul as a stream of consciousness, it is the Holy Spirit itself in us. The unadulterated Holy Spirit feeds the soul because, at the highest level, it *is* the soul in each of us. In a way, *we are what we eat*. Or in this case, *we are what feeds us*. Our soul is actually both Holy Spirit energy and our immortal body within the Christ Body because of the Universal Law All is One. In other words, since in reality we are not separate, we are both Holy Spirit Consciousness and Christ Consciousness. Just as we are not the Christ Body but rather a portion of it, we are not the Holy Spirit but rather a portion of it.

The Holy Spirit is also referenced as *God's secret wisdom*.

"…we speak of God's secret wisdom, a wisdom that has been hidden…."
1 Corinthians 2:7

The Holy Spirit is therefore the *mind of God* and *our higher nature mind* as well.

"For who among men knows the thoughts of a man except the man's spirit within him? In the same way no one knows the thoughts of God except the Spirit of God." 1 Corinthians 2:11

God, manifested as the Holy Spirit, is not only the soul in us, but is our higher nature mind as well. We are a sliver of God Consciousness, Christ Consciousness, or Holy Spirit Consciousness; they are all in effect the same. What I am really suggesting is that the Universal Law of Unity is at work here. Everything is God in one form or another, including our souls. Because we have a lower nature mind (due to our fall in consciousness) and at the same time a higher nature God-mind, we are forced to make daily choices about which one we follow. Do we choose the lower nature mind of sexual fantasy, drugs, alcohol, materialism, greed, jealousy, pride, and other sins? Or do we choose selflessness, compassion, humility, and other forms of love?

Let us now look at the definition of ego. Ego is an abbreviated form of the word *egotistical*. An egotistical person is considered to be a person that has an inflated view of his/her own self worth. The word *inflated* could be substituted by another word such as demented, exaggerated, or distorted. Sigmund Freud defined ego in another way. He divided the human psyche into three parts, the Id, the Ego, and the Super Ego, in an attempt to describe the relationship between the conscious and the unconscious.[1] For Freud, the Id is the childlike nature of the unconscious. It contains within it primary innate human drives and the repressed consciousness. Within the Id is the libido, the predominately sexual energy that underlies most human thought and subsequent action.

The Super Ego is the higher God-like level of conscience of an individual. The Super Ego is in primary opposition to the Id component. The Ego for Freud is the mediator between the Id and the Super Ego. It attempts to strike up an acceptable balance between the two opposing forces of the personality so that a person can function within society. However, these definitions of ego come more from a psychological perspective and are not always consistent with what we are talking about in terms of spiritual development.

After we are born, through much of infancy, our ego tends be somewhat underdeveloped or at least less expressive in some cases. The soul has its own distinct personality but is unable to express itself very well in an infant's body. This can prove to be very frustrating for an evolved soul. As we grow into childhood we begin to develop a deeper sense of our ego-self. Our ego-self does not, however, reflect who we truly are spiritually because it is often based on the varying perceptions and judgments of others.

These perceptions and judgments are mirrored back to us and we either reject or accept them as our reality. This ego-self reality is often skewed because no one is a perfect mirror to us. Other people will perceive us differently than whom or what we truly are due to their own biases and experiences. This is how our ego develops into a false self; the *perceived self* or *perceived personality*. Parents and childhood peers play a huge role in the early development of our own *false ego*.

As we grow into adulthood, our false ego becomes the daily masks we wear. Our false ego in time becomes our adult personality. If we truly knew ourselves, our innermost spiritual being, we most likely would be nothing like what we are today. We would have a completely different personality. In terms of spiritual development it is more helpful to think of the ego as the division between who we think we are, that which is reflected back to us by others, and the reality of who we really are, a spiritual being in a temporary physical shell. The ego, by this definition, is then our *false self* or our *lower nature personality*.

Spirituality speaking, there is more to ego than just the false ego, false self, or lower nature personality. As with all things in duality, there is a higher and lower nature. This is also true for the ego and the personality. Therefore, within the context of our ego, there is a *higher nature personality* or *true ego*. You could also look at it as our *little ego* versus the *big ego*. The lower nature personality or little ego is our own individual personality, while the higher nature personality or big ego in spirituality is our soul, our *true ego* or *true self*. All in all, I believe the term *ego* best describes the gap between how we perceive ourselves, versus who we really are underneath the facade, that being individuated points of God Consciousness.

Our own individual little ego tends to obscure the true spirit within each of us. The little ego artificially encapsulates the soul (true ego or true self) like a dirty residue conceals the brilliance of a diamond. However, the little ego serves a function. Since we don't really know who we are as yet within the context of Spirit, the little ego fills in the cracks of our personality. Otherwise there would be a void. The little ego is but one part of the mind-body-soul continuum. It is, however, at the same time a hindrance to remembering our true nature. Our goal, spiritually speaking, is to eventually eliminate the little ego or false self and to come to a spiritual realization of who we really are, that being the true ego or our true self.

When we understand that we are not our body but rather we are a soul, we better understand our true self. When we develop spiritually to a point of Christ Consciousness, we realize that we are really a member of the Supreme Personality of God. When this occurs, our little ego or little personality is extinguished. In essence, by eliminating the little ego, we recognize our divineness and become Christ Conscious. At that moment in time, we come to the realization that our soul was never separate from God to begin with since our soul is the same consciousness as the Christ Body and the Holy Spirit. Another way of looking at ego is to say that our false ego creates an illusion of separation from God, or possibly is a result of our perceived separation from God.

Likewise we have a *lower nature body* and a *higher nature body*. The physical body is a lower nature or Christ Principle representation or reflection of the higher body. The higher nature body is our immortal body within the Christ Body. The lower nature of the soul would be the Holy Spirit energy in us that we pollute by our desires for material nature. The soul should be the master of the physical body, but in reality it is in constant battle with the little ego for control. The lower nature of ego battles the higher nature of the soul. It is *our mind* that decides the victor between the higher nature mind and the lower nature mind. But the higher mind is really the same as the soul. So who is really fighting whom? Or what is fighting what? It comes down to a spiritual war between the good and evil that resides in us. But how can evil win over an aspect of God? The truth is that evil cannot be the ultimate victor because evil is not an energy consistent with the Original Source. Evil is therefore only a temporary state of dis-ease until the mind wakes up to the fact that we are an aspect or sliver of God, and that collectively we are God as the Christ Body. Until then, we are living an illusion. As long as we live in this illusion, we will reincarnate lifetime after lifetime within our ego self.

Our body, mind, and soul comprise our own little trinity full of immeasurable possibilities. In fact, we are the creators of our lives even before we are born. In other words, we plan out certain aspects of our future life even before the soul is born into the physical realm. However, once we are born we forget about the incredible greatness that lies inherent in our souls. We forget that we are mini-gods that can manifest anything once we put our minds to task. The truth is that our higher nature mind, our higher nature soul, our higher nature ego, and our higher nature personality are really many manifestations of one aspect: the Holy Spirit and Christ Body energies wrapped into the one Personal God. The Christ Body and the Holy Spirit in reality cannot be separated. They are truly one and the same. So I ask the question *Which facet of the Trinity do we wish to look at?*

As a review, the individual mind is a fragment of the mind of God and therefore is a point of God Consciousness. At the same time, our soul is a wave of consciousness just as a wave of water is a fragment of the ocean. Our original state of consciousness is *God-mind*. Anything not of pure Spirit is false ego. The soul as our *true self* is masked by our *false ego*. The body is the physical container for the soul. It is considered to be a temple because it is the container for our fragment of God. Within this container, the soul experiences duality and chooses good or evil according to its level of consciousness at the time. By choosing anything evil (sin) we only hurt ourselves. By consistently choosing the higher nature, we eventually re-enter the kingdom of heaven, our original state and plane of consciousness.

CHAPTER 32

Soul Mates and Twin Flames

There is much debate and confusion over what a *soul mate* actually is. Everyone seems to be looking for their one true soul mate, but that is a misnomer. Each of us has many soul mates. Let me explain. By now it should be clear that every one of us has a soul and as such we are all a part of the Christ Body. But remember that the Christ Body is really one soul appearing as many fragments. All souls or fragments of the Oversoul have a vibratory element to them because they are energy and consciousness. Your soul mates are actually *all souls that vibrate at the same rate of vibration as you*. Then by this definition one particular soul may then have thousands of soul mates, and we do! In other words, *all souls in your soul group are soul mates*. Of course, not all of our soul mates are going to be the one that we wish to marry and spend the rest of our lives with.

Our soul mates most likely include the people that mean the most to us in our current life one way or another. This would naturally include our mother and father, brothers and sisters, our children, our closest friends, more distant relatives, and maybe even past lovers. There may be some soul mates that we only share a brief moment with, but turn out to be very influential nonetheless. We may feel immediate love or dislike toward some of our soul mates when first introduced to them due to previous lifetime interactions. We may immediately recognize them or remember the past life injury or injustice on a soul level, while the conscious mind may not. This may also explain the concept of *love at first sight* or the immediate uneasiness we feel when we first meet someone.

As a matter of fact, the thousands of souls that vibrate the same as you are your *soul family* or *soul group*. These two terms mean the same. Each soul family has a different vibration than another soul family. Together all of the soul families make up the one Christ Body. As an analogy, soul families can be compared to bunches of grapes on a grapevine. The entire vine, including all grape bunches, is the Christ Body. The life that flows through the vine and the grapes is the Holy Spirit. Each individual bunch of grapes is a soul family (soul group). Every grape in a single bunch vibrates at the same rate as the others in the bunch. The grape bunches in close proximity to your bunch are not considered to be within your soul family, but they will vibrate similarly to, but

Soul Mates and Twin Flames

not exactly the same as, your soul group. The farther away a bunch of grapes is from your soul group, the less they will vibrate the same as your soul group. The closer a soul group is to your vibrational rate, the greater the likelihood of increased interaction in the physical world. The Universal Law of Attraction (like attracts like) plays a role in the amount of interaction that occurs between soul groups. Of course karma plays a major role as well.

In terms of reincarnation, a member of your soul group in one lifetime may have been your mother, while he/she is a cousin this life. A son in a previous lifetime may be your wife or husband in this lifetime. Gender is not important as souls will reincarnate either as a woman or a man depending upon which lessons they wish to learn in the upcoming lifetime. Some souls in our soul family will not reincarnate with us, but will stay back and will attempt to assist us from the other side of the veil. When a soul does this, it is acting as a member of our spiritual support group, or, as some may suggest, a guardian angel or spirit guide. Spiritual teachers support our life efforts as well. Our teachers are Christ Conscious souls that can appear anywhere at any time if they choose to make themselves known to us. They are not necessarily omnipresent as they remain individual souls in their immortal bodies. Omnipresence necessarily occurs within the seventh plane of consciousness when soul individuality has been surrendered. Each soul group has a group of teachers assigned to them. No one soul is without the benefits of a support group or teachers. Our teachers are also the ones that help us review our spiritual contract before we reincarnate in order to offer any advice they feel appropriate or helpful. They also may help us review our past life accomplishments and failures post death.

A *twin flame,* on the other hand, is not a term that is used widely, but describes what we typically hope for in terms of our true companion soul mate. A twin flame is *the other half of our original androgynous soul after it split between the masculine and the feminine energetic aspects.* The splitting of androgynous souls into the male and female energetic aspects of the one soul occurred early on in the Garden of Eden. It is referenced in the Bible in Genesis.

> "So the Lord caused the man to fall into a deep sleep; and while he was sleeping, he took one of the man's ribs and closed up the place with flesh. Then the Lord God made a woman from the rib he had taken out of the man, and he brought her to the man. The man said, 'This is now bone of my bones and flesh of my flesh; she shall be called woman for she was taken out of man." Genesis 2:21-23

Man was created by God and called Adam. From his rib came Eve. Another way of saying this is out of *man's womb* was created *womb-man* or *woman.* Man, before the splitting off of Eve (the feminine half of the soul) was an androgynous being or soul. As the original soul, Adam was made in the image of God, which means that

193

he had both masculine and feminine characteristics, the same as God. Ever since the androgynous energies of man, as represented by Adam, split between the feminine and masculine, these energies have remained apart. Because of this split, our own individual soul will either favor the masculine side or the feminine side because it is the half that we energetically represent. Often we will reincarnate as the opposite sex of our soul's primary energy to learn to balance out the opposing energies of our own soul. The ultimate companion soul mate for each lifetime may then be our twin flame. But just as we have multiple soul mates, we in all probability have more than one twin flame since we each may be living multiple parallel lives. Therefore not all of our twin flames may be ideal companion soul mates for us in any given lifetime.

All of this brings to mind an interesting point. If you think about it, any type of discrimination based on race, religion, or sexual preference does not hold water when you consider reincarnation, soul mates, soul families, and twin flames. It is most certain that we have all been many races over numerous reincarnations, so to discriminate because of race or sex is ignorance. The same holds true for religion. We each have been affiliated with various opposing religions over each lifetime. It is also most certain that we each have been homosexual in past lives. And there is a logical explanation for this. When a soul that is the male aspect of the twin flame incarnates into a female body, or vice versa, the result is a soul that has a physical body that contradicts the primary vibrational desires of the soul. In some cases, that desire is so strong that the soul (person) chooses a partner of the same sex. In other cases, a female may be considered to have a lot of masculine energy and a man may have a very feminine nature.

As we begin to balance out the diverging energies (feminine and masculine) over the next millennia, we will discover that we are once again becoming more androgynous in nature consistent to the original state of our souls before the split. Even today, the differences in the sexes are becoming less pronounced over time. Progressing forward in time, it follows that we may eventually come to a point in our conscious development when it will be socially acceptable to be with a person of the same gender in a mutually loving manner. That is not to say that promiscuous homosexual behavior will be tolerated by God, but for that matter, neither will promiscuous heterosexual behavior. Promiscuity will actually be less tolerated because as souls we hopefully will be more developed spiritually. Love, not lust-filled sex, will be more freely expressed to other beings because our hearts will be more open to the emotion of love. What I am suggesting is that if there is love between two people, then it is permissible for them to be together and loving in that relationship. If you look at the direction the world is heading, can you not see it happening already? On the other side of the veil, we love male-oriented and female-oriented souls equally without sexual preference because there is no sexual intercourse on the other side. However, I can only imagine that there is an incredible sharing of loving energies on the other side of the veil. We will eventually reach this same milestone on earth.

Nothing is wrong in God's eyes if it is performed out of love. Please do not misunderstand what I am saying here. I am not condoning lustful sexual behaviors. I am not suggesting that lust-filled sex with various partners is of a higher nature. It is not. What I am doing here is presenting certain possibilities within creation and humanity's progression of consciousness. If my assumptions are correct, then any judgment based on sex, race, religion, or sexual orientation would be inappropriate and sinful. Judgment is not only sinful, it is just plain foolhardy if you truly understood that *all souls in a soul group may be really one soul living many parallel lives.* If we are in fact one soul living multiple lives all at the same time, then when we judge, there is a strong possibility that we are judging another aspect of our soul living a parallel life in order to gain additional experience toward our own mutually shared enlightenment. By judging another aspect of our own soul, the net karmic result is that we are tearing down our self and hampering our own spiritual growth. It would be like the right hand of the Christ Body causing injury to the left hand of the Christ Body. Inappropriate judgments will not get us back to heaven. We will not enter heaven, not because of God's judgment on us, but because of the disharmony within our own vibration.

CHAPTER 33

Spiritual Contracts

I believe that there is no substantial reduction of karma on the upper planes of consciousness. Rather, the greatest amount of our spiritual learning via experience and karma reduction is accomplished on earth because of its denseness and the assumed realness of this plane of consciousness. Therefore a soul that is ready to do additional work in this area eventually begins to design and plan and coordinate certain events that will occur in their next physical incarnation. The soul, as it prepares for its next life in physical form, looks at the various opportunities for substantial spiritual growth at its disposal. Generally the lessons the soul wishes to learn and experience are related to the various aspects of love, i.e. generosity, compassion, forgiveness, and so forth. Having passed onto higher planes of consciousness after death, the soul will go through a past life review of his or her most recent incarnation. In this way, the soul develops a deeper understanding of where its weaknesses lie and the lessons regarding love that have yet to be mastered by the soul.

After a certain amount of earth time has passed, a soul will eventually choose the conditions of its next birth. A more advanced soul may have a greater number of options than a less advanced soul due to its cumulative positive karma. The reincarnating soul then figures out which earth family would provide the best opportunities for the type of growth it desires, most likely those being in the areas of its continuing weaknesses. The soul decides whether or not the specific body it is considering will work for the next reincarnation in order for it to accomplish its new spiritual goals. The economic status of the family may be considered. The political status of the family may also play an important role in its decision. The soul will additionally plan with whom it will reincarnate. Typically a soul will reincarnate with other souls he or she has reincarnated with in previous lives, primarily other soul group members. A soul at this time may decide with its primary companion soul mate to meet at a certain stage of his or her upcoming life mutually beneficial to both of them within divine timing.

A soul not only chooses its parents, but chooses the time it is to be born. This will place the soul in the correct position to receive the proper influences of the planets and stars it needs in order to accomplish his or her plan. The astrological influences will affect the development of the soul and will assist in drawing to the soul the lessons it wishes to learn in the upcoming lifetime. As a direct consequence, an astrology chart, if correctly produced, will reflect a soul's chosen life path.

The soul before being reincarnated in a body will also complete a spiritual contract for itself outlining what it is that it wishes to accomplish karmically in the next incarnation. It will set up in advance conditions that will further the soul in its development of consciousness. Others in the soul group may additionally decide to be reborn onto earth around the same time so that they can work together in the upcoming life. Whatever agreements they make will typically appear in the spiritual contract of each soul reincarnating if important enough to warrant it. Before the soul is reborn, the spiritual contract will be reviewed by the soul's spiritual teachers. Sometimes a soul not yet Christ Conscious will be a little too exuberant with its contract, taking on much more than is really beneficial to the soul. A soul that has decided to take on too many challenges in the upcoming incarnation may wind up terminating its lifetime by committing suicide. This will only lead to additional problems for the soul.

The problem with suicide is this: If a person commits suicide, all the soul has done is to *delay* its growth opportunities. There is no escaping what we must eventually experience in any given lifetime; only the specific details are different. If, for example, a soul needs to experience financial ruin in any given life, suicide will only cause the soul to have to face a similar scenario again in a later lifetime. It is sort of like the movie *Groundhog Day*. Bill Murray wakes up every day facing the same problems over and over again until he finally gets it right. Only then is he released from that temporary state of hell. What eventually changed in the movie is Bill Murray's attitude toward what he was facing each day. In doing so he ended his karma and was able to move forward with his life in a much more positive way. That is exactly what we must do with our own lives. We must accept what we are here to experience and learn from the experience, and in doing so, we do not have to face the exact scenario again. We will have risen above the necessity of experiencing it again in an upcoming lifetime because we completed the lesson in the current lifetime.

In any given spiritual contract, a soul may be as detail-oriented as it wishes or sees fit. The contract may be very specific early on in life with not much preplanned later in life, or it may be the reverse. It really depends upon what best suits the soul and what it plans to experience in the upcoming life. A soul may also be very specific in the lesson it wishes to learn and how it wishes to learn it. A soul may determine that it desires to learn the lesson of compassion. If this is the case, then the soul will set up the circumstances and challenges in which it will learn the lesson of compassion. It may even set up in advance an event where the soul is injured by another soul or possibly another aspect of its own soul living a parallel life in order to learn the lesson of compassion, or for that matter forgiveness, or a vast array of other lessons the soul has yet to learn.

There may also be a contingency plan placed into a contract. For example, if a soul does not learn a lesson it has placed into its contract by the time the physical body turns a certain age in earth years, the soul may have added the contingency of a disease or an accident in order for it to get back on track with its own original contract. A soul may additionally plan with another soul a reduction of its own karma or that of the other soul. The contract can become overall very multifarious and quite integrated with other contracts. In the soul's perspective it is not considered too complex since the soul has a higher degree of understanding when not in a physical body. In our earthly body with our polluted mind, it would be quite impossible to see, much less understand, all of its interwoven complexities. Soon after we are born we forget the details of our own contract. In this way, what we experience is more real.

Once the soul is born, there remain opportunities for changing the contract. We never at any time lose the opportunity to choose again as expressed in the Universal Law of Free Will. But herein lies the problem about changing your contract: how would you know what is in your contract since you are no longer conscious of it? For some people it may be possible to change it. If you intuitively receive messages regarding what your contract entails via dreams or by other means, you can then pray to alter your contract. The second method of determining what may be in your contract is by looking at what you are experiencing this lifetime. If, for example, you are experiencing something that is very traumatic in this lifetime with regard to relationships, health, or finances, it is most likely a part of your spiritual contract. Again, prayer is probably the most potent method for changing contracts. Maybe praying for strength and clarity would be a wiser prayer.

Another possibility of creating change in your life is to change the conditions of your life. If you were to develop cancer, the cure may be to change what you are thinking, feeling, or experiencing. I am not suggesting giving up on modern medicine, but rather making positive changes in your life. Figure out what is not working for you and then change it. You can do this by checking in with your feelings and emotions and screening them with your thoughts. Determine what is causing you the most distress or dis-ease in your life and then remove it if at all possible. It may be a harmful relationship or a negative behavior or pattern causing you emotional distress that you need to change. However, just because something in your life is painful, that does not mean that it is in your soul's best interest to remove it from your contract.

The pain we experience may be exactly what we set up for ourselves in order to learn the lesson we came to earth to learn. In that case, we should pray for strength to learn or minimally to accept the lesson, rather than eliminate it. The most difficult of lessons are most likely in our spiritual contract. Once the lesson is learned, the aspect of life causing the stress or dis-ease may be removed. Referencing back to our previous example, the cancer may go into remission. A spiritual contract then is our soul's plan for each lifetime that outlines our progression in consciousness for our eventual return to enlightenment and heaven.

Section VI

ENTERING INTO THE
FIFTH DIMENSION

CHAPTER 34

Material Nature – Desire and the Five Senses

❧

"The indescribable, unimaginable supreme godhead, which is pure spirit, cannot have been the creator of a world full of evil and misery. Emanations from that Oneness (in a sort of spiritual Big Bang) resulted in a hierarchy of lesser powers, one of which (often identified with the biblical creator) made the world of matter. Humankind—part matter, part spirit—must strive to cast off its gross material element and, as pure spirit, reunite with the One."[1]

The quote above not only suggests that the creation of the universe is a projection or *emanation* of God *in a sort of Spiritual big-bang* consistent with my hypothesis in chapter 21, but also seems to blame mankind for evil resulting from our seeking or residing in gross material nature. Further, it is clear that the Christ Body, as a lesser power than the Oneness, made matter. Finally, it states that Mankind's goal is to look beyond *its gross material element* (matter) to pure Spirit for salvation.

The following bullet points in part reflect our addiction to our own material nature as *materialism* while other human beings on this earth suffer immensely.[2]

- The gap between rich and poor Americans is now the widest of any industrial nation.
- One-fifth of the world's population lives in dire poverty, slowly dying of hunger and disease. Millions of others desperately need more material goods. Yet were they to consume as Americans do, the result would be an environmental disaster. Americans throw away seven million cars a year, two million plastic bottles every hour, and enough aluminum cans annually to make six thousand DC-10 airliners.
- 1.3 billion people live on less than one dollar a day. Half the world, nearly three billion people, lives on less than two dollars a day.

- According to UNICEF, thirty thousand children die each day due to poverty. And they "die quietly in some of the poorest villages on earth, far removed from the scrutiny and the conscience of the world. Being meek and weak in life makes these dying multitudes even more invisible in death."
- Some 1.1 billion people in developing countries have inadequate access to water, and 2.6 billion people lack basic sanitation.
- Less than one percent of what the world spent every year on weapons was needed to put every child into school by the year 2000 and yet it didn't happen.
- Nearly a billion people entered the twenty-first century unable to read a book or sign their names.
- Twenty percent of the population in the developed nations consume eighty-six percent of the world's goods.

The Bible suggests that *contentment* should be sought somewhere else other than materialism.

> "I know what it is to be in need, and I know what it is to have plenty. I have learned the secret of being content in any and every situation, whether well fed or hungry, whether living in plenty or want. I can do everything through him who gives me strength." Philippians 4:12-13

In previous chapters, we discovered that the Impersonal God created the lesser conscious state of form and energy (the Christ Principle) through the Personal God (Christ Body) by means of the creative energies of the Holy Spirit. We also know that the purpose of this form universe is for souls to experience form. The universe was originally created as a playground of sorts for all souls to enjoy before Adam and Eve fell from grace by committing the original sin of sexual intercourse. Once the original sin was committed by Adam there was a corresponding decrease in the Kundalini energies of all those who sinned. Souls that had committed the sin of sex moved away from God and were no longer Christ Conscious. Their consciousness had been substantially lowered and immortal man became mortal man because the act of intercourse was unnecessary. Consequently, man was cast out of the Garden of Eden, which is the same as saying that the earth was now no longer perfect either. Man and earth regressed together from a state of communion with God to a state of separation from God. Imperfection in the world whether experienced as pain, hunger, thirst, or as another misery, even inclement weather, was a direct result of man's fall from grace.

It goes without saying that within man there is a higher nature and a lower nature which is the potential for goodness and evil. They are like two sides of a coin. They go together. In the state of duality one cannot exist without the other. Something of a higher nature is *anything that brings us closer to God*. Something of a lower nature is *anything that takes us away from God*. Higher nature is anything that involves positive actions, feelings, emotions, and thoughts related to goodness and love. Lower nature is anything that involves negative actions, feelings, thoughts, and emotions such as hate, cruelty, or greed. Desires can be good or bad as well. Desire can lead us back to God or it can lead us into deeper darkness. As a result, there is *lower desire* and *higher desire* just as there is lower nature and higher nature.

Desires stem from the five senses and the subtle bodies in each corresponding plane of consciousness. The five senses and subtle bodies inherently want to be active or activated. The five senses are in a constant state of desire. At best we can only temporarily satisfy our lower desires because eventually we desire more things of a material nature. The thirst of lower desire can never be truly quenched. As humans, especially among the Western cultures, it seems that we need to be continually gratified. It appears that we are always left in a state of wanting more of everything. I recall one Black Friday (the first day of Christmas shopping which is the Friday after Thanksgiving) that one or more people were trampled to death as anxious shoppers rushed into the stores as they opened for business that day. It is clear that Materialism is a sickness and a plague for humanity. We seek constant sense gratification via sex, pornography, gluttony, drunkenness, and whatever else we can obtain to satiate our lower desires. Too many of us seek to satisfy ourselves with things associated with lower desire, but in reality we can never be satisfied with lower desire. Often we know on a soul level what is best for us, yet we choose to anesthetize our spiritual side with various types of material gratification.

Higher desire, on the other hand, is that desire that wishes to reunite with the Godhead. Some Eastern religions say it is best to eliminate desire altogether. However, I believe that they are referring to lower nature desires. Desire for reuniting with God is a higher form of desire and crucial for our spiritual development. Our soul's higher desire is what drives us to return to the Christ Body. We can't move up in consciousness without higher desire; it is almost like a base energy because we can't succeed without it.

The delusion of material nature and duality is what causes anxiety, worry, and sleeplessness. Do you toil for wealth, fame, power, or serving the Divine God? Do you desire wealth, fame, power, or enlightenment?

> "So I say live by the Spirit and you will not gratify the desires of the sinful nature. For the sinful nature desires what is contrary to the Spirit and the Spirit what is contrary to the sinful nature. They are in conflict with each other, so that you do not do what you want. But if you are led by the Spirit you are not under the law. The acts of the sinful nature are obvious: sexual immorality, impurity, and debauchery; idolatry and witchcraft; hatred, discord, jealousy, fits of rage, selfish ambition, dissensions, factions and envy, drunkenness, orgies, and the like. I warn

you, as I did before, that those who live like this will not inherit the kingdom of God. But the fruit of the Spirit is love, joy, peace, kindness and goodness, faithfulness, gentleness and self control. Against such things there is no law. Those who belong to Christ Jesus have crucified the sinful nature with its passions and desires." Galatians 5:16

Here the Bible uses the term *sinful desire* whereas I use the terms *lower nature* or *lower desire* but they are in effect the same. As members of the Christ Body, it is clear that we need to rid ourselves of sinful desires and passions because they are our lower nature even though they are seemingly inherent within each of us due to our diminished level of consciousness. Lower nature manifesting as lower desires will obviously not get us into the kingdom of heaven.

Lower desires often lead to an attachment of a particular outcome or expectation. The desired outcome associated with lower desires rarely plays out exactly the way we wish them to occur in our life. Then we are disappointed by the outcome. Disappointment will often lead to emotional frustration, which leads to a loss of discrimination, which is an important mind function. In this instance, the lower nature desire controls the mind, versus the mind controlling the desire. Desires for materialism necessitate further reincarnations for the soul. Materialism or the desire for material objects as attachment corrupts our thoughts. It corrupts our God-mind. The desire for material objects can also lead to idolatry.

The needs and desires of the body direct the body's action unless there is a conscious interrupt where the mind steps in and redirects the body and soul to a higher purpose. The mind then uses its willpower to overcome lower desires so that greater levels of consciousness can be achieved for the soul's benefit. When acting consistently with our higher nature, the body attempts to fulfill the desires of the soul. Eventually lower nature and lower desire are destroyed at which time the soul attains a point of Christ Consciousness. This is what the soul seeks to attain. Christ Consciousness is void of lower nature and lower desire because the soul has attained a higher level of consciousness. The individual mind is now purified and seeks to fulfill only the desires associated with the soul's higher nature. The individual soul's higher nature is inherent in each one of us but again is forgotten soon after our birth. However, our soul's higher purpose remains within our soul's consciousness as our truest desire for self expression. We must place our focus on our higher nature until it becomes *second nature* for us.

The material nature of this universe or Christ Principle was initially created by the Christ Body through the power of the Holy Spirit and may one day ultimately be dissolved by God. Until then, the material nature of this universe is forever changing its form into alternate forms. The mutable force of God is the feminine aspect of God (the Holy Spirit), whereas the masculine aspect (the Christ Body) is constant and never changes. The Christ Body has dominion over all material nature (the Christ Principle) just as Christ Conscious souls (souls filled with the Holy Spirit) have power over the wind, the rain, the sun, and all aspects of nature. This is demonstrated to us by Jesus when He calmed the storm.

> "He got up, rebuked the wind and said to the waves, 'Quiet! Be still!' Then the wind died down and it was completely calm." Luke 4:35-41

Anyone who fails to recognize our own divinity fails to understand the true nature of God or the mini-god in us. Sadly, it is our lower nature to doubt what we don't understand.

By repeatedly choosing our higher nature, we will become Christ Conscious once again. Jesus Christ in performing miracles did not do anything that we cannot do ourselves once we regain full consciousness. The apostles proved this by healing the sick once they were filled by the Holy Spirit. Once enlightened, their minds were consistent with God-mind, and the same will be true for us once we reach enlightenment. We will become like children again, living simpler lives steeped in faith with the knowledge that we are loved as God's children knowing full well that we will be provided for. The key to life is to live more simply seeking the higher nature within ourselves.

> "As you simplify your life, the laws of the universe will be simpler; solitude will not be solitude; poverty will not be poverty, nor weakness weakness." Henry David Thoreau

A person seeking enlightenment should understand the opposing dualities in nature (up/down, cold/hot, joy/sadness) as a part of the human spiritual experience. A person who accepts these states of nature as neither good nor bad but simply discerns between the opposites and repeatedly chooses the higher nature is on the path to enlightenment. However, this philosophy of nonattachment to material nature may take many lifetimes for a soul in physical body to comprehend and accept as its spiritual lesson. Once reunited with God as an enlightened soul, the state of all desire ceases. At this stage of consciousness we will fully recognize that All is One and separateness as a non-reality. *Solitude will not be solitude; poverty will not be poverty; nor weakness weakness.* This is the God-mind we seek. This is the state of heaven we all seek.

CHAPTER 35

Good and Evil – Devils and Angels

Why do we as God's children have evil thoughts? Is evil inherent within us? And if this is so, how can that be? Are we not made in the likeness of God? How is it that our mind is not the same mind of God? Surely God does not have evil on His mind. Surely God did not create evil. The answer is found within the Universal Law of Relativity, which states that *everything manifested has a dual nature*. In duality, since there is goodness there consequently has to be evil. Without the darkness associated with evil, how can we as souls experience the light of God? How can we choose love when there is nothing else to choose to experience? Without evil there is no choice; there is no duality. Consequently, to experience goodness, we necessarily needed to experience a fall in consciousness.

Does Satan live in us? Jesus addresses this question in the Gospel of Mark.

> "What comes out of a man is what makes him 'unclean.' For from within, out of men's hearts, come evil thoughts, sexual immorality, theft, murder, adultery, greed, malice, deceit, lewdness, envy, arrogance, slander and folly. All these evils come from inside and make a man 'unclean.'"
> Mark 7:20-23

The previous verse, as well as the next verse, indicates that evil resides in us as unenlightened souls.

> "So I find this law at work: When I want to do good, evil is right there with me. For in my inner being I delight in God's law; but I see another law at work in the members of my body, waging war against the law of my mind and making me a prisoner of the law of sin at work within my members." Romans 7:21-23

Our evils come from within, experienced within the members of our bodies. Just as we ask our own Christ within to embody us each time we perform goodness, we in essence invite evil to embody us each time we sin. Therefore we have both goodness and evil energies working within and through us. The evil in us manifesting as evil thoughts corrupts the energy of the Holy Spirit which is the life force energy within us. Did you ever notice that the reverse spelling of *evil* is *live?* Evil is the reverse of life force energy, which is by definition death. Logically, then, sin leads to death. Without evil, our bodies would never die because we would be in an unadulterated body, an immortal body. There would be consequently no false ego, sin, or evil in us.

As suggested, we have both an angel and a devil in us. However, we are not *the* devil (Satan), just as we are not *the* God. With each decision we have a choice to make. We can either serve as a vehicle for good as a child of God, or evil as a child of the devil. In any given moment we decide which force we wish to personify.

> "All things in the world are two. In our minds we are two, good and evil. With our eyes we see two things, things that are fair and things that are ugly…We have the right hand that strikes and makes for evil, and we have the left hand full of kindness, near the heart. One foot may lead us to an evil way; the other foot may lead us to a good. So are all things two, all two." Eagle Chief (Letakos-Lesa) Pawnee[1]

Evil and good are inherent in the minds of less than enlightened man. Since the fall in consciousness, man has continually sinned. We continue to sin by choosing the wrong path. Daily we each decide which path we wish to take. Do we take the path toward God or away from God? Because of the Universal Law of Free Will we are the ultimate decision maker. Do we choose goodness, truth and love? Do we listen to that little voice of God that lives within each of us as our own intuition? Or do we listen to the voice of evil? It is our choice.

The Bible is filled with references to evil. In the Gospel of Mark, Jesus heals a demon-possessed man.

> "For Jesus had said to him, 'Come out of this man, you evil spirit!' Then Jesus asked him, 'What is your name?' 'My name is Legion,' he replied, 'for we are many.'" Mark 5:8-9

This is a scary verse in the Bible, at least for me. To think that the devil has a legion of foot soldiers in this world is a chilling thought. But who or what is Satan?

> "…I saw Satan fall like lightning from heaven." Luke 10:18

This verse makes it very clear that Satan is one of God's fallen angels. It is also clear by this verse that Satan does exist. But what is an angel and what is a devil? For that matter, what is goodness and evil? The Universal Law of Vibration says all is energy. In essence, so does quantum physics. Evil, defined in the most basic of terms, is simply negative energy. Energetically speaking, sin is the same as evil just as water is the same as ice. Evil and sin also imply distance between us and God. However, one is the manifestation of the other. *Evil is the physical manifestation of the energy sin creates.* Evil is not God nature. Accordingly, negative energy is something *we* created. God did not create evil. We did. Because evil is an energy and so is negative thought, our negative thoughts and actions feed evil energies. Mankind created evil in the Garden of Eden and we continue to feed evil by our ongoing negative energetic choices. And as with most things, we like to personify them; we like to assign personal attributes just like we call nature, Mother Nature. We have done the same with evil. The personification of evil thought energy we made into a *devil*. Satan himself then is the collective evil energies that we all manifest *personified* into a being.

Devil or angel, all things created consist of form and energy. The devil is form and energy (just as God's angels are form and energy), however corrupt. By this loose definition, men and women could be considered fallen angels as well. Adam and Eve could then be considered fallen angels. You and I would then be fallen angels too. In effect, we are the angels that *volunteered* to descend unto this earth plane to experience form. If angels are simply God's energy personified, we are all His angels. However, as we often do, rather than being inclusive we tend to segment, categorize and exclude each other.

We will at times separate people by their type of employment, saying that they are plumbers, engineers, firemen, politicians, or farmers. Just as we categorize humans by job function, we have categorized angels by job function. Some angels are our spiritual teachers on the other side. Some angels are our soul mates on this side and the other side. Some serve the truest function of a typical angel as messengers of God. Some angels are perverted energetic beings we sometimes call devils. It all comes down to energy and semantics. Human beings like to categorize because categorization provides us greater meaning.

Even within the realm of angels, we separate them into categories: archangels, seraphims, cherubs, and so forth. In reality, whether angels of goodness or angels of darkness, we are energetic conscious beings. Angels are God Consciousness in energetic form. Souls are the energetic form of God Consciousness as well. Are we not all the same conscious energy? Are we not the angels that elected to fall in consciousness for God to experience form as reality?

Angels *as sinners* are referenced in 2 Peter:

> "For if God did not spare angels when they sinned…" 2 Peter 2:4

Do angels really sin? That's not what we were taught in Catholic grade school. If angels in fact do sin, then *we* may very well be the angels Peter is referring to in the passage above.

The Universal Law of Unity that says All is One means we are really one energy and one body. That fact that we are all one in the collective Christ Body says the very same thing; we are all one singular energy split into individual points of consciousness. We are all one in the Christ Body. As human beings we are then God's fallen angels carrying out His great plan.

Since we are all multidimensional beings, wouldn't it be interesting if our own guiding angels were in reality aspects of our own higher self in higher dimensions supporting our efforts in the lower more dense dimensions? In essence then, we would be *helping ourselves.*

"God helps those who help themselves." Ben Franklin

When we act as children of Satan, the sins we commit add to this negative field of evil energy that exists in the world.

"…the whole world is under the control of the evil one." 1 John 5:19

If we really do add to this negative field of energy that seems to control our world, we might better understand that the problems we face are directly related to our own sins as karma.

In the Gospel of John, Jesus calls Judas Iscariot, the apostle who betrayed Jesus, the devil.

"Have I not chosen you, the twelve? Yet one of you is the Devil!" John 6:70

Notice that Jesus did not call him Satan but did refer to him as a devil.

The apostle Paul makes a reference to a man as a *"child of the devil"* in Acts.

"Then Saul, who was also called Paul, filled with the Holy Spirit, looked straight at Elymas and said, 'You are a child of the devil and an enemy of everything that is right! You are full of all kinds of deceit and trickery. Will you ever stop perverting the right ways of the Lord?'" Acts 13:9-10

The references that are made above to children of the devil are metaphors for men who have chosen to do evil and add to the evil in the world. We are then children of the devil when we act as Satan's angels of darkness.

"He who does what is sinful is of the devil...." 1 John 3:8

Conversely, when we act in goodness, we act as children of God and subsequently as His angels of light.

However, the devil works in delusion and lies as the great deceiver. The devil will even at times appear as an angel of light.

"...for Satan himself masquerades as an angel of light." 2 Corinthians 11:14

Satan's job is to create delusion which is the illusion of separateness. His greatest tool may be doubt. Sin can lead to doubt and doubt can lead to sin. We may even doubt God. When we doubt God or our connection to God, we doubt how great we are and our own magnificence. We doubt that we will be taken care of by God and that He will *give us our daily bread* which of course is a part of the Lord's Prayer. Our daily bread represents everything we need, not necessarily everything we desire. If we knew in our hearts that we were all one, Satan would not exist. Evil is born out of our ignorance. The root word of ignorance is to ignore. To sin is to ignore the truth.

"...as it is written: God gave them a spirit of stupor...." Romans 11:8

Doesn't this mean that God created evil? *No, it does not.* God did however create the opportunity for evil to exist because as children of God we were given the freedom of choice. This freedom of choice extends to His angels which includes us.

Does God tempt us? The answer is again *No.*

"When tempted no one should say 'God is tempting me.' For God cannot be tempted by evil, nor does He tempt anyone; but each one is tempted when, by his own evil desire, he is dragged away and enticed. Then after desire has conceived, it gives birth to sin; and sin, when it is full grown, gives birth to death." James 1:13-15

Satan cannot force us into sin because we created him. He can only tempt us. When we sin we allow him entrance into our minds and bodies. The devil as evil can enter us up to the point of demonic possession. Our choice then is to either create greater evil by birthing additional sin or create greater goodness in us and the world through love and service. Evil energies increase in this world when we selfishly give additional energy to our lower nature as lower desires in order to fulfill our five senses. Choosing goodness serves to lessen evil's grip on this world. It is our choice, and consequently it is our responsibility to choose between goodness and evil wisely. Only by choosing goodness do we lessen our karmic debt. Only by choosing correctly do we return to our original state of Christ Consciousness and enter into the kingdom of heaven.

Master Eckhart makes no distinction between devils and angels as I too have suggested. Rather, he suggests that it is the devil's job to burn away sin from each of us.

> "The only thing that burns in hell is the part of you that won't let go of your life: your memories, your attachments. They burn them all away, but they're not punishing you, they're freeing your soul. If you're frightened of dying and you're holding on, you'll see devils tearing your life away. If you've made your peace, then the devils are really angels freeing you from the earth." Meister Johannes Eckhart

Some people emphatically deny the existence of Satan. In response I pose this question: *Is it better to deny that Satan exists and be caught unprepared in the final hour, or is it more intelligent to be prepared for the final hour by acknowledging the daily struggle between good and evil?*

> "Heaven and earth will pass away, but my words will never pass away. No one knows about that day or hour, not even the angels in heaven, nor the son, but only the Father." Matthew 24:35-36

In the Second Gospel of Peter the Bible offers a convincing argument as to why we should prepare ourselves.

> "But the day of the Lord will come like a thief. The heavens will disappear with a roar; the elements will be destroyed by fire, and the earth and everything in it will be laid bare. Since everything will be destroyed in this way, what kind of people ought you to be? You ought to live holy and godly lives." 2 Peter 3:10-11

Are we really living the best life we can now at this very moment?

Since my definition of evil is the total collective energies of sin, mathematically and scientifically, my definition of sin is supported by thermodynamics in that energy cannot be destroyed, only altered in its form. Therefore it might be foolish on our part to *not* believe in the existence of Satan or in our ignorance ignore Satan.

Does the presence of evil in this world explain the destructiveness of Mother Nature? I believe that there is a direct correlation. Surely it is a consequence of the evil choices we have made. Earth has a consciousness far greater than our own individual consciousness. Mother Nature is simply responding to man's negative evil energies surrounding her, the mixed energies of an imperfect world caused by our own choices, including original sin. It would not surprise me if Mother Nature were attempting to rid herself of us as a plight upon her, just as our own bodies' T-cells attack alien cells that are harmful to our bodies. I can only imagine that all life forms in the Garden of Eden before the Fall of Man were living symbiotically with earth, far from what we experience today. Because of the Universal Law of Unity or All is One, our choices affect everything in this universe. Increasing negativity in our world could be a possible explanation or causal factor for more frequent and more devastating hurricanes, floods, famine, and droughts. If you look at it, you might consider the negative reactions of the earth as simply an extension of our karma in a more global manner. In a direct sense, our weather reflects our consciousness. Who is responsible for global warming, God or us? Is it not simply the consequence of our group actions, our collective consciousness?

Could Satan as evil also be responsible for all dis-ease (disease)?

> "On a Sabbath Jesus was teaching in one of the synagogues, and a woman was there who had been crippled by a spirit for eighteen years. She was bent over and could not straighten up at all. When Jesus saw her, he called her forward and said to her, 'Woman you are set free from your infirmity.'" Luke 13:10-12

Jesus, upon performing this miracle, was questioned as to why He was healing on the Sabbath. His reply was as follows.

> "…should not this woman whom Satan has bound for eighteen years, be set free on the Sabbath day from what bound her?" Luke 13:16

Can we attribute all of our misfortune to Satan as the energetic manifestation of the cumulative energy of our own misdeeds? We certainly can. If before the Fall of Man and before the fall of the angel named *Lucifer* everything was perfect, then by default there would have been no disease or malformations. Our misfortune is only made possible by Satan along with our ongoing choice to sin. Satan, then, is the source of all imperfection. Satan is responsible for death. Satan is responsible for all sickness. Satan is responsible for all of our negative emotions, feelings, and thoughts. Without Satan we would still possess a mind consistent with God's mind or God-mind. Satan is the opposite of God-mind. However, Satan is only as powerful as the totality of the human race's negative choices since we in effect created him. Again, I am speaking energetically here, of course.

We are engaged in a constant battle between good and evil whether we realize it or not. It is a battle resulting from the Universal Law of Free Will. So what is it that we are to do? What tools do we have? The best tools for combating evil are our hearts and minds working cooperatively. However, our hearts and minds can also lead us astray since we are no longer perfected beings. Therefore it is important to test our thoughts against some sort of screening device so that we are not fooled by faulty thoughts. Here are some potential questions we can use as a screening device to test the validity and truthfulness of our thoughts:

- Who benefits from my decision?
- Is this best for all concerned?
- Is this the highest and best choice I can make?
- Is it the most loving and selfless action I can take in this situation?
- What would Jesus do in this circumstance?

In the last question you can substitute Buddha or Krishna or any other master's name for Jesus' name. By using these screening questions, and by adding a few of your own questions, you will be better able to discriminate wisely between good and evil, and between the egoic mind and God-mind.

The best defense against evil is obviously not to deny it, but rather to *resist it*. Our heads and hearts are our greatest tools for resisting evil. If we come from a loving place within our hearts and we use our heads for discrimination then we will have the greatest chance of resisting evil. By consistently making the right decisions on a daily basis, we incrementally progress to enlightenment. This is the wisdom of the Holy Spirit we seek. By resisting evil, the positive choices we make will eventually become second nature to us. When we constantly choose the path of a Christ we become the unshakable mind (God-mind). But we must be careful to not judge our self too harshly even when we fail in the moment. We are not as yet perfected souls. Spiritual evolution is sometimes taking two steps forward and one step back. It is not always possible to uphold the higher energies and consistently make better choices even though we know better. Eventually we will learn to avoid sin by mastering the energies associated with our chakras even though it may take a multitude of lifetimes to learn all of our spiritual lessons associated with this universe of material form.

The devil wants us to think that we are separate, but we are not. The devil wants us to desire for ourselves only, with little or no regard for other people. These beliefs feed the energetic consciousness of evil. Only through nonattachment to material nature can we move forward with the development of our higher consciousness. The higher consciousness associated with the Holy Spirit in us is what draws us back to God. The devil is what pulls us back into the world of delusion. As long as we keep coming back to this world of delusion, we will have to resist evil. When this world finally ends and we return back to the Godhead, there will no longer be evil; there will no longer be delusion. Until Satan is conquered, even he serves as a tool for God. Because of Satan we reach out for God. By Satan showing us darkness, we reach for the light of heaven. Strangely enough, the name Lucifer means *light bearer*. Is Lucifer in his own way pointing the way for our return to heaven?

CHAPTER 36

Judgment

"It is the Lord who judges me. Therefore judge nothing before the appointed time; wait until the Lord comes. He will bring to light what is hidden in darkness and will expose the motives of men's hearts. At that time each will receive his praise from God." 1 Corinthians 4:1-5

There are various types of judgment. There is the most obvious type of judgment, that of judging others. Then there is the judgment of our own self or self-judgment. There is judgment after our physical death, before we are again reincarnated, which I will address in the next chapter on "Beyond Death." In the Bible verses above, it is clear that we are to not judge anything before the appointed time. The appointed time is believed to be the end time when the Lord will judge the world and each of us as souls. This is discussed more in the chapter *Revelation and Armageddon*. For this chapter we will focus on the appropriateness or rather the inappropriateness of judging others and self-judgment.

In the Gospel of Matthew it speaks very clearly to judging others.

"Do not judge, or you too will be judged. For in the same way you judge others, you will be judged, and with the measure you use, it will be measured to you. Why do you look at the speck of sawdust in your brother's eye and pay no attention to the plank in your own eye? How can you say to your brother, 'Let me take the speck out of your eye,' when all the time there is a plank in your own eye? You hypocrite, first take the plank out of your own eye, and then you will see clearly to remove the speck from your brother's eye." Matthew 7:1-5

It does not take a Bible study class to understand that Jesus is saying we should not judge others since we each have our own faults. But in the real world we judge others every day. We judge people for their actions. We judge people on their looks. We judge people on their work. We judge people on the car they drive and the house in which they live. We judge others for whom we perceive them to be as individuals, even though we have no concept of what trials, tribulations, or tragedies they may be dealing with or have dealt with in their current lives.

When we come from a place of judgment, things do not flow as they should because we close our hearts. The universe has a tremendous abundance of love inherent in each and every moment. By judging ourselves or others we block the flow of love to us, in us and through us. Rather, we must learn to eliminate the negative energies that restrict this abundant loving energy. In doing so, we reopen our hearts to love. To clarify, I am not talking about criminal activities here. Criminals need to be judged, imprisoned, and when possible rehabilitated. Please understand that I am referring to judging other people's non-criminal everyday actions.

Judgment has a karmic aspect to it. As noted in the verses above, judging others is not advisable no matter what the circumstance; if we do, the measure we use to judge others will in turn be used against us. When we judge others negatively, as a consequence, we draw negative judgment back to us. When we judge others we are in effect judging ourselves since we are all one body. If the right hand judges the left hand as bad, then *the body* has been judged. When we tear down another being, we tear down the one Christ Body. Therefore we should not judge other's actions. We need to open our awareness to a higher consciousness. Judgment is directly tied to our level of consciousness. A soul with a lower consciousness will typically judge more often than a person of higher consciousness. A person with a higher consciousness understands that we all have our lessons to learn.

Generally self judgments are fear based. If we believe in scarcity, then our fear judgment becomes real, and consequently scarcity occurs in our lives. We draw scarcity into existence because of the Universal Law of Attraction. In this case, we might need to learn about the lesson of self-worth. Similarly, when we choose greed, we in effect make another self judgment. The thought behind greed is that we feel entitled to some thing we currently don't own. We think just because a friend or neighbor has something we desire, so should we. That is not necessarily the case. We are entitled to what we need to carry out our own divine purpose as a part of God's divine plan for us, and anything above that is a greater blessing. If we live our life consistent with God's purpose for us, then what we receive from God and the universe will be more than we need, that is for sure. God always provides everything we need to carry our spiritual contract, our plan. Our success is dependent upon the quality of our decisions.

When we lovingly carry out God's plan for us, the quality of life's experiences increase for us. By making judgments regarding what we think we deserve, we restrict the flow of God's loving energy to us. Because of expectation, we restrict God. We are no longer in a state of receptivity. Our focus lies in expectation and not thanksgiving. As a consequence, we may experience feelings of being emotional stuck or abandoned by God. We can likewise feel that the things we own no longer satisfy us and become burdensome like a weight around our neck. We may create a *new* negative judgment about the life we live, such as *I am a failure*. We may make judgments about our spouses or others, thinking that maybe they are to blame for the unhappiness we feel inside ourselves. Inappropriate judgments restrict our abilities to receive new loving energies and increases our negative karma. Wouldn't it be best to live in gratitude for the many blessings we have already received?

As soon as we judge, we move out of the moment of being totally present. We move into a space or place of negative evaluation and expectation. Moving into a space of evaluation is often how we handle something new or when we feel uncomfortable in any given situation. We seek to judge it rather than simply accepting it as our next challenge and opportunity for growth. This is the way we have been trained by society. The unknown for us is uncomfortable. The unknown at times can be very scary. Uncertainty causes uneasiness. Instead of judgment, it would be better to come from a place of discernment by creating a space between thought and judgment. *Discernment* is not the same as judgment. There is no emotion or feeling attached to discernment. Judgment is charged with desire and married to attachment, whereas discernment is neither. Judgment in any situation restricts options. Discernment allows things to be as they are without any negative judgment attached to it. Through discernment we let things flow naturally without interruption.

Another word for *discernment* is *discriminate*, but as some words have developed a negative connotation, so has the word discriminate. Let me give an example of a situation illustrating the difference between discernment and judgment. A couple goes out bargain-hunting for a new car. The salesman takes them to a brand-new shiny red car. The woman sees the car as red and not as another color. That is discernment or discrimination. The husband on the other hand hates the color red and thinks people who drive red cars receive more speeding tickets than people who drive cars that are blue or white.

The thought that people who drive red cars get more tickets on average than people who drive blue or white cars may even be true, but without facts and figures to prove his assumption, it is merely a judgment. Beyond that, the husband hates the color red. Possibly he associates the color red with some sort of past negative experience he had. Either way, he has attached the emotion *hate* to the color *red* and therefore he is again making a judgment. Judgments are often negative and sadly not always rational, whereas discernments typically stem from the rational mind and are typically neutral.

When you come from a place of discernment, chances are in your favor you are correct; in this case, the color red is not the color white or the color blue. Had the husband been open to the color red, he may have discovered that there was a very special rebate on red cars due to an overstock of red cars in the dealership's inventory. The universe was attempting to provide the husband with an extraordinary deal on a car, but the positive flow of loving energy from the universe was blocked due to his negative judgment of the color red. The point I am trying to make here is that negativity diminishes rational judgment and dampens the universes' attempts to provide us what we need. And in case you were wondering, there appear to be no official studies that conclusively state that red cars receive more tickets than other colored cars. However, it is very possible that red cars garner more attention due to the vibrant nature of the color.

Self-judgment can be very damaging as well, as it affects how the universe treats us. Because we send out negative vibrations to the world about ourselves that is generally what we receive in return. We are typically treated by others in the manner in which we expect to be treated by others. That is the Law of Attraction. It seems that most often we are our own worse critics. If we can't love and accept ourselves, how can we truly love anyone else? We may adopt the belief that we are not worthy of being loved. We may even test other people's love for us over and over because we can't believe that they actually love us. Eventually they will grow weary of the tests and leave, once again reinforcing the negative thoughts we have about ourselves. It becomes a self-fulfilling prophecy.

The point I am attempting to make here is that it is better to not judge at all. Discernment is fine; judgment is not. So when we have a thought about ourselves or others, use the powers of discernment. Discernment is wisdom; wisdom is not found in judgment. For example, using discernment we might say "According to my doctor, I am slightly overweight for my body type." A negative judgment may lead to someone saying "I am fat and ugly." How we react to our initial thought while avoiding any negative feeling, emotion, or attachment is key. By adopting an attitude of nonattachment through discernment we might say and do something more appropriate in response to our doctor's diagnosis such as "It appears that I am heavier than I should be for my body type and consequently I will cut back on my late night snacking." I admit that adopting an attitude of nonattachment while living in the material world is much easier said than done.

Finally, in terms of judging ourselves and others, it is important to remember that we are all on a journey. We are all in transition. We are all flawed. None of us are perfect. Therefore, we need to be a more accepting of others and ourselves. We need to stop *should-ing on* ourselves and others: "I should this" and "He should that." You get the idea. Relax and let life flow. And count your blessings. Too often we forget just how good we have it. Therefore we need to stop making negative judgments toward ourselves and others and simply discriminate. Do the best you can in any given situation given the tools you have, and then release all attachment to the outcome. Anything less leads to more negative karma and necessitates another incarnation. Only by adopting an attitude of discernment, versus judgment, can we learn compassionate understanding and ultimately reach our final destination, a place called heaven.

CHAPTER 37

Beyond Death

"Consciousness is eternal; it is not vanquished with the destruction of the temporary body." Bhagavad-Gita

Physical death is inescapable at our current level of consciousness. We are born into a physical body and as a consequence of sin the physical body must experience death. Upon death our consciousness continues uninterrupted in Spirit-form. There is never a break in our consciousness. It is our truest self. At the time of our physical death, the etheric plane is where our soul's consciousness immediately travels to upon leaving the body. The etheric plane is the plane of consciousness closest to the physical plane. Because we are immediately thrust into the etheric plane, it may seem more like a dream. Remember, the etheric plane is where our soul travels to when we dream. That is why when we dream we can make contact with people that have passed on before us. Whether we come into contact with deceased loved ones in dreams or on the etheric plane, they may appear in another form of their prior selves. They may appear drastically younger or much more physically fit than they were in their past life or as you remember them on earth. Either way, we will immediately recognize them.

Once out of the physical body, the soul as soul consciousness within the etheric plane experiences a greater degree of lightness. In near death experiences this is most often described as a very positive event. Upon death, a soul may instead become a bit confused while making its spiritual transition to the etheric plane, especially if it was a sudden transition as in a car accident or other tragedy. The soul may think that is still alive even though it passed from its physical body into its etheric body much like we see depicted in some science fiction movies. Alternatively, it may be surprised that it maintained its own consciousness outside of a physical body. If the soul is spiritually advanced in consciousness, it will make a smooth transition in the etheric plane. The soul will immediately recognize the transition it has just made. Either way, after a successful transition is made within the etheric plane, a soul is generally more conscious of its true nature, that of the soul as consciousness.

The soul may very well see others on the physical plane because their soul is still very close to the earth plane and because the veil between the earth plane and the etheric plane is thin. This is consistent with reports of near-death experiences. The soul may continue to linger for a while near its physical body and loved ones feeling some sort of an attachment. Later it will eventually begin to venture farther and farther away from its physical body as the connection to it seems to become less important. The soul may decide to move on to the higher planes of consciousness, but out of confusion, unhealthy attachments, addictions, fear, or possibly out of love for the ones left behind, the soul may stay in the etheric plane for an unspecified amount of time. Other souls, past friends or relatives, that have previously died may make contact with the newly passed soul in an attempt to assist in the transition to the higher planes. If the soul is ready to move on from the etheric plane by releasing its desires for people, places, and things left behind on the physical plane, the soul may be drawn to a tunnel of light. This tunnel can transport it to the higher planes of consciousness, or heaven as we typically think of it. Experiencing a tunnel of light is also reported in a significant number of near-death experiences.

If the soul elects to stay in the etheric plane for a while, it may begin to recreate images of its former life, either positive or negative because that is what is most familiar and comfortable to it. In the etheric plane, there is no need for sleep because there is no physical body. There is also no hunger so food intake is unnecessary. The soul may maintain an etheric duplicate (or body double) of its earthly form. In other words, the etheric body looks like the human body before death or it may take on a younger, fitter version of the body it left behind. Alternatively, it may return to the form of its immortal body, which most likely would not look like its earthly body.

The newly passed soul may create *a new world of form* out of a need for consistency. In the etheric plane there are less-limiting time and space constraints because material nature as form is less of a reality. Everything is less dense. As a result, the soul can quickly create a new reality for itself, often mimicking what the soul left behind in the physical plane. The soul generally feels more comfortable within this newly created illusion of form. However, a recently passed soul may create a space for itself that is evil, dark and gloomy because some form of hell is what the soul expects or feels it deserves.

Some souls may become temporarily trapped in the etheric plane because of some trauma or something they feel in their past life has yet to be resolved. These temporarily trapped souls on the etheric plane we often refer to as ghosts. Some souls after their death decide to stay close to earth purposely because of an addiction to something or an unhealthy attraction to someone while on earth. A soul in the etheric plane doesn't need to share its space with other souls if it doesn't wish to; however, most will share their space, possibly out of loneliness. Yes, loneliness. It may surprise you, elate you, or depress you that not much changes between this world and the next. We are not really that different other than having left the physical body. If we are entrenched in an ongoing state of sadness, loneliness, despair or anger when we die, that is most likely the environment we may unconsciously decide to create on the other side in the etheric plane. As on earth, we are drawn to souls that vibrate similarly to us. For these less advanced souls, even in a temporary hell, misery loves company. Happier, more advanced souls can create a *mini-heaven* within this plane of existence if they so desire.

An unenlightened soul within its etheric body may continually create objects of desire, just as it had on the earth plane and ethereally experience them. A soul may stay in the etheric plane indefinitely, but will eventually feel a need to move on because the etheric plane is not its real home, vibrationally speaking. In other words, a soul that resonates with a higher plane of consciousness (a higher level of vibration) will eventually feel a need to travel to a higher dimension as discussed in the chapter on planes of consciousness. Each subsequent level, whether the realm of feelings or emotions or concrete thought, still may not resonate with the soul. The soul will advance to the higher realms of consciousness until it reaches a plane of consciousness consistent with its vibration. This is where his or her soul family is most likely located. If the soul has led an exceptional life, it will venture to a higher level or plane of existence consistent with Christ Consciousness. In order to reach this plane, a soul must have broken free of the cycle of death and rebirth by having attained enlightenment. If a soul is God Conscious, it can rejoin the Christ Body in the seventh plane of consciousness as the Oversoul or indefinitely reside as an individuated Christ Conscious soul on the sixth plane of consciousness. Again, theoretically speaking, we may exist on all planes of consciousness and not realize it as less than enlightened souls.

The soul having shed its mortal form will eventually undergo a comprehensive past life review. This is not a judgment by others or by any aspect of God other than by the soul itself. The soul may review the most recent incarnation as if on a multidimensional screen, but in this movie the soul experiences the feelings, emotions, and thoughts of all the characters involved in the review. If the soul caused joy or sorrow in someone else, the soul will feel it as if it were its own joy or sorrow. If the soul caused pain or pleasure in someone else, the soul will experience it as its own pain or pleasure. The soul will know their thoughts because the soul will experience them as its own. A soul will personally judge its own lifetime as the soul reviews each and every significant interaction the soul had on earth. This will continue until the soul has completed its entire past lifetime review. It may take many earth years in which to complete this comprehensive review, but the soul has plenty of time as time is no longer important or possibly even a reality. The act of reviewing the soul's lifetime on the higher planes of consciousness does not reduce the soul's karma in any way. The review is not meant to be a hell, but it could feel like it if the soul led a less than positive life. Again, the past life review is a judgment of the soul's own actions on earth. It is not a judgment made by God but rather the god in us. This review will assist the soul in understanding what progress was made in that lifetime toward the ultimate goal of enlightenment. If the soul is already an enlightened master such as Jesus, the soul may bypass all of these processes and return directly to its point of origin; the spirit plane or possibly even a higher plane of consciousness.

If a soul, while in his or her physical body, did not fully eliminate lower desire and lower nature within its soul consciousness, the soul will eventually sense a need to return to earth once again to work on reducing karmic debt through some type of service to others. Upon regaining its original state of Christ Consciousness a soul will no longer need to return to earth and will remain in the heaven we created individually and collectively as the Christ Body. After all is said and done, the soul reengages in its primary occupation on that plane of existence consistent with the soul's individual purpose. Yes, we have the opportunity to work within whatever plane we exist, but the good news is that the work we perform is the work we love to do; and since we don't require sleep, we never get fatigued. I imagine that is what heaven would be like where even the most difficult challenges would be fun and exciting.

CHAPTER 38

Heaven and Hell

"Every man is given the key to the gates of heaven; the same key opens the gates of hell." Buddhist Proverb

If the key is the *same* for either gate, then maybe we each make the ultimate decision between heaven and hell for ourselves and not God. The key then can be defined as choice, our choice.

Heaven has been referred to as a state of mind. It is most often referred to as a place, or places as noted in the Bible. The very first line of the Old Testament references a number of heavens:

"In the beginning God created the heavens and the earth." Genesis 1:1

As a child growing up in the Catholic Church, I never noticed that this verse contained the word *heavens*, possibly implying more than one. If the Bible were referencing one heaven, why would it not read *In the beginning God created heaven and earth?* Is it possible that God created more than one heaven?

In further studying the Bible, I discovered another very enlightening passage that references more than one heaven. In a letter from Paul to the Corinthians, Paul writes about a *third heaven*, as well as a heaven he refers to as *paradise!*

"I know a man in Christ who fourteen years ago was caught up to the third heaven. Whether it was in the body or out of the body I do not know—God knows. And I know that this man—whether in the body or apart from the body I do not know, but God knows—was caught up to paradise. He heard inexpressible things, things that man is not permitted to tell." 2 Corinthians 12:2

I can only imagine Paul is referring to himself here when he speaks of being out-of-body and traveling to alternate planes of existence. He speaks of the third heaven as well as a paradise that exists where he heard beauty beyond that which human words can express. Is the third heaven he references the same heaven referenced as paradise, or is it yet another out-of-body reference where Paul experiences another heaven, this time beyond explanation?

And what about Ephesians? It mentions more than one heaven.

"He who descended is the very one who ascended higher than all the heavens, in order to fill the whole universe." Ephesians 4:10

In Hebrews there is a reference to more than one heaven.

"Therefore, since we have a great high priest who has gone through the heavens, Jesus the Son of God, let us hold firmly to the faith we profess." Hebrews 4:14

There is a verse in the Gospel of John where Jesus, when speaking to the apostles, suggests that there may be more heavens than one.

"Do not let your hearts be troubled. Trust in God; trust also in me. In my Father's house are many rooms; if it were not so I would have told you. I am going there to prepare a place for you." John 14:1-3

Could Jesus' reference to *many rooms* be a reference to *many heavens?* Could the multiple heavens be the same as the planes of consciousness discussed earlier? I believe that they are the same, that *there are seven form heavens* which correspond directly to the seven chakras. The transcendental plane of God Consciousness (where form does not exist) corresponds to the infinite God Consciousness where there is only the Impersonal God and the infinite world of possibilities. As a heaven of pure consciousness, I can't even begin to describe it because it is beyond human comprehension. Possibly the seventh or eighth heaven is the *paradise* Paul was referencing.

Either way, I believe that there are seven heavens that directly correspond to the seven main chakras and the seven planes of consciousness: the physical world, the etheric plane, the psychic plane, the emotional plane, the mental plane, the spirit plane, and finally the Plane of Logos. I believe these planes are the additional heavens referenced in the Bible and that some of these planes were corrupted by the Fall of Man, namely planes one through five, i.e. the physical world associated with the base chakra through the concrete mental plane associated with the throat chakra. The spirit plane, which is the sixth plane of consciousness that corresponds to the third-eye, is still perfect because, by definition, the sixth chakra, when fully open is the level in which a soul reaches enlightenment. The Plane of Logos, which corresponds to the seventh chakra, also remained unaffected by the Fall of Man and is still perfect.

The further a soul travels up the five corrupted levels of form heavens, the greater the separation between good and evil. Only on the earth plane do we experience the greatest interaction of evil and good. It will remain this way until *the Son of Man sits on his glorious throne.*

> "Jesus said to them, 'I tell you the truth, at the renewal of all things, when the Son of Man sits on his glorious throne, you who have followed me [speaking to the apostles] will also sit on twelve thrones....'"
> Matthew 19:28

In this verse Jesus references *the renewal of all things.* I believe Jesus is referring to *the renewal of the five planes of consciousness back to their original state.* What was corrupted by the Fall of Man by Adam (defined as mankind) will eventually be restored to its original heavenly beauty. When first created by the Christ Body the planes of consciousness were originally all perfect heavens, including the earth. Jesus is saying that all planes of consciousness will once again be un-corrupted at *the renewal of all things.* They will all be restored to perfection, back to their original state as heavens. This renewal is confirmed in Revelation as well as in Acts.

> "Then I saw a new heaven and a new earth, for the first heaven and the first earth had passed away...." Revelation 21:1

> "He [Jesus] must remain in heaven until the time comes for God to restore everything, as he promised long ago through his holy prophets."
> Acts 3:21

It is once again confirmed in Hebrews. Please notice the use of the word *heavens.*

> "At that time his voice shook the earth, but now he has promised, 'Once more I will shake not only the earth but also the heavens.' The words 'once more' indicate the removing of what can be shaken—that is, created things, so that what cannot be shaken may remain." Hebrews 12:26-27

One night I had a vision. As my visions often do, they come in an instant and then leave me. However, they remain in my consciousness for some time after I receive them. In this vision I gazed upon a pool of water, and in this pool of water was the reflection of the Kingdom of God. That was it, nothing more. Yet what my vision told me is that everything we see in form somehow reflects spiritual reality, that the earth is a reflection of the kingdom of heaven. In other words, the Universal Law of Correspondence (what is true above is true below) is again at work here. None of the seven heavens is exactly alike, but the six lower levels of consciousness as heavens, including the physical world, are all a reflection of the seventh heaven, which I believe is the highest heaven of form. All seven heavens in the original state were perfect. And as previously mentioned all seven heavens are gradually less dense as we move upwards from earth to the higher dimensions. This is consistent with my previous statement that life as we know it does not drastically change upon our physical death. Our consciousness continues in a less dense plane of consciousness above the earth plane but still one of form. And if I am correct that the dimensions above this dimension of form are a reflection of earth, how much grander would be its beauty? Why then do we hold on so tightly to this dimension of form and its materialistic ways? But when the great renewal occurs, the earth will be returned to the original state as the Garden of Eden. And all of the heavens between the physical earth and the seventh heaven will once again be perfect as well.

The corrupted planes of consciousness, as I described them earlier, will be renewed to their original state of perfection. The second plane of existence, the etheric plane, will be the etheric heaven. The third plane of consciousness will continue to be the feelings heaven where things are created to experience heavenly feelings; likewise the fourth plane, the plane of emotions, will continue to be a heaven in which we experience heavenly emotions. The fifth plane will be a heaven in which we create to experience thought patterns consistent with the concrete mind. The sixth heaven will continue as it is now, where everyone is already Christ Conscious, full of heavenly abstract-thinking perfect individual souls.

The seventh heaven, as mentioned, is the highest heaven of form where only the one Christ Body exists. The expression *I'm in seventh heaven* as well as the expression *heaven on earth* could be additional soul truisms. The fact is we often speak in terms of the higher spiritual realities within our everyday speech. Maybe that is one of the reasons why we find the number seven so integral in the history our world: seven days to create the world; seven deadly sins; seven archangels; seven heavenly virtues, seven wonders of the world; seven days in the week and so on. By the way, it is interesting to note that the Muslim religion states that there are seven heavens.

Now let's turn our attention to hell. Is hell a state of mind or a place? Well, we know that in the etheric plane we can create a hell if that is where our consciousness lies. The truth is that our mind can create a hell on earth, or immediately after our death, because hell is where we believe we deserve to go to suffer for our sins. Hell then is potentially both a place on earth and on the etheric plane we can create for ourselves if we believe we deserve it. Often times what we create on the etheric plane is most likely a recreation of our most recent experience on earth. We can create our own personal hell if it is consistent with our soul's vibrational energy. If it is true what some psychics say about the time span between lives being up to or more than a thousand earth years, then a temporary etheric hell may seem like an eternity.

Hell by any definition is *separation from God* and a disconnection from the source and therefore can be looked at as a *state of mind*. Therefore, hell can be anywhere. If a person is not Christ Conscious, then there is necessarily a void in the spiritual life of that person. On earth, a person may at first attempt to fill the void with material nature, but material nature will never fill the void. Trust me; I know this because I have personally experienced it. Only through a loving and trusting relationship with God can we ever begin to fill the void, recognizing that all else is an illusion. When I use the term *illusion* that is not to say that the earth does not exist, it does. The earth is reality. What is a truer reality is that we are mini-gods as facets of God Consciousness experiencing form.

> "Jesus answered them, 'Is it not written in your Law, I have not said you are gods?'" John 10:34

Hell is really *a choice we make* because of our lower nature mind and *a place we create* because it is justice according to our past misdeeds. We create hell by our own volition because of sin. We create a certain degree of hell no matter where we are because again hell by definition is separation from God. The intensity of the hell we create is a cumulative effect of our choices and our karma which is tied to our individual sins as well as our collective sins. Hell can be defined as *a temporary state of consequence* created by our lower nature and a result of our sins.

Since hell is our creation and not God's creation, then the concept of hell is therefore only a temporary place in which we are separated from God. We were never meant to burn in hell for an eternity, although any length of time in hell might seem like an eternity. How would God be served by condemning a part of Himself to an eternity of suffering? How can an unconditionally loving being send one of His own created souls and an aspect of Himself to hell forever because of error? Would you personally ever consider sending one of your own children to an eternity of hell no matter what they did? What about forgiveness and what about repentance? If your child committed murder, would you not forgive him if he truly were repentant? To think of hell as a permanent place of damnation is too simplistic. God is an unconditionally loving being and therefore could not and would not condemn any of His children to an eternity of hell. Again, that is not to say there isn't consequence for our actions. Universal justice or karma is one of the inescapable universal laws of God!

But how do we explain the *fires of hell* referenced in the Bible? When the Bible speaks of the fires of hell, the Bible may be referring *the purification of the soul* from its own corruption. Hell, then, would be a place of purification. The fires of hell would consequently be a reference to the burning or purification of our sinful nature. Earlier I quoted Luke 3:9, "The ax is already at the root of the trees, and every tree that does not produce good fruit will be cut down and thrown into the fire." The fire referenced here again may be referencing the purification of the soul as a consequence of not producing good works. This points to hell as a temporary place of purification. That is not to say that even a temporary hell is pleasant because it is obviously not.

The temporary hell in the etheric plane, for those who chose to create it, is the direct result of their karma, which is directly tied to their belief system. Hell is then a temporary place we create because of our negative thoughts and negative actions. Eventually a soul may leave the temporary hell he/she created on the etheric plane and be reborn onto the earth plane to once again attempt to balance out their negative karma with good karma. When we have balanced out our karma on earth, we will be released from the cycle of reincarnation; we will have attained Christ Consciousness. We will have risen above evil and all forms of hell into a state of grace.

How can I then explain the Bible references to *an eternity of hell?* First, I believe that the words when translated into English were misinterpreted from its original meaning. Just as the word *virgin* in the Bible was misinterpreted from its original meaning. The word virgin back in the days of Christ could have been defined as either a *young person* or *a person that had never experienced intercourse.* The same type of misinterpretation could have occurred with the word *hell.* The original word could have meant something completely different such as death, the grave, separation, or some type of purification. Look at the English language and how we often struggle to find the correct word when we speak. How far is *far?* How young is *young?* How deep is *deep?* These are words that explain a relationship to something else; I am attempting to do the same here with the word *hell.* I am suggesting that the word hell is a word that describes a temporary state of separation between man and God.

In the Gospel of Mark it references what lengths might be taken in order to enter the kingdom of heaven, metaphorically speaking.

> "If your hand causes you to sin, cut it off. It is better for you to enter life maimed than with two hands to go into hell, where the fire never goes out. And if your foot causes you to sin, cut it off. It is better for you to enter life crippled than to have two feet and be thrown into hell. And if your eye causes you to sin, pluck it out. It is better for you to enter the kingdom of God with one eye than to have two eyes and be thrown into hell, where their worm does not die, and the fire is not quenched. Everyone will be salted with fire. Salt is good, but if it loses its saltiness, how can you make it salty again? Have salt in yourselves, and be at peace with each other." Mark 9:43-50

Obviously these verses are again a metaphor for something else. No one should consider cutting off a hand or a foot or plucking out an eye. What is really being stated here is that we will not enter into the kingdom of heaven if there is any part of us that is impure, including our minds. But what is very interesting is the sentence *Everyone will be salted with fire*. If fire is a reference to hell as a place of purification, then hell is a place where souls regain their saltiness and *salt*, then, is consistent with goodness.

> "The wicked return to the grave, all the nations that forget God. But the needy will not always be forgotten, nor the hope of the afflicted ever perish." Psalm 9:17-18

Which of us in reality is not needy? Who is experiencing constant bliss on this earth? Which of us is not hopeful? Which of us are not afflicted by something? *The wicked return to the grave* could be referring to *the death of evil*. Satan himself is thrown into the lake of fire; again, evil is destroyed by goodness. Remember that Satan is really energy, specifically the personification of manifested evil energy. When the Bible speaks of *the gnashing of teeth*, the Bible could be referring to the evil energies that will be destroyed or the souls that will undergo the purification process.

Hell exists now because we sin. Sin causes separation from God. Without God there will always be that never-ending void in our lives we cannot fill no matter how much we try to fill it with material nature. The material world in its imperfection could be considered hell, or at least a cause for the temporary hell certain souls individually or collectively create on the etheric plane. Alternatively, heaven can be experienced by any of us instantaneously upon re-discovering the Kingdom of God within us.

> "…the kingdom of God is within you." Luke 17:21

CHAPTER 39

Revelation and Armageddon – 2012, Earth's 9/11

If I am correct in how I have decoded the Bible, the New Testament may not have been written to address a huge expanse of time yet to transpire as many of us presently assume. Rather, it is possible that Jesus, Buddha, Krishna, and other prophets were all preparing us for the time of Armageddon and Revelation as we begin to cycle out of this fourth dimension of consciousness into the fifth dimension of consciousness. As a matter of fact, I believe that we are already in the beginning of this transition and we have been for some time now. In order for us to successfully enter the next new dimension there must be a tearing down of the obsolete materialistic-based systems we humans have institutionalized into our daily lives. We must additionally let go of all types of fear in whatever form it takes, for example, racism, sexism, greed, hatred, or complacency, and replace these fears with love and compassion or our transition to the next dimension of consciousness may be worse than we could ever have imagined.

Armageddon and Revelation are obviously not the same. Armageddon is considered by many to be the final battle between good and evil. Armageddon comes from the Hebrew words *Har Meggito* which means *Mountain of Meggido* and is not surprisingly located in Israel. Megiddo is where the final battle between Jesus Christ and Satan is suggested to take place. Revelation in the Bible is believed to be about the revelation of Jesus, when Jesus will reappear or reveal Himself on earth once again.

> "At that time they will see the Son of Man coming in a cloud with power and great glory. When these things begin to take place, stand up and lift up your heads, because your redemption is drawing near." Luke 21:27

Some believe that the Bible suggests an actual return of *Jesus in one form or another* to judge us. Others believe that Jesus' return is meant metaphorically in that it represents an awakening of the personal Christ within us, within our hearts. I would place myself in the category of the latter, believing in the metaphoric symbolization of the heart (or heart chakra) opening itself to greater levels of love, which is the inner Christ in us awakening. I believe *the Son of Man coming in a cloud* suggests that His coming will be obscured, hidden, and not at all obvious in any sense of the word. Most of mankind will not realize that something very spiritual is even occurring. The events surrounding Armageddon will unfold in what will be viewed as normal, even though some of the events will be quite horrific, especially for those directly affected.

According to popular belief, Revelation includes the *final judgment* and the *final redemption,* whereas Armageddon, which precedes the Revelation, details the *physical devastation* of large portions of earth and its people in and around the end times as prophesied by Nostradamus, Edgar Cayce, the Prophet Daniel, John the Apostle, and other seers of the future.

Cayce spoke about the end times while in a self induced trance-like state. His prophetic messages are regularly referred to as the *Cayce readings.*

> "As we have seen, the Cayce readings contain many references to the biblical prophesies about the End Times. Perhaps the most amazing one is his bold statement...that *the time, times and a half time* spoken of in the prophet Daniel's vision are over! Clearly this means that the End Times are upon us....The end of the time, times and a half time means that a great battle is about to take place between the forces of the light and good and the forces of the darkness and evil. So, for Cayce, the end of the time, times and a half time is the last great battle of Armageddon...."[1]

Obviously, Cayce is suggesting that end times are upon us *now.*

John the Apostle received his prophetic visions regarding the end times as documented in the Book of Revelation while exiled (imprisoned) on an island named Patmos.

> "The revelation of Jesus Christ, which God gave him to show his servants what must soon take place. He made it known by sending his angel to his servant John...." Revelation 1:1

Additional predictions concerning the end times are linked to several ancient calendars which conclude in the year 2012, as well as being linked to Hopi prophesy.

> "The Emergence to the future Fifth World has begun."[2]

Hopi Prophecy suggests that we have lived in three previous worlds, and that the fourth world in which we currently live will soon give way to the fifth world. This is consistent with my premise that we are living in the fourth dimension which will soon give way to the fifth dimension.

The Bible states that there will be signs that serve to forecast the traumatic events of the end times, prior to us seeing the New Jerusalem, our heaven on earth. These signs will indicate the coming of the final days as spoken of by Jesus in the Gospel of Luke.

> "When you hear of wars and revolutions, do not be frightened. These things must happen first, but the end will not come right away. Then he said to them: nation will rise against nation, and kingdom against kingdom. There will be great earthquakes, famines and pestilences in various places, and fearful events and great signs from heaven." Luke 21:9-11

This is already happening in the world. Look at what we are already facing: AIDS, Bird Flu, Swine Flu, SARS, Ebola, global warming, floods, famine, terrorism, false prophets, violent crime, tsunamis, earthquakes, economic hardships, wars, revolts, and more. Possibly, the biggest threat to us currently is global warming. The effect of global warming may include bigger longer lasting droughts and an increased number of water shortages. This of course will negatively affect the world's food supply causing more frequent incidences of famine. We may also experience larger tornados, destructive winds, storms, and hurricanes of a magnitude never witnessed by mankind before. Should the polar ice caps melt along with Greenland's ice sheet the oceans may rise twenty feet or more, maybe much more. This would cause major flooding along many of the world's coastal areas and since well over half of the world's population lives on or near a coastal plain any rise in sea level could be devastating. A significant rise in sea levels could destroy major cities along our coasts and flood large areas well inland. I can only imagine that third world countries will be hardest hit because they already face so many hardships. Global warming may very well be the impetus behind Armageddon.

Whether or not we are nearing the beginning of Armageddon or not, at our current level of human consciousness, our planet cannot support the more than 6.5 billion people that call it home. It is not sustainable.

> "Earth's population will be forced to colonize two planets within 50 years if natural resources continue to be exploited at the current rate.... A study by the World Wildlife Fund (WWF)...warns that the human race is plundering the planet at a pace that outstrips its capacity to support life."[3]

And because it is not sustainable, we are already witnessing increased hostilities, war and genocide as we battle over limited resources such as oil, food, and clean water.

The signs of the end times are numerous in the Bible but none point to a specific time frame:

> "When you see Jerusalem being surrounded by armies, you will know its desolation is near. Then let those who are in Judea flee to the mountains, let those in the city get out, and let those in the country not enter the city. For this is the time of punishment in fulfillment of all that has been written." Luke 21:20

There seems to be an enormous amount of conflict in the Middle East currently, with intermittent conflicts occurring in and around Jerusalem. Luke also infers in the passage above that Armageddon is a *time of punishment*. Could this be referencing the accelerated cleansing of our negative karma?

The Bible warns us to be ready for the end times.

> "Be always on the watch, and pray that you may be able to escape all that is about to happen, and that you may be able to stand before the Son of Man." Luke 21:36

When the time of Armageddon arrives there will be unleashed upon the earth numerous tribulations, all with horrific results. The first seven tribulations are set into motion as each of the seven seals of the heavenly scroll are opened in sequence by the Lamb of God, acknowledged as Jesus. When the first seal was opened the Bible references the appearance of the first of four horsemen, also known as the *Riders of the Apocalypse*. The first horse was white in color while the rider held a bow and was given a crown.

> "...he rode out as a conqueror bent on conquest." Revelation 6:2

This rider may represent the antichrist coming into power on earth.

When the second seal was opened a rider on a red horse was unleashed upon earth to make war. The third seal unleashed a rider on a black horse. He was holding a pair of scales in his hand. The fourth seal unleashed a rider on a pale horse. The rider of this horse was named death.

The second, third and fourth riders represent war, famine and pestilence, respectively.

> "They were given power over a fourth of the earth to kill by sword, famine and plague, and by the wild beasts of the earth." Revelation 6:8

It doesn't get any better for us as the rest of the seals are opened.

The seventh seal refers to seven trumpets as additional devastation that will be inflicted on the inhabitants of the earth.

"The first angel sounded his trumpet, and there came hail and fire mixed with blood, and it was hurled down upon the earth. A third of the earth was burned up, a third of the trees were burned up, and all of the green grass was burned up." Revelation 8:7

Could the reference to *hail and fire mixed with blood* be describing nuclear fallout? Could the reference to *a third of the earth was burned up, a third of the trees were burned up, and all of the green grass was burned up* be a reference to global warming or yet another reference to the consequence of nuclear war?

"The second angel sounded his trumpet, and something like a huge mountain, all ablaze, was thrown into the sea. A third of the sea turned into blood, a third of the living creatures in the sea died, and a third of the ships were destroyed." Revelation 8:8-9

Something like a huge mountain, all ablaze, could be describing a large meteorite landing in one of our oceans or the eruption of a super-volcano.

The Bible is consistent with at least one of the prophesies of Nostradamus.

"After great human misery a greater approaches,
The great motor of the centuries renewed:
Rain, blood, milk, famine, weapon, and pestilence,
In the sky fire seen, dragging long sparks."
Quatrain 2.46

According to researchers, there exists thousands upon thousands of comets we know little or nothing about. Should a significantly sized meteorite strike the earth it would be enough to create global havoc.

"The third angel sounded his trumpet, and a great star, blazing like a torch, fell from the sky on a third of the rivers and on the springs of water—the name of the star is Wormwood (which means bitterness). A third of the waters turned bitter, and many people died from the waters that had turned bitter." Revelation 8:10-11

This, too, sounds like a description of devastation possibly caused by a meteorite striking our earth, polluting or possible poisoning our waters; or might it be describing a warhead armed with chemicals, biological warfare?

"The fourth angel sounded his trumpet and a third of the sun was struck, a third of the moon, and a third of the stars, so that a third of them turned dark. A third of the day was without light, also a third of the night." Revelation 8:12

The *lack of light* mentioned in the above passage could be caused by the smoke of a meteorite hitting the earth, smoke and ash resulting from nuclear war, or a significantly sized volcanic eruption.

The next passage speaks of yet another star falling to earth causing the sun and moon to be once again darkened by smoke; this time out of the smoke come a torrent of locusts to torment the earth.

"The fifth angel sounded his trumpet, and I saw a star that had fallen from the sky to the earth. The star was given the key to open the Abyss. When I opened the Abyss, smoke rose from it like the smoke from a gigantic furnace. The sun and sky were darkened from the smoke of the Abyss. And out of the smoke locusts came down upon the earth and were given power like that of scorpions of the earth. They were told not to harm the grass of the earth or any plant or tree, but only those people who did not have the seal of God on their foreheads." Revelation 9:1-5

Is the reference to a *star* describing a nuclear warhead as it descends to earth? Are *locusts came down upon the earth* a metaphoric reference to squadrons of jet fighters descending upon the earth or armies of soldiers entering battle? Is the *power like that of scorpions* referring to the sting of a bullet or other more advanced weaponry?

Here are three more biblical references, one of which clearly suggests war.

"A third of mankind was killed by the three plagues of fire, smoke and sulfur that came out of their mouths." Revelation 9:18

Is *fire, smoke and sulfur that came out of their mouths* a reference to cannons or tanks?

"They had breastplates like breastplates of iron, and the sound of their wings was like the thundering of many horses and chariots rushing into battle." Revelation 9:9

The *sound of their wings* resembling *the thundering of many horses* could easily be describing the sound associated with helicopters. It may have been difficult for John the Apostle to explain his visions of the apocalypse any other way.

This next verse is more straightforward.

"The number of mounted troops was two hundred million."Revelation 9:16

Did Nostradamus write any quatrains that might relate to predictions of a third world war?

"From brick to marble, the walls will be converted,
Seven and fifty peaceful years:
Joy to mankind, the aqueduct renewed,
Health, abundant fruits, joy and honey-making times."
Quatrain 10:89

If Nostradamus is suggesting fifty-seven years of peace following the Second World War, we would be facing the advent of another world war in or around 2002 since World War II ended in 1945.

"On September the 11th, enemies of freedom committed an act of war against our country." President [George W.] Bush, September 20, 2001[4]

The Iraq War, also known as Operation Iraqi Freedom, began in March 2003. This quatrain may be implying that the Iraq War, which is causing substantial instability in the Middle East, may eventually result in a third world war or at least be the impetus for one. Nostradamus, as with other great prophets, could not specify exact dates because as our consciousness changes so does our future. There are any number of significant events that could lead to another world war including a global economic collapse. Only in hindsight will we know for sure.

The Hopi elders have made some very specific predictions concerning a third world war as well:

"World War III will be started by those people who first received the light [the divine wisdom or intelligence] in the other old countries [India, China, Egypt, Palestine, Africa]. The United States will be destroyed, land and people, by atomic bombs and radioactivity....Bomb shelters are a fallacy. It is only materialistic people who seek to make shelters. Those who are at peace in their hearts already are in the great shelter of life. There is no shelter for evil. Those who take no part in the making of world division by ideology are ready to resume life in another world....The war will be a spiritual conflict with material matters...."[5]

In the book *The Hopi Survival Kit,* author Thomas E. Mails writes about Hopi prophesy:

"Many of the prophets who forecast future problems and a great 'war to end all wars' say that only one-third of mankind will survive these. The Hopi attach no numbers to their predictions, but the general terms they use to describe them seem to agree with the estimate. They even pose the possibility that no one will survive. It all depends on how the 'ifs' work out."[6]

As you can see there are a number of prophesies concerning the possibility of a third world war coming from various sources.

Getting back to the Book of Revelation, the sixth trumpet releases four angels that are to kill one-third of mankind.

"The rest of mankind that were not killed by these plagues still did not repent of the work of their hands; they did not stop worshiping demons, and idols of gold, silver, bronze, stone and wood—idols that cannot see or hear or walk. Nor did they repent of their murders, their magical arts, their sexual immorality or their thefts." Revelation 9:20-21

The above passage speaks directly to our desires for worldly pleasures as various evils, *worshiping demons, sexual immorality,* and materialism as our false *idols of gold, silver, bronze, stone, and wood*. Is this not true of our society today?

Later in Revelation it speaks of the seventh trumpet.

"…when there came flashes of lightning, rumblings, peals of thunder, an earthquake and a great hail storm." Revelation 11:19

Clearly this will be a traumatic time for those on earth.

"And there was a war in heaven. Michael and his angels fought against the dragon, and the dragon and his angels fought back. But he was not strong enough, and they lost their place in heaven. The great dragon was hurled down—that ancient serpent called the devil or Satan, who leads the whole world astray. He was hurled to earth, and his angels with him." Revelation 12:7-9

Could the Law of Correspondence be at work here, suggesting that there is actually a battle being waged between good and evil in heaven as well as on earth? There is clearly a war between good and evil being waged on earth. That much we know for sure.

In Revelation chapter sixteen, the Bible speaks of seven more plagues referred to as the *seven bowls of God's wrath*.

"Then I heard a loud voice from the temple saying to the seven angels, 'Go, pour out the seven bowls of God's wrath on the earth.'" Revelation 16:1

The first bowl causes painful and ugly sores to appear on people who have the mark of the beast upon them. Clearly, this is a reference to pestilence. Scientists suggest that a world pandemic is going to occur at some point or another. They say it is only a matter of time before it does.

The second bowl turns the seas to blood and every living thing in it died. The third bowl causes the rivers and springs to turn to blood. Could the second and third bowls be a reference to the effects of a specific strain of red algae known as the Red Tide that robs water of its oxygen causing all things in it to die?

"The fourth angel poured out his bowl on the sun, and the sun was given power to scorch people with fire." Revelation 16:8

Could global warming become such a runaway problem that we cannot even go outside without being scorched by the sun? Or is it a reference to the ever-increasing depletion of our ozone layer and the subsequent increase in radiation from the sun hitting the earth?

The fifth bowl causes darkness. The sixth bowl causes drought and speaks of demons that perform miraculous signs that in turn gather men for a great battle.

"Then they gathered the kings together to the place that in Hebrew is called Armageddon." Revelation 16:16

The seventh bowl speaks of an inconceivable earthquake.

"Then there came flashes of lightning, rumblings, peals of thunder and a severe earthquake. No earthquake like it has ever occurred since man has been on earth...." Revelation 16:18

Over the generations we have become very complacent about prophecy to the point of disbelief. These days we are much more influenced by materialistic society. But it is not as if we haven't been warned.

"Pray that your fight will not take place in winter or on the Sabbath. For then there will be great distress, unequaled from the beginning of the world until now—and never to be equaled again. If those days had not been cut short, no one would survive, but for the sake of the elect those days will be shortened." Matthew 24:20-22

The verses in Matthew above imply that *if* Armageddon takes place in winter or on the day of the Sabbath, it will be only through the grace of God that any of us survive the final days. This is an ominous warning that would be foolish to ignore.

There will come a time when Satan's hold on the world will come to an end; however, this is only a temporarily situation. A period of peace is prophesied to last a thousand years once Satan is bound by an angel.

> "Then I saw an angel coming down out of heaven, having the key to the Abyss and holding in his hand a great chain. He seized the dragon, that ancient serpent who is the devil, or Satan, and bound him for a thousand years." Revelation 20:1-3

It is clear in the following verses that not everyone turns to God as a result of these tribulations (Armageddon) as foretold in Revelation.

> "They came to life and reigned with Christ a thousand years. The rest of the dead did not come to life until the thousand years were ended. This is the first resurrection. Blessed and holy are those who have part in the first resurrection." Revelation 20:4-6

What is referenced above in Revelation as the *first resurrection* isn't spoken about much, maybe because it is one obscure verse. However, this verse is critical because it suggests *two sets of resurrections* for the souls on the earth. Many will turn to God in the first set of tribulations and resurrect. But many will not. Those that do not turn to God in the first set of tribulations will remain dead during the thousand years of peace. The phrase *The rest of the dead did not come to life* may be suggesting that their hearts remained closed and are *dead in Spirit*, not necessarily dead physically speaking. They may be dead in terms of their conscious awareness but quite possibly still alive on earth. This may necessitate a second set of tribulations as in another Armageddon.

A second set of tribulations would be another opportunity for *the rest of the dead* to come to life, as in spiritual redemption. This is apparently the reason why it is necessary for Satan to be released from his bondage.

> "When the thousand years are over, Satan will be released from his prison and will go out to deceive the nations in the four corners of the earth—Gog and Magog—to gather them for battle. In number they are like the sand on the seashore. They marched across the breath of the earth and surrounded the camp of God's people, the city he loves. But fire came down from heaven and devoured them." Revelation 20:7-9

The tribulations will prove to be very trying physically, emotionally, and spiritually.

> "During those days men will seek death, but will not find it; they will long to die, but death will elude them." Revelation 9:6

Eventually all evil is destroyed. This is referred to as the second death.

> "The sea gave up the dead that were in it, and death and Hades gave up the dead that were in them, and each person was judged according to what he had done. Then death and Hades were thrown into the lake of fire. The lake of fire is the second death." Revelation 20:12-14

Let's stop here for a moment and reflect on the time sequence the Book of Revelation is suggesting. It is obvious that Armageddon may last for many years into the future, well beyond the year 2012, with some potentially horrific tribulations coming to fruition. If so, we will suffer the consequences of our sins over what could be a very long period of time. During the time of Armageddon we may be hit by a large meteorite or multiple meteorites. We may experience a super-volcano. We may experience a mega-quake, or as some people call it, *The Big One* which by a number of scientists' calculations is overdue. We may witness our sea levels rise twenty feet or more and destroy many coastal and inland areas. We may experience a third world war. All of these are possibilities. But I need to be clear here; I am not suggesting that all of these events will occur. It would only take a third world war along with the effects of global warming to fulfill most, if not all, of the prophesies in one way or another. If any additional tribulations come to fruition—more possibilities are listed later in the chapter—Armageddon will be that much more traumatic for us all. Once Armageddon comes to a conclusion, there is prophesized 1,000 years of peace for those that come to life during the first resurrection; and they will reign with Christ for 1,000 years.

> "The second death has no power over them, but they will be priests of God and of Christ and will reign with him for a thousand years." Revelation 20:6

Could *they will be priests of God and of Christ and will reign with him for a thousand years* indicate that for those that open their hearts—the Christ within them awaken, also defined here as the Revelation of Christ—they will live in peace upon the earth for 1,000 years? If Armageddon is as bad as it sounds, living in peace may be essential for the future survival of mankind, especially if we engage in another world war.

After the conclusion of the 1000-year period of peace, Satan will be released from the Abyss. Those that did not turn to God during the first set of tribulations may suffer additional tribulations. This could equate to the onset of a second Armageddon (Revelation 20:7-9).

Clearly, the Bible is referencing a substantial period of time before the final judgment occurs and the renewal of all things in heaven and on earth.

> "He who was seated on the throne said, 'I am making everything new!'"
> Revelation 21:5

At the end of time evil is destroyed and the souls are judged. Again, the souls being judged may infer a self judgment by the Christ Body.

> "If anyone's name was not found in the book of life, he was thrown into
> the lake of fire." Revelation 20:15

Since everything is energy, good or bad, is it possible that evil can manifest itself as a person as implied by the existence of an antichrist? If so, then is it possible that evil can manifest itself within a human body as if a soulless being, a child of the devil? If this is correct, then there may very well be evil entities roaming this planet in human form. Given the atrocities we witness in our lives, this may very well be the case. Then the verse above should be taken literally in that evil beings in human form will be thrown into the lake of fire.

Either way, as implied by the following verses in Revelation, it appears that there is a predetermined number of souls that will ultimately reach heaven. That number sealed as God's chosen people is limited to 144,000, the twelve tribes of Israel.

> "Do not harm the land or the sea or the trees until we put a seal on the
> foreheads of the servants of our God. Then I heard the number of people
> who were sealed: 144,000 from all the tribes of Israel.
>
> From the tribe of Judah 12,000 were sealed,
> from the tribe of Reuben 12,000,
> from the tribe of Gad 12,000,
> from the tribe of Asher 12,000,
> from the tribe of Naphtali 12,000,
> from the tribe of Manasseh 12,000,
> from the tribe of Simeon 12,000,
> from the tribe of Levi 12,000,
> from the tribe of Issachar 12,000,
> from the tribe of Zebulun 12,000,
> from the tribe of Joseph 12,000,
> from the tribe of Benjamin 12,000."
> Revelation 7: 3-8

"And he said, 'These are they who have come out of the great tribulation; they have washed their robes and made them white in the blood of the Lamb." Revelation 7:14

These 144,000 souls *who have come out of the great tribulation,* sealed as God's chosen people, appear to be the *only* souls that will eventually reach heaven.

However not all is grim. I believe that I have some *great news* for you. I believe that there are only 144,000 souls on this earth. For that matter, there are only 144,000 souls in this universe. Therefore *we* are all members of the twelve tribes of Israel!

Let's look at my reasoning here. First, if you attempt to explain the twelve tribes of Israel literally, it doesn't make any sense. If there are twelve tribes with twelve thousand people living in each tribe, what happens if a baby is born into one of the tribes? Would one of the tribe members have to die at the exact same moment in order to keep the tribe's population at precisely twelve thousand members, assuming reincarnation is a reality? It is ludicrous to think so. Assuming reincarnation is *not* reality, then not even all members of the twelve tribes of Israel are going to heaven, because the number of its own descendants surely number more than 144,000. Therefore the concept of only 144,000 tribe members going to heaven cannot be taken literally in the sense of the total number of tribal members living and/or deceased.

Consequently, we must look to *the total number of souls* as the key to defining who goes to heaven. Since hell is a temporary place, which by definition means everyone goes to heaven, the only logical explanation is that the billions of souls that seem to exist on earth beyond the chosen 144,000 are all part of 144,000 soul groups living multiple parallel lives. It makes perfect sense that there are only 144,000 souls (soul groups) on this earth plane, which again equates to the fact that we all necessarily go to heaven. When I say soul groups, I am really referring to each soul group as *one collective soul.*

If what I say is correct, a more accurate definition for a *soul group* or *soul family* would be *one soul living multiple parallel lives with all facets necessarily having the same vibrational rate.* In other words, there are only 144,000 soul groups, which are in reality only 144,000 souls collectively acting as if they are billions of individual souls. Consequently, there are a plethora of *you's and me's* running around this earth thinking that we are all separate souls. This is very consistent with quantum physics in that there may be a plethora of you's and me's living in a multitude of parallel dimensions or universes. I admit that this might be a little *ego-shattering* for some of us in that we all want to think that we are whole individuals in and of ourselves, but are we not in reality simply an aspect of the one Christ Body? Why would one soul living parallel lives on earth be that much more a stretch of the imagination?

So, if there are only 144,000 souls on earth, what does this say in terms of all the other beings on this planet? Since there are approximately 6.5 billion people living on earth then each soul on average is living approximately 45,139 parallel lives. Think about that for a moment. If what I suggest is true, your soul on average is living approximately 45,139 parallel lives all at the same time. What does that say to you? How does this affect you? How might this affect the way we judge other people around us? If I were you (and I might be), I would begin to wonder if the people closest to me are the same soul as me living a parallel life.

Now let's take this same concept in a slightly different direction. If we are individually only one aspect of the roughly 45,139 aspects of our own soul, then it is quite possible that our soul may be experiencing life on many different human levels. Your soul (for that matter, any soul) may be experiencing life as a homeless person, a radical Islamic cleric, a poor mother in India with three children, a drug addict bouncing in and out of rehab, a politician, a rich man, a person in prison, a recluse, a homosexual suffering from full-blown AIDS, a starving child in Africa, an elderly person living in a nursing home all at the same time all for the sake of experience and returning to our original state of consciousness. Finally, if we are one aspect injuring another aspect of our own soul for the betterment of our own collective soul (to learn the lesson of love), it puts the necessity of forgiveness in a new light. We are in essence forgiving ourselves. Mind-boggling, isn't it? Let's get back to 2012 prophecy.

Armageddon may also be rooted in astronomy and consequently linked to several ancient calendars such as the Tibetan calendar, the Aztec calendar, and the Egyptian calendar, but maybe most notable of all, the Mayan calendar. What the Mayan calendar represents is a timetable that measures or tracks the movement of the planets and stars, and quite possibly the development of consciousness of the human race as it progresses over time. Let me backtrack a little here to provide some supporting documentation. Today we use the Gregorian calendar which was established by Pope Gregory XIII in the year 1582. It is based on a twelve month year, a twenty-four hour day, and a sixty-minute hour, etc.[7] The Gregorian calendar proved to be a slightly more accurate measure of time replacing the Julian calendar (named after Julius Caesar) which had been used since its inception in 45 B.C.E (Before Common Era).

The Mayans similarly used a number of varying cycles or periods in concert with each other to measure time. Each period or cycle was based on natural phenomena within astronomy. The portion of the Mayan calendar that marks off one-year segments has thirteen months with twenty days in each month. The monthly portion of the calendar is based on the cycles of the moon and consists of 20 days. The total number of days in a year for the Mayans was therefore 260 days which may have been tracking the movement of the planet Venus.[8] Together the Mayan time periods or cycles work like gears of a watch. There are larger gears that move more slowly and smaller gears that move more quickly. The smaller gears (cycles) track shorter segments of time which are tied to the distance the stars or planets travel across the sky. The larger gears (cycles) track huge vast amounts of time and greater distances of stellar and planetary travel across the sky.[9] These longer cycles of time are referred to as the Mayan Long Count Calendar.

The Mayan Long Count Calendar is based on a number of somewhat complex increments of time: 7,200 days; 52 years; 144,000 days; 5,125 years; up to 26,000 years.

> "Even *longer* dates with more components have been found. This includes enough additional base 20 components to write dates millions of years in the past or future.... Imagining that kind of chronological depth to the universe is another Mayan accomplishment...."[10]

Beyond the obviously huge successes the Mayans had in tracking time in sync with the stars and planets, I personally find it significant that the Mayans chose to measure one of their cycles of time in 144,000 day increments. Is it a mathematical coincidence or based on a higher truth?

By using these cycles in concert with each other, the Mayans were able to make predictions about the future based on the past because they believed that everything in nature repeats itself. Correspondingly, they believed that the progression of human consciousness is also cyclical. It is believed that their calendar represents the *cycles of man as we progress in evolutionary consciousness*. Overall, the Mayan calendar was amazingly accurate in tracking the pathway of the stars and planets. It must have taken the Mayans thousands of years of intense study and observation to better understand the relationship of the stars and planets to major events on earth as they experienced them. Or possibly they received assistance from more advanced beings, who knows?

As mentioned, one of the largest cycles within the Mayan calendar is the cycle that marks off time in increments of 26,000 years. This cycle of time is once again tied to astronomy, specifically the *Precession of the Equinoxes*. It takes 26,000 years for the earth to transition through the *Precession of the Equinoxes*, or in layman's terms, *the time it takes for the North and South poles to complete one full wobble through the signs of the zodiac.* [11] Yes, our planet earth wobbles, just like a top as it begins to decelerate. At the point in which we complete the next 26,000 year cycle there will occur a very significant astrological alignment. The writings of John Major Jenkins describe this astrological alignment in detail below. Please note that the bracketed definitions inserted by me within the next quote are credited to John Major Jenkins.

> "The Galactic Alignment is the alignment of the December solstice sun [The sun, on the December solstice] with the Galactic equator

[The precise mid-line running down the Milky Way. Analogous to the earth's equator, it divides the galaxy into two hemispheres, or lobes]. This alignment occurs as a result of the precession of the equinoxes.

The Galactic Alignment occurs only once every 26,000 years, and was what the ancient Maya were pointing to with the 2012 date of their Long Count Calendar.

We can have a more general discussion of galactic alignments in history if we consider that the solstice axis aligns with the galactic equator every half precession cycle. Likewise, the equinox axis aligns with the galactic equator every half precession cycle....

In terms of Mayan astronomy and mythology, the Dark Rift feature (which the Maya called the Black Road or Xibalba be) lies along the galactic equator (the Milky Way) in the place where the December solstice sun will be in 2012.... Thus, in terms of Mayan mythology, we can also describe the Galactic Alignment of era-2012 as the alignment of the December solstice sun and the Dark Rift. This entire region is targeted by the cross formed by the Milky Way and the ecliptic between Sagittarius and Scorpio. This Cross was also recognized by the Maya, and was called the Crossroads or Sacred Tree. This entire region is embraced by what astronomers call the 'nuclear bulge' of the Galactic Center or the center of our Milky Way galaxy [A bright and wide region of the Milky Way, visible to the naked eye and between Sagittarius and Scorpio]. As any amateur astronomer or naked eye star gazer knows, this nuclear bulge is recognizable without the aid of radio telescopes. It is wider and brighter than other parts of the Milky Way. So, in a general sense we can also say that the alignment in 2012 is an alignment between the December solstice sun and the Galactic Center. However, since the nuclear bulge is quite large, this definition is not as precise as saying "the alignment of the December solstice sun with the Galactic equator," which occurs in the range 1980 - 2016."[12]

The alignment occurring between the years 1980 and 2016 may suggest that we are already in the transition to the next dimension as I too have suggested. If the lengthy quote above left you a little confused don't be alarmed. What is prophesized to occur in the year 2012 will hopefully become clearer as you continue to read on.

The length of time for the earth to complete one full wobble is approximately 26,000 years and marks off a period of time sometimes referred to as a *World* or *World*

Cycle.[13] According to the Mayans, each time we progress through one World Cycle we enter a new world and correspondingly reset the time clock back to zero. Marking time in concert with the Winter Solstice, the Mayans believed that we would begin a new World Cycle on December 21, 2012.

To summarize, on December 21, 2012 as our earth completes one 360 degree wobble, there will be a significant galactic alignment with our sun in relation to the center of the Milky Way Galaxy known as the Dark Rift. When this occurs we will have completed one more World Cycle. As you can see, the Mayans were not predicting the end of the world but possibly the end of the world as we know it now. I believe the Mayans were attempting to alert us by their calendars to the possibility that in year 2012, specifically on the winter solstice, the human race would enter a new dimension of consciousness and that this transition may be linked to a significant degree of devastation. This devastation may occur over many years as mentioned previously.

There are a number of scientific possibilities that could coincide with the end of this World Cycle. As we near (or pass through) the Dark Rift of the Milky Way, there very well may be a drastic increase in the number of sun spots (solar flares), and consequently an increase in the amount of solar radiation that hits the earth. We could be hit by huge gamma ray bursts that might disable the electrical power grids that supply us with electricity for many years into the future. We may experience a major shift in the magnetic polarity of this planet which by the way appears to have happened to our earth in the past. A rapid shift of the poles would cause floods, droughts, earthquakes and tsunamis of greater magnitude than ever before witnessed by man. Passing through the Dark Rift may even affect the rotation of the planet or shift the earth on its axis.[14]

Due to an already weakening heliosphere (the sun's protective bubble) the earth is becoming increasingly unprotected against intergalactic cosmic radiation. "Without the heliosphere the harmful intergalactic cosmic radiation would make life on Earth almost impossible by destroying DNA and making the climate uninhabitable."[15] As we pass through the Dark Rift of the Milky Way Galaxy we may also observe a greater number of objects in space of significant mass that could collide with earth resulting in the earth being bombarded by multiple meteorites. This ironically coincides with what is potentially prophesied in Revelation. It would take only one significantly sized meteorite to hit the earth for one-third of the world to be devastated. The meteorite that hit the earth approximately 65 million years ago wiped out the dinosaurs and paved the way for mankind to take dominion over the earth.[16]

It has been speculated that as a result of this galactic alignment there may occur a huge burst of light emanating from the black hole located at the center of the Milky Way that will engulf our earth. Some believe that every 5,125 years (a Mayan Long Count cycle) we are hit with this burst of light versus every 26,000 years:

"They say that at the beginning and end of these cycles, which is to say, every 5,125 years, the central sun or light of the galaxy emits a ray of light so intense and so brilliant that it illuminates the entire universe. It is from this burst of light that all of the Suns and planets sync. The Mayans compare this burst to the pulse of the universe, beating once every 5,125 years. It is these pulses that mark the end of one cycle and the beginning of the next. Each pulse lasting 20 years...."[17]

Could the reference to 5,125 years (versus 26,000 years) be consistent with the length of time it takes to complete a transition to the next higher dimension? Could the ray of light represent a quantum leap in our consciousness each time we cycle into a higher dimension? Could the 20 year pulse also be a reference to the length of time for the upcoming Armageddon?

Whether this burst of light occurs every 5,125 years or every 26,000 years the point is moot as we are now reaching a point where both cycles end in 2012 which may usher in a new dimensional reality for mankind. As stated, the height of the transition through the Dark Rift is reportedly to occur in 2012 on the winter solstice, specifically on December 21, 2012. In terms of the traditional zodiac, this occurs in the sign of Sagittarius. Sagittarius in the zodiac is the archer. Do you recall what the definition of sin is in archery terms? It is missing the mark. Is this simply another coincidence or the conscious wisdom within the universe continuing to display itself as synchronicity?

According to a special that aired October 28, 2007, on The History Channel, Nostradamus believed that there are thirteen signs in the zodiac.[18] The thirteenth sign is Ophiuchus, a Greek term meaning *the serpent holder*. The serpent holder could ironically be representative of the rising Kundalini energy necessary to make the transition to the fifth dimension. Continuing on, the constellation of Ophiuchus exists between Sagittarius and Scorpio, the two more traditional signs of the zodiac. This mostly unheard of sign literally points to the Dark Rift within the center of the Milky Way galaxy. Is the reason the Mayans broke one year into thirteen months due to their tracking thirteen celestial bodies which we commonly refer to as the zodiac? Did we somehow miss one of the significant constellations referred to above as Ophiuchus?

In the *Great Celestial Conjunction Crosses, Part I: Crosses in the New World*, Jan Wicherink writes the following about the 2012 galactic alignment:

"The ancient Maya understood that the zodiac cross (cross formed by the solstice and equinox axis) revolves against the backdrop of a fixated cross during a precession cycle. The first cross, the zodiac cross is the

Earth Cross while the second cross is the Galactic Cross. The Galactic Cross is the intersection of the Galactic Equator with the ecliptic and the axis perpendicular to this intersection. When the Earth Cross and the Galactic Cross are superimposed they form an eight-pointed cross. The two separate crosses become conjunct and form a single four-pointed cross during the moments of a Great Celestial Conjunction. After the Great Celestial Conjunction the individual crosses separate again to form an eight-pointed cross again."[19]

John Major Jenkins and Jan Wicherink seem to agree that this alignment is an auspicious time for us.

What did Edgar Cayce have to say about the 2012 transition? Here below is an excerpt from an article entitled *2012—Mayan Year of Destiny*, written by John Van Auken, editor of the *Ancient Mysteries Newsletter*.

"...the end of the Mayan Calendar is simply the end of the present World Age. And, important to us, it simply marks the beginning of the next cycle of rebirth, renewal.

...December 21, 2012, signals the end of this 5,125-year age that we've been living in and the commencement of a new Earth Age.

When asked what the New Age means to humanity, Edgar Cayce replied: 'By the full consciousness of the ability to communicate with the Creative Forces and be aware of the relationships to the Creative Forces and the uses of same in material environs. This awareness during the era or age in the Age of Atlantis and Lemuria or Mu brought what? Destruction to man, and his beginning of the needs of the journey up through that of selfishness.'

Cayce is informing us that in a previous time cycle, humanity had a level of consciousness and relationship with the Creative Forces that allowed us to live at higher levels of material, mental, and spiritual activity in the Earth and beyond. Unfortunately, we misused this consciousness and the power that came with the close relationship to the Forces. This misuse brought on the destruction of our great cultures and a long, karmic soul journey through the pain and confusion that resulted from our selfishness and self-centered focus on our will without regard for the will of the Creator and others. Now, as the cycles come around again, we are nearing a time when the level of consciousness and relationship with the Creative Forces will allow us once again to regain these powers. How will we use them this time?"[20]

Cayce is stating here, similar to what might be occurring today, that past civilizations misused their conscious intelligence and consequently what was created by mankind was destroyed. Lemuria (Mu) was destroyed approximately 26,000 years ago (one Precession of the Equinox) while Atlantis was destroyed 13,000 years ago (the midpoint of a Precession of the Equinox). The destruction of Atlantis occurring 13,000 years ago may be consistent with John Major Jenkins when he wrote "We can have a more general discussion of galactic alignments in history if we consider that the solstice axis aligns with the galactic equator every half precession cycle."

The higher levels of radiation or solar flares we may experience as we pass through the Dark Rift could create a higher vibrational frequency for our planet and our physical bodies, specifically our endocrine system, which is energetically tied to our chakras. More so, the pineal gland, which is considered to be a gateway to higher levels of consciousness, may become increasingly active or activated. If I am correct, there will be a heightened level of psychic phenomena as I suggested earlier. This is also known as *Kundalini rising*. An increase in the body's vibrational rate will cause our Kundalini energy to rise to higher chakras within the body. A rise in our Kundalini energy will increasingly open up our hearts to love as the higher vibrational energies move upward along the spine to our higher chakras. Not surprisingly, for some individuals it may cause the throat chakra or third-eye chakra to open even more.

As the Kundalini energy rises each time we go through a major astrological alignment, with it may arrive the amount of devastation necessary for us to raise our own vibrational energy to remain consistent with the new outer vibrational energy. The reason that as much as one-third or more of the earth's population may be killed this major cycle is because we have so densely populated the earth along major fault lines and shore lines. In previous cycles the earth was substantially less populated and possibly more fragmented, geographically speaking. With each major rise in consciousness there must be a tearing down of the old to bring in the new; this time there are more of us present on earth to experience the end of this age, possibly because of the benefits of being present for the transition. As suggested by the Mayan calendar, what emerges out of each major cycle is a mankind with a higher level of consciousness. Soon enough mankind will face the end of another 26,000 year cycle and the beginning of a new one.

The year 2012 obviously marks a very auspicious time in terms of our spiritual evolution as it not only designates the end of a smaller Mayan Long Count cycle (5,125 years), but designates the end of a major World Cycle (26,000 years). What will emerge for us after we pass through this Dark Rift once again is a mankind with a higher consciousness. When we have completed this round of transformation, we will have necessarily mastered the chakra energies associated with the heart chakra. This change in our consciousness will represent our entrance into the fifth dimension associated with the energies of the concrete mind. We will have left behind us the fourth dimensional lessons associated with learning the lesson of love. We will, of course, still experience emotions; what is different is that we will have sufficiently mastered them, hopefully.

For those of us who *do not* master their emotions, what will become of them? For those of us who *do* sufficiently master their emotions, what will become of them? Will they need to suffer along with those that do not master their emotions when the transition occurs in 2012? Is it possible that there may be a quantum split in our universe where those souls that mastered their emotions will somehow be transported to another dimension? Is it possible that this evolutionary change in consciousness may lead to the creation of another dimension altogether? Could another higher dimensional earth be created where spiritually elevated souls move forward into the fifth dimension while the souls that failed to make the transition stay back on the fourth dimensional earth? Does a fifth dimensional earth already exist? A splitting of dimensions may or may not be an explanation for the *supposed* Rapture. I use the word *supposed* since the word Rapture never appears in the Bible. The term Rapture is often associated with the verses that appear in Thessalonians.

> "For the Lord himself will come down from heaven, with a loud command, with the voice of the archangel and with the trumpet call of God, and the dead in Christ will arise first. After that, we who are still alive and are left will be caught up together with them in the clouds to meet the Lord in the air." Thessalonians 4:16-17

If the Rapture were to occur, the Rapture might occur in a later Mayan cycle or World Cycle than the one we are about to experience in 2012. Or maybe the Mayans believed that a Rapture occurs every major World Cycle. This would explain the disappearance of certain lost civilizations. If the winter solstice in 2012 is the time of the Rapture, will the Rapture be obvious, or will it appear to us as a normal event where huge numbers of people die due to natural causes, or natural disasters, with those dying transitioning to another higher dimensional reality? Will the souls that do not make the transition to the higher dimension understand that the Rapture just occurred? Will they understand that they are about to suffer through Armageddon? Will the souls that transition to the higher dimension understand that they just experienced a quantum event?

In the chapter on "Quantum Theory and Thermodynamics" where I discussed parallel universes, research indicates *that during a quantum event, one reality may split into a superposition of many realities, and that the observer (you and me) would individually experience this splitting merely as a slight randomness; we would not perceive a splitting of realities as alternate dimensions.* According to quantum physics then, we may very well experience a Rapture, but we would most likely not even realize it. The Rapture would appear as a non-event! However, even though the Rapture appeared as a non-event, there could have been a quantum split in realities with the old earth remaining in the fourth dimension, and a *New Earth* transcending into the fifth dimension.

The net effect may be the addition of a new thirteenth dimension. Could a new thirteenth dimension correspond to the thirteenth sign of the zodiac, Ophiuchus? Either way, everything might seem quite normal in terms of our physicality, even though spiritually and scientifically the entire human race experienced a quantum event with one dimension splitting into two separate dimensions. If this is true, then the New Testament of the Bible, in particular the Book of Revelation, addresses a much smaller span of time that we could have ever imagined. Specifically, it addresses our transition from the fourth dimension into the fifth dimension which is set to occur in 2012. And if so, are ready for this next transition?

So what does this mean for us? How do we prepare? Should we store food? Should we build more underground shelters? The fact of the matter is the best way to prepare is to open our hearts to the emotion of love by utilizing our concrete minds which is associated with the lower mind function. Our concrete mind associated with the fifth chakra provides us the tool we need to open our hearts. We each decide if we take the higher or lower path and how much we will each individually suffer in which dimension. We must use our minds to open our hearts. We must learn to control our thoughts through constant diligent observation of our thoughts. So the answer to the question above *How do we prepare?* is to prepare spiritually.

The end times as we tend to think of it does not signify the end of mankind but rather it marks a new beginning for us. What will it take to get us there? Will it take great devastation to get each of us to the point of compassionate loving understanding? Will we all make the transition? The answer is up to us. What will we do? Will we open our hearts or will we choose to keep them closed? By choosing the latter, I mean *seeking for our own benefit only*, we increase the likelihood of mass devastation. In choosing *fear*, some people may turn to violence during this tumultuous time in an attempt to obtain sufficient food and water much like what occurred in New Orleans as a result of hurricane Katrina. Those choosing *love above fear* will understand that we are all in this together, and that only in *community* and acting in each other's best interest can we survive this next phase of mankind's evolutionary spiritual development.

"'Love your neighbor as yourself.' Love does no harm to its neighbor. Therefore love is fulfillment of the law. And do this, understanding the present time. The hour has come for you to wake up from your slumber, because our salvation is nearer now than when we first believed." Romans 13:9-11

The best response to this newly acquired knowledge about 2012 is to make positive changes within ourselves now. We must look within our hearts and ask what we can do for humanity, not necessarily for ourselves. We mustn't get caught up in selfishness or self-full-ness. We mustn't get caught up in the material nature of this earth. We must rather prepare by opening our hearts to love now before it is too late.

"Since you have kept my command to endure patiently, I will also keep
you from the hour of trial that is going to come upon the whole world
to test those who live on earth." Revelation 3:10

Here we have God's promise that the faithful will be saved *from the hour of trial*, but only those who kept His command will be saved. Unless we choose to love others more and be less selfish, it is going to get increasingly difficult for us. The *greed bubble* is about to burst. We must let go of our materialistic ways. It is divine timing to move into the next dimension, and time may be running out for many of us. What do we have to lose by choosing love? It is clear what we have to lose if we don't. It may be earth's 9/11. It may be our spiritual wake-up call. We can make this transition much smoother, but it will take a reawakening or remembrance of who we really are. We are the children of God. We are all one connected within the Christ Body. But what can we each do now to move toward this goal of opening our hearts to love? The answer may be Immortal Life Yoga.

CHAPTER 40

Immortal Life Yoga

Understanding now that there are at least seven form heavens each associated with one of the seven chakras and at least one non-form heaven associated with the transcendental chakra, what will it take for us to get to heaven? Maybe a better question to ask is *What it will take for us to regain our original state of Christ Consciousness so that we can regain full access to all form heavens and alternate heavenly dimensions beyond form?*

Once again let's look to the Bible for clarification.

> "But seek first his kingdom and his righteousness, and all things will be given to you as well." Matthew 6:33

From the above verse it seems as if there is a prerequisite for our return to heaven, specifically the process of *seeking*. However, we each seek heaven in our own way, and as we now know *all roads lead to heaven*, though some faster than others. Sin is a detour for all of us, and we each sin in our own way and in varying degrees. It seems from the verse above that when we make seeking heaven our first priority, God responds by giving us everything we could desire and subsequently all things will be given to us. But is that really the case? Can we desire to be rich or lust and still seek God first? Too often it seems that we seek things of this earth first, placing a higher emphasis on material nature. I strongly suggest that what we need to seek is a greater depth of spirituality. In seeking God first and foremost, we as a result desire appropriately while not yearning for things of a material nature beyond what is necessary. If so, then the verse above is correct in that we should neither have to endure poverty nor should we possess great riches beyond a deep richness in Spirit. Therefore, to return to our original state of enlightenment and our immortal bodies we must *seek first His kingdom and His righteousness*.

> "And he said: 'I tell you the truth, unless you change and become like children, you will never enter the kingdom of heaven.'" Matthew 18:3

This verse states that we must *change and become like children* to get to heaven. But how do children act? From what I have witnessed in very young children, there exists in them a certain level of innocence, often accompanied with absolute honesty. Children appear to very much live in the moment. As with most children they have parents or guardians who nurture them and provide for their every need. Children are most often happy, playful, generous, and loving. They seem satisfied with little or nothing, unless taught otherwise. As a child I often played with nothing more than my imagination. As a child, a stick became a rifle. An old can became the focal point of a game called "kick the can." A nearby field became a jungle where we would build an imaginary fortress. Not surprisingly, young children do not see color, race, or disability as a barrier to love. Perhaps most importantly, young children have little or no ego, at least in the negative sense of the word. By becoming more like children we grow closer to Spirit.

The Bible is chocked full of *do's and don'ts*, so to list them all here might be a little overwhelming and most likely unnecessary. So what is the quickest way to get to heaven? I believe the shortest path is yoga, but not just any type of yoga.

For the majority of my adult life, I didn't have any interest in yoga, until one night I had a very extraordinary dream that opened my eyes to the importance of yoga. In the dream I was talking to a man about a very pleasant-looking blond-haired woman about thirty years old standing about ten feet away from us. The man told me that the woman's name was Alice Bailey. Alice Bailey was speaking with an entirely different person altogether. The man I was speaking with then explained to me that Alice Bailey was very influential in the development of a certain type of yoga, even though she was not the person who created it. After I received this brief explanation, the dream abruptly ended and I awoke. That was the entire dream. However, the dream was so very vivid it struck me as peculiar, so out of curiosity I did an internet search using the words *Bailey Yoga*. As a result of my search, many websites popped up on Alice Bailey and a certain style of yoga called Raja Yoga.

As it turns out, Alice Bailey was an author that lived from 1880 until her passing in 1949. I was intrigued to read that although she did not create Raja Yoga, she was very influential in its development, just as my dream had suggested. She was also a prominent figure in Theosophy, which is a religious philosophy originating with Helena Blavatsky. A key component of Theosophy is that *all religions hold a portion of the truth within Divine Wisdom and that mankind is ever evolving in search of spiritual perfection.* I found this to be very interesting and an enlightened nonjudgmental approach to religion and life.

After reviewing several websites, I intuitively decided which one of Alice Bailey's books I would read. I chose the book *The Light of the Soul,* which outlines and interprets the original *Yoga Sutras of Patanjali*.[1] Patanjali was a man who lived thousands of years ago, sometime before Christ, and is considered the Father of Yoga. He compiled

195 sutras, which are brief instructive guidelines for life, detailing how to live a life that ultimately leads to personal enlightenment. In this way, the sutras are considered a guide to achieving greater spiritual awareness and growing in Spirit. Overall, I found this all to be quite remarkable, especially since I had never heard of Alice Bailey, Raja Yoga, or Patanjali before my dream.

Previously to reading Alice Bailey's book *The Light of the Soul*, I did not understand the essence of *true yoga*. I thought yoga was primarily stretching exercises. I understand now that yoga, as it was initially intended, is what I would call a *true religion*; it is about living a good, honorable, spiritual life. True yoga, as it was originally intended, is not based in any dogmatic teachings, churches or synagogues, codes, religious fervor, or even exercise. True yoga stretches the mind and the soul, not just the body, and is meant to be a method for returning to our original state of enlightenment.

Having studied the yoga sutras of Patanjali and various other religions and philosophies of the world, I created my own philosophy as to how to best live a good, honorable, spiritual life and attain personal enlightenment or rather regain the state of enlightenment that was our original state. I call it *Immortal Life Yoga*. I chose the name Immortal Life Yoga because that is what I believe we, as spiritual beings in material nature, are attempting to become once again, that is, immortal. By becoming enlightened or Christ Conscious, we return to our original perfect state as a pure immortal being in our pure immortal body unencumbered by lower nature thoughts and desires.

Immortal Life Yoga is a systematic way of life that incorporates several styles of yoga that exist today: Hatha, Bhakti, Jnana, Karma, Kundalini, and Raja—just to name a few.[2] For the most part, all yoga styles practiced today include the basic exercises of stretching and strengthening the body. But Immortal Life Yoga is much more than exercise as you will soon see.

Here is an overview of the various primary styles of yoga that play an integral role in Immortal Life Yoga.

Hatha Yoga focuses primarily on specific exercises that add to the participant's strength and flexibility. This is what most people consider to be traditional yoga (physical exercises), with few people understanding the true purpose of yoga. Additionally, this style of yoga recognizes the body as the temple or vehicle for the soul. It is believed that through physical exercise via specific posturing called *asanas* and breathing techniques, purification of the mind and body is eventually achieved.

Bhakti Yoga focuses primarily on the *emotional body*, specifically on love and devotion to God. Bhakti Yoga's focus is on controlling our feelings and emotions. Bhakti Yoga approaches God through the heart and not through the mind. It can include prayer, chanting, singing, certain rituals, and of course asanas. It is believed that by opening up to greater levels of love, we eventually rejoin with God.

Jnana Yoga conversely focuses on *the mind* (mental body) in order to realize our truest nature, and in doing so, we discover God and the God within us. Jnana Yoga discovers God through acquiring knowledge with the intent of expanding the mind. This yoga places a heavy emphasis on contemplation, study, and analysis. It is believed that by obtaining greater levels of wisdom, the veils of ignorance are lifted and we regain our original state of enlightenment.

Karma Yoga focuses primarily on taking *proper action* and a commitment of *devotional service* to God and others. The name of the yoga itself says it all; karma is the key to spiritual enlightenment. It is believed that our negative karma is reduced through selfless work until liberation from reincarnation is attained.

Kundalini Yoga focuses on raising the *Holy Spirit life force* (Kundalini energy) that resides latent within the spinal column. This process of seeking enlightenment is augmented by maintaining the specific intent of raising this energy, postures, visualizations, mantras, and breath work. It is believed that enlightenment is reached when this energy is raised to the seventh chakra from the base chakra and continually flows up and down the spine unrestricted.

Raja Yoga teaches *self-control*. Raja means *kingly* or *royal*. Raja Yoga focuses on controlling the emotions as well as the mind's thoughts. It focuses on *right mind* and *right action*. Meditation is a primary component of Raja Yoga. Mindful concentration and breathing exercises are an important part of this style of yoga as well. It is believed that by exercising proper control over our emotions and our mind's thoughts, we purify ourselves and return to a state of enlightenment.

What is fundamentally missing from the individual yoga styles mentioned above is the understanding of the interrelatedness of the body, the mind, and the soul. Each individual style of yoga attempts to reach God and enlightenment independently of the other, which is not possible. It is like preparing for a triathlon but only focusing on one of the three segments of the race ignoring the other two segments. Each one of the various yoga styles practiced independently of the other will help us grow in Spirit but does not fully prepare us by balancing the various energies associated with the body, mind, and soul.

Historically, Patanjali appears to be the first person to speak of yoga and teach the science of yoga to others. Patanjali meant for his yoga sutras to be a step-by-step process back to the state of enlightenment and the Creator. Over hundreds or thousands of years the true science of yoga has become corrupted from its original version, just like everything else, including religion. Even today, the few that practice yoga correctly may still be practicing yoga with the wrong intent. They are practicing it with the purpose of personal enlightenment. Surprisingly, that is the wrong intent. Yoga is not about the self; it is about being selfless. If we seek anything for the self it will hold us back from reaching the goal of enlightenment and our ultimate reunion with the Creator. Only by becoming selfless can we eventually merge back into the Godhead. Yoga is actually a very old science. You may or may not know that the word *yoga* is derived from the Sanskrit word *Yuj* which means *yoke* or *union*. Union or possibly *re-union* with God is the primary purpose for our existence beyond our original intent to *experience form*. And for those of us who desire to reach a more immediate state of enlightenment, Immortal Life Yoga could possibly be the most direct way.

Immortal Life Yoga is a more complete spiritual way of life. It is based on the sutras of Patanjali, the primary styles of yoga already presented, and the basic tenets behind all religions before man corrupted each of them. The basic tenets of religion are based on love, service, balance, surrender, and remembrance of whom and what we really are. That is to say we are souls or fragments of one *form* body or Christ Body. Just as there is a thread of truth that runs through all religions, there is a thread of truth that runs through all styles of yoga. Immortal Life Yoga combines the truth in the various styles of yoga into one yoga style. And because of this, I would go so far as to suggest that Immortal Life Yoga is the *fast track* to heaven as it promotes a life devoid of sin.

What defines the Immortal Life Yoga fast track specifically? Immortal Life Yoga is not just about the exercise of yoga (asanas), it is about how we live our lives and how we live in relationship to others recognizing that we are all one within the Christ Body. There are many styles of yoga today but they are merely fragments of what we need to be doing with our lives. Immortal Life Yoga integrates the various styles of yoga into one practice. In this way Immortal Life Yoga integrates the head with mind, the heart with love, and the body with the soul. And yes, it includes the exercise component of asanas as well. The various yoga styles practiced together in unison as Immortal Life Yoga leads to an integrated lifestyle balancing the physical world with the spiritual world.

In relationship to the development of the body, mind and soul, which is inextricably tied together, we must place our primary focus on these four main aspects: *the physical, the emotional, the mental,* and *the spiritual.* As previously mentioned, we cannot ignore any of the above in favor of the other and reach enlightenment. In Immortal Life Yoga we focus on these four aspects by integrating all of the above-mentioned yoga styles into one complete style. When coordinated into a cohesive practice these four aspects lead to three all-important outcomes: *right thought, right desire,* and *right action.* The following is how it is accomplished.

The *physical aspect* of Immortal Life Yoga pertains to *right action* as witnessed primarily in Hatha Yoga. Hatha Yoga prepares the body as a vehicle for the soul through asanas.

The physical exercises of yoga are meant to loosen up the body and prepare it for longer periods of meditation. It can be quite trying on a body to sit for a time without stirring. More importantly, the asanas open up the chakras allowing the Kundalini energy to move more freely up and down the body. Regarding caring for the physical body, a healthy organic diet free of pesticides and hormones mixed with a diet of live foods can be important facets of attaining enlightenment. If you are not preparing the body for enlightenment, the mind and soul cannot become enlightened. The body needs to be purified along with the mind and soul. The Holy Spirit can only fully enter a body that is adequately prepared for it. If the vibration of the body is too low, the Holy Spirit cannot add to the soul's vibrational rate. The body would not be able to handle the increase in vibrational spiritual energy. Eating correctly and exercising play important roles on the vibrational rate of our bodies. If we eat poorly and don't exercise, the vibrational rate of the body may remain too low for major spiritual advancements to occur.

Putting drugs, alcohol, or unhealthy foods in our bodies is an offense against the body and likewise offends the Holy Spirit. This is true because our body is the temple of the Holy Spirit. How do you feel when you walk into a public restroom and it is disgusting? You would prefer not use the facilities, correct? How do you feel crawling into a bed that has freshly washed sheets? Do you see the difference? How do you think the Holy Spirit feels when we defile our body with impure things? Would you defile a church of God? We defile our own temple when we eat unhealthy foods, drink alcohol to excess, take illicit drugs, and think unholy thoughts. In addition to *right action*, progress down the spiritual path cannot be maintained without *right desire*.

The *emotional aspect* of Immortal Life Yoga as seen in Bhakti Yoga pertains to love, which leads to *right desire*. Desires stem from emotion and are an integral part of the three-step creation process. The first step in creation is ideation. An idea is formed within consciousness. The next step of creation is emotion, which leads to desire. Without emotion there would not be any creation. Nothing would be created because there would be no desire to create. Ideation is the masculine aspect of the universe while the emotional component is the female aspect of the universe. The merging of the male and the female is the action that needs to take place as the third step in the creation process. In our physicality, the action of creation can be witnessed by sexual intercourse because it is the active merging of the female and the male aspects. As it sometimes happens, the result is the formation of a child, another *being*. It is in the merging of the mind and the heart that we create all that is in this universe. It is thought and emotion, desire with action that formed the cosmos. Just as we need thought, we need desire. But the *right desire* is critical to reaching heaven. So what is it that you desire? Is your primary desire spiritual transformation? Is it enlightenment? Is it heaven? Or are your desires for the material nature? When we create we should create in love and service. This is right desire.

The feminine aspect of God is the Holy Spirit in the spiritual realm and is represented by Mother Earth in the physical realm. But the Holy Spirit is really everywhere and in everything because it is the vibration of life itself. Therefore the Holy Spirit is omnipresent within creation, not just God the Father. The three aspects of God in this universe are truly inseparable as I have mentioned many times now. Therefore, in Immortal Life Yoga, we recognize that *everything has value*. In other words, *right desire* includes a healthy respect all people, places, and things as a part of the Divine. Desire contains within it *recognition;* a recognition that *everything is Spirit* and that Spirit lives within each of us. This recognition leads to a desire to live in oneness and to live a good, honorable, spiritual life with respect, recognizing Spirit in all things.

The *mental aspect* of Immortal Life Yoga pertains to *right thought* as witnessed in Jnana Yoga, Karma Yoga, and Raja Yoga. Jnana Yoga focuses on increasing knowledge through spiritual study to expand the mind. Karma Yoga stresses the necessity of correct thought; otherwise we incrementally increase our negative karma. Raja Yoga promotes self-control of the mind in order to maintain proper thoughts. Altogether the mental aspect of yoga is intended to raise our consciousness back to its original God-mind.

> "Always aim at complete harmony of thought and word and deed. Always aim at purifying your thoughts and everything will be well."
> Mahatma Gandhi

Anything less than God-mind is ego-mind. Ego-mind is steeped in thoughts related to fear and other less desirable emotions. God-mind is steeped in thoughts of love. To develop God-mind, we require discipline. Discipline is necessary to control our mind as we have many competing thoughts that vie for our attention; some good, some bad. Proper thoughts raise our consciousness and our soul's vibrational rate. Discipline helps us stay in *right mind*. Discipline helps us to focus on positive thoughts and to consistently steer clear of negative thoughts and our sinful nature. Discipline overall is about choosing the higher nature within us which is the higher nature of God. Discipline, of course, implies right mind. In Immortal Life Yoga, we strive to be constantly vigilant by maintaining an awareness of our thoughts and redirect negative thoughts back to our higher nature, our God-mind. Right mind (God-mind) coupled with right desire then leads to *right action*.

> "You must be the change you want to see in the world." Mahatma Gandhi

The *spiritual aspect* of Immortal Life Yoga as seen in Karma Yoga, Kundalini Yoga, and Raja Yoga pertains to developing and maintaining a spiritual outlook on life and keeping in mind God's purpose for us. Remembering that we are individual beings of light leads to *right thought*. Raja Yoga, through discipline, infers not only right thought, but *right action*. Karma Yoga implies that through *devotional service* we reduce and eventually eliminate our bad karma. Devotional service is therefore vitally important for obtaining enlightenment. Devotional service is taking the right action in life. Devotional service can occur in many ways and serves to lessen or reduce our karmic debt. By reducing our negative karma we are one step closer to being released from the cycle of reincarnation. What generally increases our karma is doing things for ourselves that tend to satiate our lower desires for material form. Excessive desire for material form is materialism. Wealth in and of itself is not a sin. But attachment to wealth is a sin. Attachments, whether to an outcome, a possession, or a person, create the opportunity for misery and suffering and separate us from God.

The spiritual aspect of Immortal Life Yoga comes with an understanding that we walk in both the physical and the spiritual worlds and that there is a constant interplay between the two. However, life is not about how much wealth we can accumulate. It is not about manipulating the spiritual laws and principles available to us to increase our physical abundance. That is materialism, and it's the biggest problem mankind faces today. How is it that we can come into possession of so much more than we need yet we allow children in Third World countries to starve to death? It is not possible to hold our possessions above service to others and God and regain heaven.

Souls that have awakened to this understanding feel the yearning within their souls for something more purposeful than accumulating wealth. Our true individual purpose is found within the *DNA of our soul* as a part of the God DNA in each of us. Our soul's DNA defines our soul's personality. As such, we can begin our journey to discovering our true purpose by living life under certain guiding principles or spiritual tenets, Immortal Life Yoga. These guiding principles or tenets open us further to the discovery of our soul's purpose. When we take a step closer to God, God opens up Himself to us and our purpose becomes clearer. When a person travels toward a mountain, the view of the mountain becomes clearer, doesn't it? Did the mountain change? Of course it didn't. What changed was the proximity of the person to the mountain, and subsequently the view of the mountain.

The same is true for God. As we move closer to God via living a good, honorable, spiritual life, our perception and consequently our understanding shifts. Our soul's purpose becomes clearer and who we are in relationship to God becomes clearer. However, moving closer to God does come with a cost, that is, the cost of leaving the old self behind as false ego and stepping into our new truer self. Once we come to a point of recognition of our soul's purpose, we must become the truer expression of our soul's purpose, otherwise we depress it. On a physical level, we then experience depression often not even realizing why.

One of the more important steps to enlightenment is spiritual study. Spiritual study is very important for ongoing spiritual growth. I suggest beginning your journey by reading scripture and other spiritually-based books. It is important to study other religions with an open mind. I would further suggest attending lectures or joining an open-minded spiritual study group. Then apply what it means to you. And by all means, ask questions! Question *why*. It's not just about intellectual study. It is about understanding the spiritual concepts concerning love and then living it. In living it, we experience it and become it. Spiritual study is important because we attain wisdom. By studying scriptures we learn the wisdom of the great spiritual leaders. Through the attainment of wisdom, we make better choices which then reduces karma. For me, my journey included the study of many religions, philosophies, science, and metaphysics. In my research I discovered a much deeper understanding and as a result developed the concept of Immortal Life Yoga.

Right action, as a part of the spiritual aspect of Immortal Life Yoga, necessitates a daily meditation practice. I believe one of the purest ways to enlightenment is through meditation as suggested in Raja Yoga. The soul in you is the god in you. By developing an ongoing deep meditation practice, we quiet the mind and come to know the god in us by traveling inward. In this way, we seek the Kingdom of God within us. You can also think of meditation as taking time to get to know your truest inner you. Via meditation we come into contact with God Consciousness through our soul. Overall, I would say that meditation is one of the most important components of Immortal Life Yoga. Therefore any amount of meditation during the day will greatly augment our spiritual journey back home. Meditation coupled with mantras and visualizations serve to raise the vibrational rate of the body to make it more in tune with the soul.

As possibly suggested in Kundalini Yoga and as definitely suggested by me, one of the fastest ways in which to raise the level of spiritual energy within us is to withdraw from having any and all orgasms permanently, or simply for a period of time. This creates an opportunity for rapid spiritual advancement for you and your partner (if you have one); but it must be integrated with increased spiritual effort such as Immortal Life Yoga. Abiding by the tenets of Immortal Life Yoga or a similar spiritual practice may be very necessary in order to channel this energy into productive outcomes.

By successfully moving this energy up my spine I felt as if my heart and mind were opening to increasingly greater levels of joy, love, and mental clarity. Often I would feel a physical tingling on the back of my neck or on the top of my head as if being tickled by a feather while I meditated. This occurred because of the increased levels of energy stimulating and activating my fifth and seventh chakras. They were in effect opening. I also notice flashes of white light around the outer edges of my third-eye area. These flashes looked very similar to the flashes of light I experienced after two or three hours of sitting in meditation. I can only assume that these flashes of light were indicative of my third-eye chakra opening.

For me, Immortal Life Yoga balances my life. It is a way for me to live my life while integrating the physical, emotional, mental, and spiritual aspects of my being. I believe it to be a systemic way of life that will return my being back to God, heaven, and enlightenment most quickly. But it all takes effort, patience, and endurance to grow in Spirit. The way of enlightenment is a constant battle. It is not the easy way. There is no easy way. But neither does it have to be a way of intense suffering. The difficult changes we make in our life will become easier over time with continued practice. What might appear initially as fantasy or maybe even heresy will become our new reality as we move forward on our spiritual path. What initially was a state of ignorance that necessitated reincarnation will once again return to a state of perfection, that of Christ Consciousness. We must first begin with *surrender* to the notion that there exists an infinite world of possibilities. There is an incredible being of light within us, which is our soul. It is eternal. By growing in Spirit we develop a greater connection to our soul, which can only lead to greater levels of love and joy. This is real peace of mind. Creating anything less only leads to impermanence and suffering. Only by giving up our attachment to the material world and turning our lives over to God can we even begin to hope for an escape to suffering.

Are we nearing Armageddon? The answer is yet to be seen; only time will tell. What is certain is that we are moving now into a time of mastering the fourth chakra energies of love as we begin to enter the fifth dimension.

Jesus Christ taught that we should love and that time is now.

"This is my command: Love each other." John 15:17

That is our next step of spiritual evolution, to open our hearts to experiencing greater levels of love. Some devastation will naturally occur within this physical plane of consciousness as we begin our transition and many may deny that there is even a spiritual transition of any type occurring. But the Law of Correspondence is at work here. What is shifting within the spiritual realm will cause shifting in the physical realm, whether we recognize it or not. The physical and the spiritual worlds are constantly interacting. They are integrally tied together, and a spiritual shift is sometimes fueled by physical devastation.

The return to enlightenment and our immortal bodies can be a long, painful, and arduous process, or it can be made much easier. It is our choice. By raising our consciousness even a little bit just maybe we can collectively change the direction in which this earth is heading. Rather than the destruction that is forecast in the Bible in the book of Revelation, which I believe is our current transition to the next dimension, the transition will hopefully come in like a lamb rather than coming in like a lion. Those souls that are able to raise their soul's vibrational energy, even if only partially, will assist those who are not as willing to awaken spiritually, because the raising of the spiritual energy of one positively affects us all. No matter which yoga style we choose, the net effect of raising our spiritual energies will naturally have a positive impact on the world's overall consciousness. Very soon our souls will *need* to vibrate at an elevated rate consistent with having sufficiently mastered the fourth chakra associated with our emotions or there may be incredible suffering. It is vitally important we begin this process of raising our consciousness before it is too late. The critical issue we face is not whether or not we will return to our original point of consciousness as enlightenment, but rather how quickly we return and how much we suffer before we return to our original state of enlightenment. The choices we make today determine our fate. The choices we make today determine how long, how difficult, and how far our journey is back to our original state of enlightenment.

As I was about to finish this book, I asked my higher self a question and wrote it down in my dream book before I went to sleep. I asked if there was anything else I missed or needed to add to this book. That night I had a surprising dream. I dreamed that I was in a spaceship. I was standing in front of the spaceship's computer and I was inputting numbers as if creating some mathematical formula. What I was attempting to do was to save the world, but I was running out of time and I knew it. There was a woman standing behind me and she reminded me that I needed to add twelve hours to the time sequence I was working on due to a galactic time shift. That was the end of the dream.

As soon as I awoke, my mind began to race with alternate interpretations. Did my dream indicate that there would be a galactic shift forward in time splitting our dimension into two separate dimensions? Did my dream suggest or even go as far as to verify that a Rapture will occur in 2012 where a portion of the world's population will be catapulted forward in time into a new dimension parallel to our current world, another parallel universe? Could this galactic time shift create another dimension, perhaps a twelfth or thirteenth dimension, yet to be discovered by scientists? Was my dream suggesting that the transition to the fifth dimension will occur on December 22, 2012 rather than the highly anticipated date of December 21, 2012 which is the winter solstice?

Of course I asked for further clarification before my next dream. I lay awake in bed for what seemed like hours with my eyes occasionally tearing up thinking about what could be the future of the earth and the people left behind after the Rapture, assuming some type of Rapture were to occur. Eventually I fell back asleep and had another dream. In the dream I walked up to a ticket booth to exchange tickets to a concert for new tickets because the time and date of the concert had changed. Initially I did not have enough tickets for everyone in our group to attend the concert. After returning my tickets to the person working inside the ticket booth, I mistakenly received a greater number of tickets in return. I received more tickets than the number I originally needed so now everyone in the group could attend the concert.

Everyone now getting tickets to attend the concert could be interpreted to mean that there will not be a Rapture. Everyone then will experience a shift in dimensions, from the fourth to the fifth. This of course means that we would all suffer Armageddon together if it were to unfold in our time. As stated in my dream, the concert day and time had changed to a new time and a new day. After I received the new set of tickets, I asked the ticket handler for the revised concert date and time. He said that it was now going to occur on Saturday at 11:00 a.m. Then I woke up.

I quickly turned on the light and dashed to my appointment book to see if it contained a calendar for 2012. I wanted to see if December 21, 2012 (the winter solstice) is a Friday. It is. I remember saying to myself, "Oh my God! Saturday is December 22nd!" I realized that my dream was informing me that the shift into the fifth dimension was going to occur on Saturday, December 22, 2012 at 11:00 a.m. instead of Friday December 21, 2012 as previously suggested in Chapter 39 of this book. My dream was indicating to me that the actual time of the transition to the fifth dimension is scheduled to occur one day later than anticipated. What this means is that the transition to the next dimension is set to occur on a Saturday which is the day of the Sabbath, versus a Friday which is not. I recalled immediately the warning contained within the Bible, specifically in Matthew.

> "Pray that your fight will not take place in winter or on the Sabbath. For then there will be great distress, unequaled from the beginning of the world until now—and never to be equaled again. If those days had not been cut short, no one would survive, but for the sake of the elect those days will be shortened." Matthew 24:20-22

If we are about to experience Armageddon, it may very well be horrendous because the transition to the fifth dimension is set to occur not only in winter, but also on the Sabbath. If I interpreted my dream correctly, we are in for a whole world of trouble. Mankind collectively may have chosen the more difficult path.

Days later I had another dream I believe is related to the 2012 transitional shift. In the dream I was on an island with a number of other people. There was a small airplane there that we were going to use to escape the island. In the dream I was one of the people who were going to be rescued. A number of us got on the plane and we flew off into the sky leaving the island behind us. I was relieved to know that I was being rescued. Then in the same dream I was back on the island. I was in my home, which in the dream was nothing more than a hut that contained all of my possessions. I was in my hut looking at the possessions I had accumulated over time, wondering what I could bring with me on the plane. I then ran out of the hut toward the plane. This time the plane had left without me. I watched as the plane flew into the sky. I felt sickened that I had missed it. I was not going to be rescued this time.

In this part of the dream, I watched the plane leave from *a totally different perspective* than the first part of the dream in which I had made the plane. This time I was left behind on the island. The island at that moment cracked into two pieces. In my dream I both *made the plane* and *missed the plane,* each time from a different viewpoint. In the first part of the dream, I was elated that I was being rescued. In the latter part of the dream, I hesitated leaving because I felt an attachment to my belongings, and consequently I was left behind on the island. In the dream I personally felt sickened by the thought of not being rescued without actually experiencing the destruction that I naturally assumed would have followed. Could the island cracking into two pieces suggest a splitting in the dimensions? Either way, the reference in my dream to my attachment to material possessions is obvious in that any attachment to material possessions will cause greater suffering for those of us that are not able to let go of them. It is a choice we must all ultimately make. More so now than ever, I believe that all of the major prophets that came to earth in this fourth dimension (Jesus, Krishna, Buddha, etc.) descended from heaven to teach us about love and the evils of materialism.

Once again I asked my higher self if there was anything else I needed to add to this book before I went to sleep. Immediately upon falling asleep, I had another very vivid dream. Possibly it may have even been a vision. Either way, it was quite remarkable. What I saw was a wristwatch or pocket watch. It was so large it encompassed my entire view. In the vision or dream, it shattered into a million tiny pieces, and then I awoke. To me, this may have meant a number of things. First, it is possible that it may have been completely unrelated to my question, but I highly doubt it as it seems to correlate quite well to a shift in our consciousness. I believe that this dream could mean that once we enter into the fifth dimension, we will be entering a dimension associated with the lower mind, i.e. concrete mind and the fifth chakra; and as we enter into this dimension, we will come to a realization that time is not real and that time is an illusion man created. The *illusion of time will be shattered* just as the watch in my dream shattered into a million pieces. This particular dream interpretation reminded me of when I left my body through my third-eye, which is associated with the sixth dimension, abstract mind, and devoid of time. I naturally wondered if the fifth dimension was the same as the sixth where time does not exist. Could the reference to *end times* be *the end of tracking time*, another soul truism? Will time become less important or less real as we become increasingly psychic and more cognizant of other dimensions?

A significant amount of time elapsed before I received additional information from Spirit concerning the 2012 transition by means of another prophetic dream. The message contained within my dream was surprisingly straightforward. I was told *"There will be a lot of destruction, but not right away."* As a result of my dreams and the information that Spirit provided me one way or another, I believe that we are transitioning to the next dimension on Saturday, December 22, 2012 at or around 11:00 a.m.; this is one day later than all other predictions. I cannot say for certain whether or not the appointed time is California time or Greenwich Mean Time. Spirit did not specify in the dream. However, I am not a fool. I do realize that it is possible the transition to the fifth dimension may go down in history as a *non-event* as was our transition into the new millennium on January 1, 2000. I also realize that our transition into the next dimension *may only appear as a non-event* when something spiritually amazing is actually occurring! As for me, I do not believe there will be a Rapture where people suddenly disappear from the face of the earth. However, we could very well experience a splitting of dimensions, but how would we even know it occurred? The *earth changes* we are already experiencing are just the beginning. I believe that there are many more disasters to come; many of them will be horrific, and sadly many people will die—over time, possible up to two-thirds of the world as predicted. Can we avoid the destruction that has been prophesized by so many? What will it take for us to experience the Revelation?

In the Bible it says that no one will know the exact time or day of the Revelation. With this in mind, I would like to make it clear that I have not suggested that I know the exact time or even the day of the Revelation.

"No One knows about that day or hour, not even the angels in heaven, nor the Son, but only the Father. Be on guard!" Mark 13: 32-33

What I have stated is that I know the approximate time and day of our transition into the fifth dimension. This dimensional shift may or may not accompany an ongoing cleansing of our sinful nature known to us as Armageddon, although I have strongly suggested it will.

As for me, I believe the biggest danger we face is ourselves and seemingly our inability to love our neighbors as ourselves and to live symbiotically with our earth and all its inhabitants. Our problems (past, present and future) stem from our lack of consciousness. But I have hope, because in the most difficult of situations we do come together demonstrating love and compassion for each other. Do you still recall experiencing a shift in consciousness after 9/11 even though short lived?

The transition to the fifth dimension is *not* something to be feared. It is rather something to prepare for. If you are ready for the transition I believe that it will go well for you. For those that are not prepared, it will possibly be a very difficult and painful transition. For those of us tied to our false ego living in fear, anger, jealousy, lust or greed, it will be a much more difficult transition. For those tied to this form universe and the material gratification the world has to offer, it will be a more difficult transition. In order to make the necessary changes we seek, we must first change our consciousness. For those of us that are striving to increase our soul's consciousness, we will as a consequence be more open to love and will be operating at a higher vibrational frequency. We are in effect creating a *consciousness revolution*.

Immortal Life Yoga will help us prepare for this conscious awakening. It is a way of life that is consistent with the vibration of a higher dimension and a greater understanding. Immortal Life Yoga is the way of love. The choices we make today determine our future, individually and collectively. We have but one question yet to answer, *How much must we suffer before we come to the realization that we are all a part of the one Christ Body?* The fact is we are slowly waking up to this new awareness, that we, collectively, are the Personal God, and that we determine our own fate. But is the transition within us occurring fast enough?

Armageddon or not, the human race will survive. This is not the end. Rather, this is the dawning of a new dimension. We must change the dream of the modern world from one of materialism to one of spiritualism. To grow in Spirit is to grow in love. Move forward now in loving consciousness. Go forth, letting the Christ within you awaken.

"Follow the way of love...." I Corinthians 14:1

And know that you are not alone on your journey!

About the Author

❦

Gary J. McDonald holds dual Bachelor of Business Administration degrees in Marketing and Finance from the University of Wisconsin in Milwaukee and a Master of Arts in Counseling from the University of Colorado in Colorado Springs. A Licensed Professional Counselor in Colorado, the author is well versed in spiritual subject matter, trained in past life regression, and has worked with Celtic, Native American, and Peruvian shamans. A businessman and entrepreneur, McDonald has dedicated his life to humanitarian work both nationally and internationally.

McDonald's study of philosophies and ancient religions such as Christianity, Buddhism, Hinduism, Theosophy, and the Kabbalah greatly assisted him in his work more so than any particular author. It was only by studying the Bible, the Bhagavad-Gita, the Kabbalah, the Yoga Sutras, Theosophy, Buddhism, and Hinduism that Gary discovered that it is purely linguistics that separate mankind's religions and philosophies.

To contact the author, order additional books, or order books in bulk, please log onto www.EverythingYouNeedToKnowToGetToHeaven.com.

References

Footnotes/Additional Sources:

Chapter 1

1. Scripture taken from the Holy Bible, New International Version (Zondervan Bible Publishers, Grand Rapids Michigan) Copyright © 1973, 1978, 1984 International Bible Society. Used by implied permission of Zondervan Bible Publishers.

Chapter 3

1. Tekla, Nee S., *The Everything Baby's First Year Book*. Adams Media, an F+W Publications Co. Avon, MA. USA, 2002

Chapter 5

1. Website: Nautalex—Interesting Information
   http://www.nautalex.com/interestinginfo.html

Chapter 7

1. Website: Unity of Salt Lake
   http://www.globalsvcs.com/karen/webfolio/UnitySLC/about_unity.html

2. Website: What is a Mantra and How Does It Work?
   http://www.sanskritmantra.com/what.html

Chapter 12

1. Ehrman, Bart E., *Misquoting Jesus: The Story Behind Who Changed the Bible and Why*. Harper San Francisco, a Division of Harper Collins Publishers, New York, NY, 2005

2. Ehrman, Bart E., *Misquoting Jesus: The Story Behind Who Changed the Bible and Why*. Harper San Francisco, a Division of Harper Collins Publishers, New York, NY, 2005

3. Ehrman, Bart E., *Misquoting Jesus: The Story Behind Who Changed the Bible and Why*. Harper San Francisco, a Division of Harper Collins Publishers, New York, NY, 2005

4. Hillerbrand, Hans J., General Editor, *Christianity, Illustrated History.* Duncan Baird Publishers, London 2008

5. Hillerbrand, Hans J., General Editor, *Christianity, Illustrated History.* Duncan Baird Publishers, London 2008

6. Website: Creeds and Documents From the Seven Ecumenical Councils http://members.aol.com/theclarion/creeds_confessions/seven_councils.html

7. Website: The Third Ecumenical Council http://www.goarch.org/en/ourfaith/articles/article8066.asp

8. Website: Immaculate Conception Defined by Pius IX http://www.ewtn.com/library/papaldoc/jp2bvm23.html

9. Lampe, Stephen M., *The Christian and Reincarnation.* Millennium Press, Legacy Edition, Ibadan, Nigeria, 2008

10. Website: Fifth Ecumenical Council (Second Constantinople) – Anathemas against Origen http://www.comparativereligion.com/anathemas.html

11. Pollack, Robert, *The Everything World Religion's Book.* Adams Media Corporation, an F+W Publications, Inc. Avon, MA, 2002

12. Website: Past Forward: Inspirational Quotes on Reincarnation http://www.healpastlives.com/pastlf/quote/qureincr.html

13. Website: Reincarnation – Famous People http://www.reincarnation.ws/famous_people.html

14. Lampe, Stephen M., *The Christian and Reincarnation.* Millennium Press, Legacy Edition, Ibadan, Nigeria, 2008

15. Lampe, Stephen M., *The Christian and Reincarnation.* Millennium Press, Legacy Edition, Ibadan, Nigeria, 2008

16. Sanderfur, Glenn, *Lives of the Master, the Rest of the Jesus Story.* Fourth Printing, A.R.E. Press, Virginia Beach, VA., 1994

Chapter 16

1. Website: Common Sanskrit Terms – [RMIC]
   http://www.sriramakrishna.org/sanskrit.html

Chapter 18

1. Website: The Nazarene Way of Essenic Studies
   http://www.thenazareneway.com/yeshua_jesus_real_name.htm

2. Website: The Holy Name: Yahweh & Yeshohua
   http://www.pickle-publishing.com/papers/holy-name-yahweh-yehoshua.htm

3. Website: Inquisitive Atheists, God – Men like Jesus
   http://www.geocities.com/inquisitive79/godmen.html

4. Website: Mithras = Christianity?
   http://jdstone.org/cr/files/mithraschristianity.html

Chapter 20

1. Al-Khalili, Jim, *Quantum: A Guide for the Perplexed*. London, Weidenfeld & Nicholson, Wellington House, 2004

2. Al-Khalili, Jim, *Quantum: A Guide for the Perplexed*. London, Weidenfeld & Nicholson, Wellington House, 2004

3. Bohm, David, *Quantum Theory*. Dover Publications, Inc. New York, 1989

4. Website: Superstring Theory: Definition and Much More from Answers.com
   http://www.answers.com/topic/superstring-theory

5. Kaku, Michio, *Physics of the Impossible*. Anchor Books, A Division of Random House, Inc., New York, 2008

6. Website: M-Theory, the theory formally known as strings
   http://www.damtp.cam.ac.uk/user/gr/public/qg_ss.html

7. Website: Hamilton, Wm., The Mutiverse
   http://www.astrosciences.info/Multiverse.htm

8. Website: Parallel Universes
   http://space.mit.edu/home/tegmark/multiverse.pdf

9. Website: Parallel Universes
   http://space.mit.edu/home/tegmark/multiverse.pdf

10. Website: Parallel Universes
    http://space.mit.edu/home/tegmark/multiverse.pdf

11. Website: James Prescott Joule – Encyclopedia.com
    http://www.encyclopedia.com/doc/1E1-thermody.html

12. Website: James Prescott Joule – Encyclopedia.com
    http://www.encyclopedia.com/doc/1E1-thermody.html

Chapter 21

1. Website: The Expansion of the Universe and the Discovery of the Big Bang
   http://www.e-articles.info/e/a/title/The-Expansion-of-Universe-and-the-Discovery-of-the-Big-Bang/

2. Website: Creation of the Universe – Harun Yahya
   http://www.creationofuniverse.com/html/bigbang_01.html

3. Website: The dawn of time – after 13 billion years in the darkroom...
   http://www.smh.com.au/news/science/dawn-of-time—after-13-billion-years-in-the-darkroom/2006/12/19/1166290545385.html

4. Website: Harvard Gazette: History of life on Earth is largely microbial
   http://www.hno.harvard.edu/gazette/2004/10.07/15-origins.html

Chapter 22

1. Website: The Origin of Species by Charles Darwin
   http://www.talkorigins.org/faqs/origin.html

2. Website: What Is An Evolutionist?
   http://www.allaboutphilosophy.org/what-is-an-evolutionist-faq.html

3. Website: Survival of the fittest – Wikipedia, the free encyclopedia
   http://www.answers.com/topic/survival-of-the-fittest

4. *Time* Magazine, "What Makes Us Different?" October 9, 2006

5. Website: Creationism vs. Intelligent Design By Daniel Engber
    http://www.slate.com/id/2118388

Chapter 23

1. Website: Hebrew word: adam
    http://www.Bibletexts.com/terms/heb-adam.html

2. Kotter, Thomas Boken, *A Concise History of the Catholic Church*. Image Books, Doubleday, a Division of Random House, Inc., 2004

3. Prophet, Elizabeth Clare, and Erin L. Prophet, *Reincarnation: The Missing Link in Christianity*. Summit University Press, Summit Publications, Inc., 1997

4. Prophet, Elizabeth Clare, and Erin L. Prophet, *Reincarnation: The Missing Link in Christianity*. Summit University Press, Summit Publications, Inc., 1997

Additional Sources:

Website: Origin and History of the Doctrine of Original Sin
http://www.gospeltruth.net/menbornsinners/mbs03.html

Chapter 24

1. Website: HyperDictionary.com
    http://www.hyperdictionary.com/

2. The Merriam-Webster Dictionary, Merriam-Webster Inc., An Encyclopedia Britannica Company; Springfield, Massachusetts; 2005

Chapter 25

1. Website: PBS Frontline - From Jesus to Christ
    http://www.pbs.org/wgbh/pages/frontline/shows/religion/maps/primary/thecla.html

2. Website: PBS Frontline - From Jesus to Christ
    http://www.pbs.org/wgbh/pages/frontline/shows/religion/maps/primary/thecla.html

3. Website: Excerpts from the Gospel of Mary
    http://www.sacred-texts.com/chr/apo/marym.htm

4. *Catechism of the Catholic Church*, Second Edition. Doubleday, A Division of Random House, Inc., 1997 p. 624

Chapter 26

1. Website: Comparison of Eastern and Western Art
   http://www.sanatansociety.org/vedic_astrology_and_numerology.html

2. Website: Comparison of Eastern and Western Art
   http://www.sanatansociety.org/vedic_astrology_and_numerology.html

3. Website: Comparison of Eastern and Western Art
   http://www.sanatansociety.org/vedic_astrology_and_numerology.html

4. Website: 12 Around 1 Geometry – Crystalinks
   http://www.crystalinks.com/12around1.html

Chapter 27

1. Mercier, Patricia, *The Chakra Bible: The Definitive Guide To Working With Chakras*. Sterling Publishing Company, Inc. A Hachette Livre UK Company, 2007

2. Mercier, Patricia, *The Chakra Bible: The Definitive Guide To Working With Chakras*. Sterling Publishing Company, Inc. A Hachette Livre UK Company, 2007

Additional Sources:

Website: Chakras: Cerebrospinal centers or chakras also represent…
http://www.sanatansociety.org/chakras/chakras.html

Website: The Seven Major Chakras – Study of the chakras
http://healing.about.com/od/chakratheseven/a/study7chakras.html

Website: The Chakras
http://www.journey-to-self.com/chakras.html

Website: The Endocrine System
http://www.4dshift.com/products/html/endocrine.html

Website: The Endocrine System
http://biology.clc.uc.edu/courses/bio105/endocrin.html

Website: The Endocrine System
http://www.vivo.colostate.edu/hbooks/pathphys/endocrine/index.html

Website: Crystalotus.com–7 chakra–welcome to shana's amazing world of…
http://www.crystallotus.com/chakra/7chakra.html

Chapter 28

1. Website: Kundalini means 'coiled energy' and it refers to a power which…
http://www.adishakti.org/subtle_system/kundalini.html

2. Trainor, Kevin, General Editor, *Buddhism The Illustrated Guide* Oxford University Press, Inc. NY, NY 2004

Chapter 29

1. Website: Akif, Manif J., Comparative Cosmology—the Vedic Concept of the Universe
http://www.newagepointofinfinity.com/NAU/vedic_concepts.htm

Chapter 30

1. Robinson, Lady Stearn, and Corbett, Tom, *The Dreamer's Dictionary.* New York, Warner Books, 1994

Chapter 31

1. Website: Id, Ego, and Super Ego in the Unconscious in Psychology 101 at…
http://allpsych.com/psychology101/ego.html

Chapter 34

1. Merillat, Herbert Christian, *The Gnostic Apostle Thomas, The Twin of Jesus.* Xlibris Corporation, 2007, p. 14

2. Website: Affluenza Teacher's Guide
http://www.pbs.org/kcts/affluenza/treat/tguide/tguide7.html

Additional Sources:

Website: Global Issues: Causes of Poverty
http://www.globalissues.org/TradeRelated/Facts.asp#fact1

Chapter 35

1. Website: Some of My Favorite Quotes
   http://www.cs.iastate.edu/~honavar/quotes.html

Chapter 39

1. Van Auken, John, *The End Times—Prophesies of Coming Changes.* A SIGNET Book, Published by New American Library, a division of Penguin Putnam, Inc., 2001

2. Waters, Frank, *Book of the Hopi.* Penguin Books, Published by the Penguin Group, 1977

3. Website: *The Observer*
   http://www.guardian.co.uk/uk/2002/jul/07/research.waste

4. Website: The President Declares "Freedom at War with Fear" – The White House
   http://www.whitehouse.gov/news/releases/2001/09/20010920-8.html

5. Waters, Frank, *Book of the Hopi.* Penguin Books, Published by the Penguin Group, 1977

6. Mails, Thomas E., *The Hopi Survival Kit—The Prophesies, Instructions, and Warnings Revealed by the Last Elders.* Penguin Compass, Penguin Putnam, Inc., 1997

7. Website: Wikipedia - The Free Dictionary
   http://en.wikipedia.org/wiki/Gregorian_calendar

8. Website: Beyond 2012
   http://www.diagnosis2012.co.uk/1.htm

9. Website: Mayan Calendars and Cosmology
   http://www.kachina.net/~alunajoy/94aug.html

10. Website: Mayan Calendar
    http://www.sacred-texts.com/time/cal/mayacal.htm

11. Website: What is the Galactic Alignment?
    http://alignment2012.com/whatisga.htm

12. Website: What is the Galactic Alignment?
    http://alignment2012.com/whatisga.htm

13. Website: Harmonic_Convergence
   http://rahelio.homestead.com/Harmonic_Convergence.html

14. Website: 2012 Warning article on the Mayan Prophecy of 2012
   http://www.2012warning.com/mayan-prophecy-2012.htm

15. Website: Sun's protective 'bubble' is shrinking - telegraph
   http://www.telegraph.co.uk/news/worldnews/northamerica/usa/3222476/Suns-protective-bubble-is-shrinking.html

16. Website: Reuters - After dinosaur demise, mammals late to the party
   http://www.reuters.com/article/idUSN2833662620070328

17. Website: Mayan Prophecy 2012: Entering Our Galactic Day
   http://www.2012planetalignment.net/229/mayan-prophecy-2012-entering-our-galactic-day/

18. The History Channel – *The Lost Book of Nostradamus*; program aired 10-28-07

19. Website: Great Celestial Conjunction Crosses
   http://www.soulsofdistortion.nl/great%20celestial%20conjunction%20crosses.html

20. Website: Edgar Cayce's A.R.E.
   http://www.edgarcayce.org/2012.asp

Chapter 40

1. Bailey, Alice A., *The Light of the Soul: The Yoga Sutras of Patanjali*. New York, Lucis Publishing Co.

2. Hewitt, James, *The Complete Yoga Book*. Schocken Books, New York, 1977.

8385016R1

Made in the USA
Lexington, KY
28 January 2011